Economic forecasting and policy –
the international dimension

International Library of Economics

Economic forecasting and policy – the international dimension

John Llewellyn, Stephen Potter and Lee Samuelson

Routledge & Kegan Paul
London, Boston, Melbourne and Henley

First published in 1985
by Routledge & Kegan Paul plc

14 Leicester Square, London WC2H 7PH, England

9 Park Street, Boston, Mass. 02108, USA

464 St Kilda Road, Melbourne,
Victoria 3004, Australia and

Broadway House, Newtown Road,
Henley on Thames, Oxon RG9 1EN, England

Set in Linotron Times 10 on 12 point
by Text Processing, Ireland
and printed in Great Britain
by Billing & Sons Ltd., Worcester

© John Llewellyn, Stephen Potter and Lee Samuelson 1985

Library of Congress Cataloging in Publication Data

Llewellyn, G. E. J. (Graeme Ernest John), 1944–

Economic forecasting and policy—the international dimension.
(International library of economics)
Bibliography: p.
Includes index.
1. Economic forecasting. 2. Economic policy. 3. International economic relations.
I. Potter, Stephen, 1940–   II. Samuelson, Lee. III. Title. IV. Series:
ILE.
HB3730.L56   1985   338.9   84-27659

British Library CIP data also available

ISBN 0-7102-0600-3

Contents

Tables and charts

Tables

Charts

Preface

We were motivated to write this book by the evident increased difficulty of managing economies in recent years, and by the feeling that our own experience might enable us to provide a perspective on some aspects of current problems that may not always be available in national discussions of economic matters.

The book covers a range of topics, from international economic concerns to general questions of economic policy-making and more technical issues of economic forecasting. This reflects the view that effective macroeconomic management needs to draw upon, and blend appropriately, a wide range of techniques and skills. We have various audiences in mind, and recognize that any individual reader may not be equally concerned with all chapters. One target group consists of interested general readers with a taste for practical applied economics; another consists of those in business or government who are involved, directly or indirectly, in the analysis and assessment of the international economic outlook, or in the formulation of economic policies; we also expect the book to be of interest to advanced undergraduate and graduate students who, having followed courses in, for example, macroeconomics or international economics, are seeking to deepen their knowledge of recent economic history and to gain practical insights into how economic analysis can be applied to current issues.

It will be clear that we would have been in no position to write the book had we not spent a major part of our professional lives in the OECD Secretariat. We owe a general debt of gratitude to the Organization, to colleagues past and present, and to a large number of national officials with whom we have been brought into contact by our OECD work. But this book is in no sense officially-sponsored. We have written it in our (scarce) spare time. Views expressed are ours, and do not necessarily correspond to those of the Organization or its Member governments.

Some more specific acknowledgements are also needed. A particular debt is owed to John Fay, who made extensive comments on the book as a whole, and helped provide an overall balance. And we were fortunate to be able to draw upon discussions with Emile van Lennep of a number of the key postwar economic policy episodes.

Chris Higgins and Flemming Larsen were a continuing source of stimulation and encouragement, commenting critically on the drafts of many chapters. Gordon Hughes, David Henderson and Gerry Holtham helped at various stages. Michael Feiner and Flemming Larsen contributed importantly to chapter 4. Derek Blades helped us with parts of chapter 5. Haruhito Arai, Marie-Odile Louppe, Yoshiro Nakajo, Andras Racz and Peter Richardson contributed important parts of chapter 6. Nick Vanston assisted with chapter 10. Byron Ballis helped on many parts of the book. We are also grateful to Serge Devos, Basile Gondicas, Eliane Betout-Mossé and Jean-Pierre Tuveri for help on specific points.

Data for the tables and charts were prepared by Anick Bouchouchi, Raoul Doquin de St. Preux, Anne Keeling and Chantal Nicq, and the charts were drawn by Michel Houlle. Marie-Blanche Koromzay compiled the index.

The whole was typed with unfailing cheerfulness and accuracy by Ruth Mariette, assisted at various times by Priscilla Field, Angela Gazaroglu, Anne Hamilton and Virginia Kurlansky.

An earlier version of parts of chapters 3, 4 and 6 has appeared in OECD's twice-yearly publication, *OECD Economic Studies*. We acknowledge permission from the Organization to re-use this material.

The text can be taken to reflect developments through 1983, the latest year for which data were available at the time the book was finalized.

John Llewellyn
Stephen Potter
Paris, September 1984   Lee Samuelson

Part I
Policy-making in an open world economy

1 Introduction: prosperity and recession

Until a few years ago, it would have been understandable for most people in the advanced industrialized world, including most policy-makers, to consider rapidly-growing prosperity the natural order of things. For people in their mid-fifties today, who entered the labour force after the second World War, the dominant memory of economic matters is of the quarter-century of rapid growth from the late 1940s. Over this period, average living standards rose to an unprecedented degree. But for people now in their mid-twenties, whose awareness of economic events is concentrated on the last decade, things may be viewed very differently. A high standard of living tends to be taken for granted. But the overriding impression, particularly in Europe, may be of some of the apparent consequences of recent slow growth, including the increased difficulty of finding a job. And whereas the middle-aged person would be likely, perhaps to an exaggerated extent, to attribute high and rising living standards to the success of government policy, the younger one, more influenced by the recent climate of opinion, is quite likely to believe that today's problems can largely be laid at the door of excessive government involvement in the economy.

Rapid economic growth has not always been the norm. Between 1870 and 1913, 16 of the largest economies of the world grew on average by about 2½ per cent per year (Table 1.1). There was, naturally, significant variation both between countries and from year to year, but this average figure provides a reasonable overall summary. Considering then the next epoch, the level of real GDP in these countries in 1950 would seem, when taken in relation to the figure for 1913, to imply an average rate of growth that was rather lower, at not quite 2 per cent per year, although of course the significance of this figure is somewhat dubious, as there had been two world wars in the interim. By contrast, average GDP growth for the same group of countries proceeded at nearly 5 per cent per year over the post-war epoch 1950 to 1973, virtually twice as fast as had previously been seen.

Employment grew in all three epochs. Although there were differences from one epoch to the next, these were less than the differences in the rate of growth of output, so that, as a matter of simple arithmetic, labour productivity growth, and thereby the growth of the standard of living of the workforce and indeed the population as a whole, fluctuated considerably. Again, the most dramatic change took place between 1950 and 1973. Unemployment was far lower on average in this period than it had been earlier; and those who were unemployed were generally better protected by social insurance programmes.

The inflation differences between the three epochs are particularly striking. Between 1870 and 1913 there was virtual price stability, prices rising on average by less than ½ per cent per year. But over the period 1913 to 1950 considered as a whole prices rose very rapidly, at nearly 9 per cent per year on average. This average figure masks quite disparate movements within the period, however – sharp rises during both world wars, with an actual fall in the price level in between. During the third epoch, from 1950 to 1973, inflation proceeded at an intermediate rate, of just under 4 per cent per year on average.

Between 1870 and 1913 overall real living standards grew on average by a little under 1½ per cent per year. And between 1913 and 1950 the growth of living standards may have been slightly slower than this. The problems in providing a reliable quantitative estimate are considerable, because the period includes two world wars, which brought with them large changes in technology, patterns of demand and the structure of production. On the best estimates available, which rely heavily on terminal levels, it seems that real per capita income may have grown by about 1¼ per cent per year. At such rates of growth, living standards double about every fifty years. The average grandparent, recalling at retirement the real wage at which he or she started work at fifteen, would see his or her grandchild start work at a real income that was about twice as high. During the epoch from 1950 to 1973, however, productivity and general living standards grew much faster – at about 3¾ per cent per year. The phenomenon of compound growth being what it is, at that sort of rate living standards take less than twenty years to double;

and the starting income of the average new entrant to the labour force is about six times higher than that of his or her grandparents. By the late 1960s, the OECD world had seen two decades of spectacularly successful economic performance. Furthermore, it seemed to many that, short of war or extreme natural disaster, little of economic significance was likely to go wrong. Much of the credit was attributed to economic policy. The problems of ensuring a satisfactory, and indeed continually improving, performance from the modern mixed economy seemed to have been largely overcome. Students of economics were taught, and many people believed, that through the correct application of economic policy it was possible not only to achieve full employment, but also to iron out all but the most minor fluctuations in activity. Inflation was generally not thought a serious problem, and such difficulties as manifested themselves through the balance of payments could usually be dealt with relatively straightforwardly.

The comparatively poor performance of the last decade has come as something of a shock, therefore. First of all, growth has dropped back to a modest 2¼ per cent rate on average, little better than during the 1913 to 1950 period, and less than in the 1870 to 1913 epoch (Table 1.1). Employment has grown, but not sufficiently to prevent unemployment from rising significantly. Furthermore, the growth of living standards has generally slowed down, to its more customary historical 1 to 2 per cent rate. And throughout, most economies have proved more inflation-prone than before. What were the main reasons for this deterioration in economic performance? With the benefit of hindsight, it seems clear now that, during the high growth epoch, a number of economic clouds were gathering on the horizon.

Inflation was building up, albeit slowly and from rates that today would be regarded as low. The world energy balance was changing, with the United States switching from being a net exporter to a net importer of oil and the net energy imports of the OECD area as a whole growing rapidly. The system of pegged exchange rates was becoming harder to maintain. There was a strengthening feeling, hard to substantiate but no less real for that, that the supply side of OECD economies, particularly those in Europe, was becoming less responsive.

Other changes were occurring too, although in the prevailing environment of virtually full employment these did not seem to

Table 1.1. *Economic performance, major epochs, 16 major countries*[a]

	1870–1913	1913–1950	1950–1973	1973–1983
1. Real GDP growth, per cent per year	2.5	1.9	4.9	2.3
2. Total employment growth, per cent per year	1.1	0.7	1.2	0.4
3. Productivity growth, per cent per year[b]	1.4	1.2	3.7	1.9
4. Unemployment rate, per cent		7.8[c]	2.6	5.3
5. Capital stock (non-residential) growth, per cent per year[d]	2.9	1.7	5.5	4.0
6. Export growth (merchandise volume) per cent per year	3.9	1.0	8.6	4.8
7. Consumer price increase, per cent per year	0.4	8.9	4.1	9.3

[a]   The figures are unweighted arithmetic averages of the figures for Australia, Austria, Belgium, Canada, Denmark, Finland, France, Germany, Italy, Japan, Netherlands, Norway, Sweden, Switzerland, United Kingdom and United States. These countries account, at present weights, for 95 per cent of the total output of the OECD area. Data for the period 1870 to 1973 are taken from Maddison (1982). Data for the period 1973 to 1983 are taken from OECD sources.
[b]   Figures for the growth of output per head of population, not shown here, are very similar.
[c]   1926–1938.
[d]   United States, Japan, Germany, France, United Kingdom, Italy and Canada only.

present any insuperable problems. Important new industrial poles emerged not only within the OECD but also in the newly-industrializing countries of South America and the Far East. International trade grew rapidly – about twice as fast as GNP – so that OECD economies became progressively more intertwined, and thereby progressively more affected by developments in partner countries. Financial integration too proceeded apace, reinforcing international interdependence. And in virtually all countries the government sector grew continually in relation to the economy as a whole.

While this description is a stylization, most of these elements are characteristic of most OECD countries. They have generally figured in discussions of the problems of conducting economic policy in OECD countries over the last decade or so. A number of these factors – and perhaps others too – came to a head in the early 1970s with the 1972-73 commodity price boom, the 1973-74 quadrupling of the price of internationally-traded oil, and a dramatic increase in nearly all countries in the rate of inflation.

There followed a decade of change. This decade saw not just the first but also a second great oil shock, a massive rise and then an even larger fall in non-oil commodity prices, large swings in countries' external current accounts, volatile exchange rates, stubbornly high inflation, high public sector deficits, record rates of bankruptcies, near-financial collapse of several big developing countries, a resurgence of protectionism, prolonged OECD recession, and high and rising unemployment.

It is therefore perhaps not surprising that this became a decade of disillusionment, including disillusionment over the ability of economic policy in general to bring forth an adequate performance from the modern economic system. Earlier optimism on the part of national economic policy-makers about their ability to control their national economic destiny seemed to fade. The system of pegged exchange rates could no longer be maintained. The role and the effectiveness of the two main levers of macroeconomic policy – fiscal and monetary policy – began to be fundamentally reappraised. Rigorous attempts were made to check, and then reverse, the growth of the government sector. And in a number of countries policy-makers, after three decades of apparent belief in the central role of aggregate demand policy, seemed to swing towards believing that there was little if anything that such policy could or should do, apart from seeking to provide a framework of financial stability. 'Fine tuning' of demand was dismissed, the 'automatic-stabilizer' element of fiscal systems fell into disrepute, and simple non-discretionary rules were tried instead.

Some at least of this response may have been an over-reaction. The balanced view may be that, while policy and policy-makers cannot take all the credit for everything that went right over the quarter century after World War II, neither should they take all of the blame for what went wrong subsequently. In matters of economic performance it pays to beware the single all-embracing explanation. In the case of the 1970s deterioration in economic performance it is almost certain that the origins have been both numerous and complex, with the relative importance of the various causes differing both from period to period and from country to country.

A key question is whether the epoch from 1950 to 1973 will prove, in retrospect, to have been unique, or whether it will be possible for economies to perform in that sort of way again. This book does not attempt to consider the whole range of possible reasons for the deterioration in economic performance over the last decade, or all the elements that will determine economic performance in future epochs. Nor does it discuss the particular problems of the developing countries and the centrally-planned economies. To cover all these issues would be a mammoth undertaking, and even provisional answers are probably years away.

Rather, the book concentrates on one particular, but apparently important, reason for the deterioration in the performance of the Western industrialized world over the last decade. This is that, collectively, national economic policies did not deal adequately with influences that were transmitted internationally. Some of these were shocks originating within OECD countries. Others came, at least proximately, from the non-OECD world. But all were rapidly transmitted among the very open OECD economies. This made policy-making more difficult, and perhaps also made policy appear less effective. And this state of affairs could well continue. Openness of the international trading and financial system is the modern-day environment; it goes far in underpinning current standards of living, but at the same time it carries with it an increasing vulnerability to external shocks.

However, it may be possible to do something about these difficulties. It may well be that more attention should, and can, usefully be paid to devising coordinated policy for the OECD countries as a group. And because, inescapably, policy has to be made on the basis of projected, rather than actual, conditions, this implies in turn putting effort into improving further the accuracy and quality of the international·and thereby national analysis and forecasts upon which policy has to be based.

This book therefore considers first the major successes and

failures of policy over the post-war period. It then explains how international forecasts are currently made. Various ways are suggested in which it may prove possible to improve national economic forecasts through improving international forecasts, and achieve better national policy through more international cooperation in determining national policy settings. The aim at no point is to suggest that any country should take action that is not in its national self-interest. Rather, the point is that, in many situations, it will be possible for countries to take individual actions which, taken together, lead to a better outcome, for all together and each separately, than would result from non-cooperative policy-making.

2 The contribution of policy in the 1950s and 1960s

Summary

The government sector today is large, having approximately doubled in most OECD countries over the last thirty years. Governments' spending decisions have, for this reason alone, a significant impact on the economy. Governments have generally chosen to exercise these decisions so as to influence the economy in the way they want. Sometimes they have sought to stabilize activity, by offsetting unwanted fluctuations originating in the private sector or abroad. On other occasions the level of economic activity and employment have been the main concern, and sometimes inflation, the balance of payments, or public sector deficits. During the period covered by this chapter, countries acted as necessary to stabilize their exchange rates against the dollar. This also served to contain inflation in the world at large as long as it was low in the United States. For much of the period, most countries were also able to devote fiscal policy to stabilizing the level of economic activity and to promoting a rate of growth sufficient to maintain a high level of employment.

Introduction

The government sector nowadays is large. Thirty years ago government consumption represented about 12 per cent of the total quantity of goods and services produced in the OECD economy. By the early 1970s, the proportion was 16 per cent and by the early 1980s had reached 20 per cent. And if account is taken also of the government's role in transferring resource claims from one group to another, its measured involvement is higher and has risen faster, from 20 per cent in 1950 to 30 per cent in 1970 and 40 per cent in 1980.

The fact that the government sector has become so large carries with it both obligations and opportunities. At a minimum, government has to take care to ensure that its expenditure and taxation decisions mesh appropriately with what is, and is expected to be, going on in the rest of the economy. For example, government needs to ensure that the total of the resource claims that it and the private sector are jointly making on the economy will not exceed the economy's productive capacity. If government fails in this, resulting pressure on capacity would create or exacerbate domestic inflationary pressure in product markets, and quite possibly push up wage rates also. Any *ex ante* excess demand not choked off in this way would not only spill over into imports, but also lead to a deterioration of international competitiveness, thereby worsening the balance of payments and perhaps causing depletion of reserves or currency depreciation, depending on the exchange rate regime in operation.

In addition to this essentially passive policy of merely ensuring that total resource claims are not excessive, however, governments have on occasion wished to go further. They have sought to exercise their influence more actively, framing their taxation and spending decisions so as to improve the macroeconomic performance of the economy when it was doing badly, and stabilize its performance whenever it was doing well. The aim has variously been to change the level of activity, or to stabilize it about its trend.

Attempts by government to influence the level of aggregate demand in the economy are, however, not in themselves the main reason why the public sector has grown so much. The public finance literature traditionally distinguishes three branches of government activity: allocation, distribution and stabilization.[1] With the assumption by government of greater responsibilities for economic management after the Second World War, all three branches grew in importance. The three are of course not independent. As a broad generalization it might, however, be said that the growth in the share of public spending was largely attributable to the allocation and distribution objectives of government, particularly large increases having occurred for health, education, social transfers and income maintenance programmes. Meanwhile, the stabilization ('demand management') objective may often have affected the timing of the growth of particular programmes. To some extent, the growth of public spending represented the disposal of the 'fiscal dividend' (the growth of tax revenues associated with rapid economic growth) but, particularly in the more recent period, tax rates have tended to increase also.

By the 1970s, many governments and observers of the economic scene had become concerned at the implications of the size or the rate of increase of the public sector share in their economies. This chapter covers the years from post-war reconstruction up to the beginning of the 1970s, a period over which such concerns were largely absent.

The pegged exchange rate regime

Before attempting an assessment of the success of policy it is necessary to determine what it was that policy was seeking to achieve. During the period in question, countries were faced with two kinds of macroeconomic policy requirement. Domestically, there was an explicit or implicit commitment to high levels of employment. Internationally, countries were bound by the Bretton Woods 'rules of the game', as embodied in the Articles of Agreement of the International Monetary Fund.

The key international obligation was the maintenance of the exchange rate within margins of ±1 per cent around its parity vis-à-vis the U.S. dollar. Changes of parity were seen as an instrument of adjustment, but only in cases of 'fundamental disequilibrium', a state of affairs in which it was judged impossible, at the existing parity, to bring the current account into line with sustainable (or underlying) net capital flows by an acceptable degree of deflation of aggregate demand (in the case of a weak currency) or reflation (in the case of a strong currency). In practice, parity changes among the industrialized countries were rare, perhaps surprisingly so. Over the 18 years between the wide-ranging realignment of 1949 and the sterling devaluation of 1967 which was the beginning of another, more protracted, realignment, the only parity changes among major currencies were devaluations by France in 1957 and 1958 as part of a major stabilization effort and a small revaluation by Germany and the Netherlands in 1961. The Canadian dollar floated for much of the period, generally not fluctuating much.

Does the fact that countries were generally so successful in holding parities unchanged mean that they had to be prepared to accept wide deviations of aggregate demand from desired levels? It appears not. Over the years 1955 to 1972, the average annual deviation of GNP from trend in eighteen OECD countries was less than 1½ per cent (from Boltho and Keating, 1973). There may have been one or two cases of 'repressed' fundamental disequilibrium: the United Kingdom authorities certainly considered at times that they were holding back the growth of the economy for balance-of-payments reasons (though in fact the margin of unused resources seems to have been fairly low throughout); and the German authorities may occasionally have felt that they were running their economy at higher levels than they would have desired in order to avoid an embarrassingly strong external position. Japan undoubtedly had policy-induced cycles in activity related to balance-of-payments fluctuations, but around an extraordinarily high average growth rate.[2] Overall, however, as described in chapter 1, the average level of activity over this period was historically high, and the amplitude of fluctuations around that average historically low – see Chart 2.1.

Once the immediate post-war reconstruction phase was over, inflation was less of a problem than it was to become in the 1970s. To be sure, economic commentary often mentioned inflation as an issue, and it tended to be cited as a reason whenever policy took a restrictive tack. But counter-inflation policies were seldom pursued with vigour for any length of time. Economies were evidently not as inflation-prone as they were later to become.

This is shown most clearly by the behaviour of inflation during and after the Korean War. The outbreak of the war in June 1950 led to an immediate and sharp increase in the world demand for most internationally-traded primary commodities, both by the private sector and for government stockpiling. Prices of primary commodities, particularly the fibres and metals, rose over the next nine months more rapidly than at any time over the previous hundred years, except during the two world wars. They reached their peak around March 1951, and declined thereafter, albeit somewhat less rapidly than they had risen.[3] In annual terms, the import prices (unit values) of the industrial economies rose on average by about 15 per cent in 1950 and a little over 25 per cent in 1951. In terms of the initial shock to the price level of the OECD economy, this increase amounted to 2½ to 3 per cent, and hence slightly more than that caused by each of the two oil price shocks, in 1973-74 and 1981-82.

In the United States there was a swift response of policy. Taxes were increased, mortgages were restricted, and a general wage and price freeze was enacted. Profits had expanded considerably in 1950, so that within the price control ceiling there was probably room for a significant increase in primary commodity prices. Consumer prices, which had scarcely increased in 1950, rose by 8.1 per cent in 1951 and by a further 2.1 per cent in 1952. But as commodity prices started to fall, these controls were lifted progressively, the last by early 1953. Over the period of price control, the prices of many goods in fact fell below their ceiling, and with the final abolition of controls the overall price index grew very little – by just 0.8 per cent in 1953. Similarly U.S. export prices, which had risen by about 18 per cent in 1951, then stabilized at that new level and in aggregate rose only very slowly thereafter until the mid 1960s.[4]

Although there were some differences from country to country, overall the other industrial countries too responded similarly to the Korean War commodity price shock. By and large the resulting higher import prices fed temporarily into wages, but thereafter wage inflation decelerated quite quickly – a markedly different response to that which was to follow the 1973-74 oil price rise, when wage rates rose rapidly in nearly all countries, and for a much longer period. By 1953, consumer price inflation in the industrial world as a whole was down to 1.3 per cent.

More generally, the inflation experience over the Bretton Woods period seems to fit quite well the textbook story of fixed exchange-rate blocks. By pegging their currencies to the dollar, countries had broadly the U.S. rate of inflation, and were in the main satisfied with this. They remained broadly satisfied until inflation in the United States started to accelerate at the time of the stepping-up of the Vietnam War in the mid-to-late 1960s (Table 2.1). In other words, adherence to the obligations of the pegged rate regime constituted an anti-inflation policy all the time the U.S. inflation rate was acceptably low.

Table 2.1 *Inflation in the United States*
Per cent per year

	1953–58	1958–65	1965–73
Consumer prices	1.6	1.2	4.4
GNP deflator	2.2	1.2	3.9
Export unit values	1.3	0.4	1.9
Compensation per man-hour	4.6	4.2	6.8

Sources: Shapiro (1977) page 276, and IMF *International Financial Statistics*, 1980.

The fact that exchange rates could stay pegged for such a long period without major slack in some countries and excess demand in others remains remarkable. A number of explanations might be offered. First, there may have been an element of luck – possibly combined with good judgement – in the setting of the 1949 parities, even if with the benefit of hindsight a few European countries may have devalued somewhat too much. Second, there was no doubt a tendency for countries in incipiently strong payments positions, such as Germany, to liberalize current account transactions, and particularly capital movements, more rapidly than those in weaker positions, such as the United Kingdom and France. Third, over the medium term there was a tendency anyway for countries' relative growth rates and competitiveness to adjust into line with each other.[5] Fourth, the period can be considered to have been relatively free of major shocks, at least in retrospect; the main ones were the wars in East Asia already referred to. Fifth, the United States was fully prepared to play the role of 'nth country', thereby significantly easing the task of countries (each individually small in relation to the United States) seeking to achieve a particular payments position. This last point is returned to in chapter 12.

The full-employment commitment

In this environment there was agreement in many countries that a prime aim of policy – including fiscal and monetary policy – should be to stabilize the level of activity and employment at a high level. This commitment represented a fundamental change from the doctrine which had prevailed quite generally before the second

World War. Furthermore, the commitment to full employment became enshrined not only in the policy of many countries, but also, in a number of them, in the law of the land. Given the significant natural growth of the labour force in the majority of countries, which was augmented in some of them by immigration, the full-employment commitment translated into a *growth* commitment, so that achieving high and reasonably steady growth in turn became a commitment, formal or informal, in many countries.[6]

Governments soon were setting themselves growth objectives that seemed ambitious when judged against the rates seen in previous eras. Yet in fact these objectives were for a time often exceeded. At a Ministerial Council meeting in 1961, OECD countries adopted the target of increasing their combined national output by 50 per cent during the decade from 1960 to 1970. They recognized that 'rapid growth facilitates the harmonious development of the world economy, helps to promote a liberal world trading system, provides a necessary foundation for rising living standards, and ensures a high level of employment'. This output target was in fact surpassed. As noted in the McCracken Report, 'In the early 1960s there was a tendency to under-estimate the potential for growth. By the mid-1960s projections of growth had been revised upwards to levels close to those actually achieved in the second half of the decade. .... This led to the projection of even higher growth rates at the beginning of the 1970s and for a while it looked as though these might be achieved ...'.[7]

Fiscal policy was seen as having an important role in this regard. In 1968 an international panel of economists, drawn from the United States and Europe, concluded that 'In all industrial countries, over recent decades, it has increasingly been felt that a primary duty of governments is to maintain conditions appropriate to steady growth, full employment and balance in the economy. Simultaneously, there has emerged the realization that fiscal policy is a major instrument whereby these functions could be fulfilled both in the long-term – by favouring investment, improving education and in other ways – and in the short-term – by maintaining an appropriate balance between demand and supply.'[8]

And as regards monetary policy, an assessment by the OECD Secretariat, based upon a study of six major OECD countries over the period 1960 to 1971, concluded that '... though there was some acceleration of prices towards the end of the period, it would not be much of an exaggeration to say that the main internal task of monetary policy was seen as one of stabilizing real demand at a level commensurate with current productive capacity'.[9] Further, while it was recognized that the task would not in general be particularly easy, there was fairly general confidence in a number of countries in the ability of aggregate demand policy to achieve its objectives.

The discussion which follows concentrates mainly on the effectiveness of fiscal policy in stabilizing real activity. The appropriateness of such a study depends critically upon the extent to which this was indeed the central aim of fiscal policy. As discussed in the previous section, this objective stood to be overridden by external policy requirements. There are two reasons, however, why this may not constitute a major qualification to the results. First, to the extent that economies were 'well-behaved' and not in fundamental disequilibrium, domestic and external requirements would have tended to point in the same direction anyway: external deficit (and possibly inflation too) would tend to be associated with excessive activity levels, and surplus with deficient activity levels. Second, the instrument 'assigned' to external balance was typically monetary policy; to the extent that the stance of monetary policy nevertheless continued to be broadly accommodating, as was usually the case, the workings of fiscal policy may have been little affected.

The type of policy that it is technically feasible to make is shaped in significant part by the accuracy of the forecasts upon which the policy is to be based, the extent to which the likely effects of policy changes can be correctly assessed, the precision with which policy changes can be applied, and the political will of governments to apply such changes, especially when they are liable to be unpopular. In the 1950s and early 1960s, economic forecasting was not particularly widespread, but the effects of policy changes were considered to be adequately well understood, and in some countries at least the institutional framework was such as to permit policy changes to be applied fairly precisely. The strength of political will varied over time and from country to country, but in general the number of 'unpopular' policy changes that would have been considered appropriate by economists but were not made was probably fairly small. One important case, however, was the delay by the United States in enacting tax increases to neutralize rising defence expenditure in the late 1960s. This episode had far-reaching implications: while it was not the only cause of the events which followed, it contributed to the acceleration of inflation both in the United States and abroad, to the emergence of a U.S. current account deficit in 1970, and to the breakdown of the Bretton Woods system of fixed exchange rates.

The evidence of the more recent period, particularly from the mid-1960s to the present, suggests that typically it is possible to predict the level of year-ahead GNP for a single country only to within 1 to 1½ percentage points. (The question of the accuracy of forecasts is taken up in chapter 6.) Furthermore, even for an economy as relatively insulated and well studied as the United States, the experience so far is that it is probably not possible to predict accurately more than about half the turning points in the level of activity. In other countries an even lower proportion may have to be accepted. This suggests that it never has been practicable, at any time over the post War period, to attempt to eliminate all the fluctuations in the level of activity in OECD economies. On the other hand, given the prevailing level of forecasting accuracy, it may well have been that policy was able to reduce, on average, the size of the fluctuations in the economy.

Thus it is useful to make a distinction, not always clearly made in the literature, whether of the time or more recently, between 'fine tuning' and 'stabilization policy'. To clarify this issue, fine tuning (which as defined was seldom an objective of policy but nevertheless served to make critical points in the literature) is taken here to mean an attempt to reduce *in each and every year* the deviation of the level of activity from its trend. Stabilization policy (which by contrast was fairly generally pursued) is taken to be the attempt to reduce the *average* deviation of activity from its trend *over a run of at least several years*, although not necessarily in every single year. In terms of these definitions, it is conceptually possible for policy to have been destabilizing in some individual years, while nevertheless to have been stabilizing over the cycle taken as a whole.

The degree of commitment to stabilization policy as defined differed between countries. Those most committed were probably the United Kingdom, France, Austria, Australia, Finland, New Zealand, Norway and Sweden. Most other countries were not so committed, but nevertheless took measures on occasion to stabilize activity.

Detailed studies of the effectiveness of stabilization policy are not particularly numerous, and certainly less so than the number of pronouncements that have been made on the effectiveness or otherwise of the policy. Very likely the relative paucity of careful investigations reflects the intrinsic difficulty of reaching a definitive empirically-based conclusion on the issue. Initially the debate was most active in the United Kingdom, perhaps reflecting the fact that this was one of the first countries to enter into an explicit full-employment commitment, immediately after the second World War.[10] It is worthwhile examining with some care the early studies made of that economy, in part because it has become apparent over recent years that judgements reached about the success or failure of stabilization policy depend importantly upon the methods used. And, more generally, the methods pioneered in the study of that economy were later taken over into the study of other economies.

Output stabilization policy – the evidence

The first major study of the effectiveness of stabilization policy in the United Kingdom, and certainly the most influential, even up to the present day, was by Dow (1964) for the period 1948 to 1960. His basic method was to estimate for each year the impact of fiscal policy changes on real total final expenditure. On the basis of these estimates Dow, in an oft-quoted passage, concluded that 'The major fluctuations in the rate of growth in demand in the years after 1952 were ... chiefly due to government policy. This was not the intended effect; in each phase, it must be supposed, policy went further than intended, as in turn did the correction of these effects. As far as internal effects are concerned then, *budgetary and monetary policy failed to be stabilizing, and must on the contrary be regarded as having been positively destabilizing*' (emphasis added).[11]

In terms of the definitions proposed above, it is clear that Dow was appraising the success of fine tuning, rather than stabilization policy. The conclusion that fiscal policy was 'positively destabilizing' was cautiously supported by Prest (1968), whose main evidence (working with the same implicit definition, for the period 1955 to 1966) was a modest negative correlation between the deviations from trend of a quarterly series of public expenditure on goods and services and an index of capacity utilization.[12] Writing at much the same time, and also looking at matters in essentially a year-by-year fine-tuning sense, Musgrave and Musgrave (1968) concluded that discretionary changes in central government taxes, which were the main fiscal mechanism for achieving stabilization objectives in the United Kingdom, were over the period 1950-66 '... such as to be perversely related to current growth rates, thus tending to emphasize the growth cycles'.[13]

But these judgements did not go unchallenged. One criticism was that, by considering only fiscal policy, and not also monetary policy, these studies did not examine the effects of aggregate demand policy as a whole. Another was that they paid too little attention to the impact on the economy of fluctuations in exports resulting from changing levels of world trade. Neither of these seems to have been a particularly serious omission over the period in question.[14] The more serious criticism was that the conclusions of Dow, the Musgraves and Prest were reached only on the basis of the direction of year-to-year changes in the policy variables, and that this was not the appropriate way to approach the policy-assessment issue. Thus Little (1962), implicitly making the sort of distinction proposed above, argued that Dow's results did not mean that monetary and fiscal policy was positively destabilizing in the sense that the actual fluctuations were greater overall than would have occurred under some 'neutral' policy held unchanged throughout the period. Essentially the same point was made by Worswick (1971) in relation to the findings of Prest and the Musgraves.[15] And Bristow (1968), concentrating on the effects of changes in taxation, concluded that certain individual changes may well have been destabilizing – thereby supporting Dow - but that nevertheless over the period 1948 to 1960 as a whole tax changes 'had a stabilizing effect'.[16]

Despite this intensive interest in the issue, however, a fundamental problem is that the apparatus necessary to examine the question in the appropriate way does not exist for the 1950s and 1960s. As relatively recently as 1969, for example, Hansen (1969) writing about OECD countries in general, observed that '... if sufficiently detailed well-specified and quantified models ... were available the problem of estimating the effects of budgetary policy would be reduced to simulating the interventions made during the period under survey. However such models do not exist ... even for the United States they do not give an answer to all fiscal policy problems of the period, and for ... other countries model building is much less well developed'.[17]

Accordingly, in order to examine the effects of fiscal policy in a number of countries – Belgium, France, Germany, Italy, Sweden, the United Kingdom and the United States – Hansen built his own model. The approach[18] was to attach instrument-specific multipliers to the changes (discretionary, automatic and total) of various expenditure items, thereby purging the annual series of actual GNP for the changes that were attributable to changes in policy. The amplitude of this so-called 'pure' series was then compared with the amplitude of the actual series. A summary statistic measured the success or failure of stabilization policy. A figure of 100 indicated perfect stabilization: actual GNP lay on a straight trend line. The further the figure is below 100, the more imperfect the stabilization was. At a value of 0, there had been no stabilizing effect whatever over the period as a whole, and at negative values the budget had been destabilizing.

While there are conceptual limitations to Hansen's approach, as indeed there are with any attempt of this sort, it was a considerable advance on earlier methods, explicitly meeting the Little point that it was appropriate to assess the degree of stabilization not year-by-year, but over a run of several years. Furthermore, because a uniform method was applied to each of seven countries, using standardized national accounts data, the study made cross-country comparison much more possible.

Hansen found that the six countries studied fell into three distinct groups. The United Kingdom was unique in being the only country having on balance destabilized the level of activity through the budget, both through discretionary measures and those changes occurring automatically. (This conclusion was later challenged, however, as is discussed below.)

Policy in France and Italy was considered to have destabilized the economy through discretionary measures, but the effects of the automatic stabilizers were sufficiently strong that the net effect was nevertheless a certain stabilization. In the third group, Belgium, Germany, Sweden and the United States, both discretionary measures and automatic effects were considered to have stabilized the economy, albeit to very different degrees.

An alternative method of analysing the effects of stabilization policy is to measure the degree of stabilization in relation to estimated levels of potential (or full capacity) output, rather than the trend of actual output. This procedure was adopted by Snyder (1970) for three countries – Sweden, the United Kingdom and the United States. The results were, in Snyder's judgement, 'strikingly different'. For Sweden, Snyder calculated that 'The total impact of budget changes ... eliminated nearly two thirds of the gap between the pure cycle and potential GNP and helped create a level of demand that was virtually identical with potential output during a majority of the years'. For the United Kingdom, Snyder also found that stabilization performance when assessed in relation to the path of potential output was better than when considered in relation to actual GNP: 'The United Kingdom's performance also is improved, from a generally destabilizing pattern to one where about one-quarter of the potential stabilization was achieved.'[19] The assessment of the performance of the United States was rather different. While the annual budget impacts 'unquestionably' helped to damp fluctuations of actual GNP, they did not prevent the economy from slipping below 95 per cent of its estimated full employment potential during half of the years. Hence the amount of stabilization achieved relative to potential output was estimated as a mere 17 per cent.

More recently Boltho (1981), taking the examination of the United Kingdom yet one stage further, has pointed out that Hansen's conclusion was based on a relatively wide definition of the public sector, which includes investment by public corporations. Boltho shows that if this expenditure, which was not used in Britain as an instrument of stabilization policy, is excluded from the measure of fiscal stance, demand management in the United Kingdom over the 1955-65 period can be assessed as having been marginally stabilizing. Interestingly, Boltho reaches the same conclusion for the later period 1966-71, and hence for the period 1955-71 as a whole. Thus by adopting the standard definition of 'general government' as suggested by Boltho, or by taking potential rather than actual output as the reference path using the method of Snyder, it is possible to argue that fiscal policy was at least moderately stabilizing of output, even in the United Kingdom.

The most recent estimates of the success of policy in stabilizing

Table 2.2   *Effects of fiscal policy on GNP*

(stabilization of GNP growth around trend or potential)

	percentage stabilization achieved by general government				
	including public enterprises	Excluding public enterprises			
	(around trend)	(around trend)	(around potential)		
	1955–65	1955–65	1955–65	1966–71	1955–71
France[a]	12[b]	2[b]	53	39	50
Germany	..	35	52	8	27
Italy[a]	31	42	35	17	26
U.K.	−11	7	18	20	18
Spain[a]	..	..	..	31[c]	40[d]
Belgium	31	29	32	..	..
Netherlands	..	..	..	11	23[c]
Sweden	31	33	45	29	40

[a] Measured on non-agricultural GNP
[b] 1958-65
[c] 1966-70
[d] 1963-79
[e] 1962-71
Source: Boltho (1982).

GNP, in relation either to its trend or to potential and both including and excluding public enterprises, are given for European countries in Boltho (1982) – see Table 2.2.

Conclusions

Any assessment of the degree of success of stabilization policy has to be cautious, for there are numerous difficulties, both conceptual and empirical. First, there is the problem of defining what is meant by 'stabilization policy'. It has been argued that the most helpful definition is the reduction of the deviation of output from its trend over a run of several years, the alternative concept of 'fine tuning' – the reduction of the deviation of output from its trend in each and every year – being an inappropriately narrow definition, and not in reasonable accord with what most governments realistically hoped to achieve. Second, there are innumerable problems in determining what the level of activity would have been had other policies been pursued. Third, there is the problem that, while many countries had the broad objective of stabilizing the level of activity, this was of course not the only objective. Other immediate short-term concerns included variously an appropriate balance of payments (however defined), and a satisfactory inflation performance. Furthermore, these objectives at times conflicted.

Nevertheless, the broad conclusion seems to be that in a number of major countries fiscal policy in the 1950s and 1960s was stabilizing, by an amount which varied from modest in some countries to near total in others. Indeed, Heller *et al.* (1968) were able to reach the judgement that 'Governments have, to a large extent, succeeded in subduing or overcoming the rhythmic fluctuations which used to be called the trade cycle. This makes it increasingly appropriate to speak of "stabilization" or "conjunctural" rather than "counter-cyclical" policy'.[20]

Certainly it is the case that, taking the majority of OECD countries together, the fluctuations in the (growth of the) level of activity were markedly smaller after World War II than they had been ever since national accounts or other measures of the level of activity began to be kept (Chart 2.1).

There is a further respect in which stabilization policy may have contributed significantly to the relative smoothness of activity in the 1950s and 1960s, and indeed to have constituted a 'growth policy'. The argument, advanced notably by Matthews (1968), is that, because economic agents in general, and entrepreneurs in particular, believed that policy-makers had it within their power to control the level of activity fairly precisely, and would indeed exercise their power to that end, the private sector invested on the scale, and with the smoothness, that steadily-growing high employment levels of demand would warrant. In so doing, the argument runs, they thereby *caused* the level of activity to be relatively stable. There may well be truth in this. Certainly, relative to earlier decades and, indeed, relative to the decade of the 1970s, the general mood in the 1950s and 1960s would seem to have been optimism about the technical ability of governments to shape countries' overall economic destinies. And equally certainly there was in many of them a strong political commitment to do so. But the extent to which such belief was in fact self-fulfilling is practically impossible to test.

The conclusion that for the decades of the 1950s and 1960s the policy of stabilizing output was, in a number of major OECD countries, apparently quite successful is, however, subject to an important caveat. While it is probably impossible to be sure, it seems quite likely that the very success of output stabilization policy in securing not only relatively stable activity, but also a high average level of activity in relation to productive potential, may have slowly but steadily built up an inflation problem which was to manifest itself fully only in the decade of the 1970s. To the extent that that was so, stabilization policy may have been less, perhaps significantly less, successful when judged over a period of several decades than appears the case when it is considered cycle by cycle.

Policy-makers in the 1970s frequently found inflation the most pressing problem of all, to the point where the term 'stabilization policy' took on a totally different meaning in some countries, namely the reduction of inflation. Furthermore, balance of

Chart 2.1 Year-to-year GDP growth of 16 economies

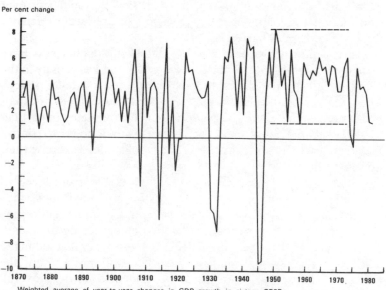

Per cent change

Weighted average of year-to-year changes in GDP growth in sixteen OECD economies: Australia, Austria, Belgium, Canada, Denmark, Finland, France, Germany, Italy, Japan, Netherlands, Norway, Sweden, Switzerland, United Kingdom, United States.

Source: Maddison (1982).

payments problems were acute in a number of countries at various times throughout the 1970s, and public sector deficits also became a growing problem. Faced with this multiplicity of problems, policy-makers found themselves seriously short of instruments, so that monetary and fiscal policy had to be directed forcibly to problems other than stabilization of the level of activity. And the achievement of other policy goals, most notably the reduction of inflation, frequently conflicted directly with the aim of stabilizing output.

Hence any belief that there may have been by the end of the 1960s that stabilization policy would be able to deal with virtually any disturbances to which individual economies, or the OECD economy as a whole, were likely to be subjected was almost certainly misplaced. The question of what kind of policy it proved feasible to make over the decade of the 1970s is addressed in the next chapter.

3 Policy successes and failures since the early 1970s

Summary

Whereas many governments were able to direct policy during the 1950s and 1960s towards the stabilization of output, the problems throughout the 1970s were more numerous, and the aims of policy more diverse. Important additional or enhanced concerns included the reduction of domestically-generated inflation, reducing or eliminating current account deficits on the balance of payments, preventing currency depreciation and hence an acceleration of imported inflation, and reducing the size of public sector deficits. These problems had become larger in most countries individually but also for the OECD countries as a group. Furthermore, the exchange rate regime had changed to one of much greater flexibility. Because policy was directed variously at the different objectives, with degrees of emphasis that differed from country to country and from time to time, it is difficult to make even the sort of tentative technical assessment of the effectiveness of policy that was made in chapter 2 for stabilization policy in the 1950s and 1960s.

One reasonably clear lesson of the period is that inflation can relatively easily reach a rate where its reduction necessarily becomes the prime aim of policy. There is little evidence that such reduction can be achieved in most countries without a substantial loss of output.

Introduction

Compared with the two earlier decades, the 1970s were an extraordinary period. The decade as a whole presented problems for economic policy-making that were markedly more difficult than those which had gone before.

The decade began with a brief growth recession, which quickly gave place to an exceptionally rapid boom. Domestically-generated inflation accelerated, and was capped in 1973 by a major commodity price boom. On the heels of this came a quadrupling of the price of oil, with sympathetic increases in the prices of other fuels. The OECD economy went into massive deficit on the current account of the balance of payments. Recession followed, accompanied – most atypically – by accelerating inflation. Recovery began in 1975 and lasted in hesitant fashion for several years, but before it was consolidated there was a second oil shock, nearly as large as the first. This again put the OECD current account into substantial deficit, boosted inflation anew, and again was followed by recession, which saw the decade out. Indeed, this recession was to prove longer-lasting than the one that followed the first oil shock.

Taking the decade as a whole, the scale of problems confronting policy-makers was markedly greater than before. The system of pegged exchange rates was abandoned. For OECD countries as a whole, unemployment was significantly higher on average than in earlier cycles, yet inflation was also much higher. The current account of the balance of payments was on average in large deficit over the ten-year period, with very substantial deficits in some years, a novel development. And public sector accounts moved sharply into deficit, also a new phenomenon.

The problem of policy-making was compounded by a marked increase in uncertainty about how economies were working. Forecasting errors became large in the early 1970s, generally larger than at any time since the end of the Second World War and, in countries which had started forecasting after the mid-1950s, the largest ever – this matter is considered in detail in chapter 6. Furthermore, the coexistence of high unemployment and rapid inflation was unique. Against this background, alternative and at times quite radical theories began to be propounded about how economies function. And because of the newness of many facets of the underlying situation, there were insufficient historical data to make it possible to establish which of the theories were the more likely to be correct. Over this decade there was much experimentation, and much was learned.

This chapter considers first the major events in the decade, and the major policy responses to them. It is difficult in many instances to establish precisely what the underlying aims of policy were, but an attempt is made to evaluate, in the light of actual performance, how successful policy may have been in stabilizing output, reducing inflation, and containing current account and public sector deficits.

The change of international regime

One of the key policy features of the period is that the international system was operating under new rules – or, closer to the truth, in the absence of the old rules, the new ones not yet being clear.

First, the dollar was devalued. This was the centrepiece of the Smithsonian realignment of end-1971 (an episode discussed in detail in chapter 12). However, the United States continued to run a huge overall payments deficit; more generally, the volume of highly mobile capital in the world was growing fast; and inflation and inter-country differences in inflation had increased. The political will to maintain a fixed-rate system was waning, with many thinking that the system conferred undue seignorage advantages on the United States while that country was ultimately no longer prepared to accept the obligations of the system either. Since March 1973, the major currencies have floated, though the authorities of most countries have on occasion intervened heavily in the exchange markets in an attempt to influence rates. More recently, a group of European countries have sought to maintain a block of fixed parities among themselves.

Few developments in economic history have been as warmly welcomed by the economics profession as the move to flexible exchange rates. Many policy-makers seem at the time to have shared the profession's enthusiasm, feeling that they were being liberated from what had become a serious constraint on their freedom of policy manoeuvre – the need to defend a particular exchange rate. After a decade of experience of floating rates, the centre of gravity of opinion on the issue has become a good deal more negative – perhaps unduly so. While the regime of floating rates has not resulted in the degree of national policy autonomy that had been hoped for, it is nevertheless difficult to envisage any other system accommodating at all satisfactorily the shocks and inter-national differences of economic policy and performance that have characterized the last ten years.

Without attempting an assessment of the floating system, two particular points are relevant here. The first is that in the final years of the fixed rate system, massive intervention was carried out in defence of the dollar, only partly sterilized and therefore entailing a big boost to the money stock for countries other than the United States. Meanwhile, money creation in the United States accelerated, so that overall the combined money stock of the seven major OECD countries (M2) rose 36 per cent between 1970 and 1972. This was no doubt an important ingredient in the inflationary boom of 1972-73.

The second point is that in the early years of floating rates some countries were slower than others to realise that although flexible rates freed monetary authorities from some obligations, they imposed others. With the fixed exchange rate no longer there as an 'anchor' for the nominal values in the economy, an alternative had to be found. Monetary autonomy, now available, had to be used. Germany and Switzerland did so almost immediately, from 1973 onwards. But France, Italy and the United Kingdom did not follow non-accommodating monetary policies until some years later, when forced to by the rude disciplines of the financial markets.

The early 1970s: inflation and recession

As the OECD world entered the 1970s inflation was accelerating. Some of this acceleration was domestically-generated, and had been taking place for at least five years. And that it might be developing into a potentially serious problem had already been recognized. A 1970 OECD report, for example, had noted that 'The general price level will have risen this year by at least 5 per cent in most OECD countries; this is more than double the rate in the early 1960s. And, for the first time in a decade, prices in world trade have been rising as fast as the general domestic price level. ... Some signs of a slowdown in price rises are now emerging and a more significant improvement is expected over the next twelve months. But there are also disquieting signs that the problem of inflation may have got worse in the sense that, where traditional restrictive policies have been applied, the effect on prices has been less rapid and less long-lasting than in the past. Several European countries have experienced something like a "wage explosion"; and in the United States and a number of other countries it is an open question whether, when a normal growth is resumed after a period of cooling off, prices may not accelerate again more quickly than expected.'[1]

That is in fact what happened, but the scale was not predicted, even by the most pessimistic observers. The OECD economy, after modest (3.3 per cent) GNP growth in 1970, picked up progressively; the growth rate for 1973 was 6 per cent, and between mid-1972 and mid-1973 growth was at the extremely vigorous rate of over 7 per cent. Virtually all OECD countries shared in this. The rapid monetary expansion was one contributing factor. Another was a move towards fiscal expansion. For the seven major countries considered as a group the fiscal swing over the three years 1971 to 1973 was about 1 percentage point of their combined GNP (Table 3.1). At first OECD inflation slowed slightly. It fell in 1971 to 5.3 per cent, and further in 1972, to 4.7 per cent, being helped by a near 8 per cent growth of productivity – GDP per person employed – over the two year period, as well as (temporarily) by wage and price controls in the United States. The OECD GNP deflator grew throughout 1971 and 1972 at an essentially unchanged rate – between 5¾ and 6 per cent per year. But in 1973 inflation accelerated sharply, to 7.8 per cent, and in 1974 it accelerated yet further, to reach 13.4 per cent for the year as a whole. This acceleration was caused by an acceleration both in the growth of the prices of primary commodities (Chart 3.1) and oil, and then in the growth of wages and hence unit labour costs.

There is a fairly general consensus that the first part of this commodity price rise was a straightforward reflection of the high level of demand in the OECD economy as a whole, and of supply interruptions and low stock levels in particular markets.[2] However, the second phase of the commodity price boom, from about the end of the first quarter of 1973, and lasting for about three quarters, would seem to have been due in large part to speculation – in the sense of purchase for purposes other than reasonably-immediate final use – rather than to the normal interaction of supply and demand. There are various reasons for believing this. First, OECD industrial production weakened sharply in early 1973. Under these circumstances the boom in primary commodity prices would, on past relationships, have reversed almost immediately. But this did not happen (Chart 3.1). Instead commodity prices climbed much further, this rise continuing until March 1974, and thereafter they fell back only slowly, despite the recession into which the OECD economy had by then fallen.

The second reason for considering speculation to have been important in this second phase of the commodity price boom was a substantial increase in the volume of movement trading – the taking of market positions on the basis of following price movements,

Table 3.1 *Discretionary changes in general government financial balances*
A negative number indicates an increase in the (cyclically adjusted) budget deficit, and hence a stimulus to aggregate demand. (Percent of potential GDP/GNP)

Year	United States	Japan	Germany	France	United Kingdom	Italy	Canada	Seven major countries
1971	−0.5	−0.2	−0.1	−0.2	−1.4	−1.5	−1.3	−0.6
1972	0.5	−1.1	0.2	−0.3	−2.4	−1.7	−0.3	−0.2
1973	−0.2	−0.3	1.3	0.0	−2.8	0.1	0.4	−0.2
1974	0.9	0.4	−1.8	0.3	−0.1	0.2	0.9	0.4
1975	−1.6	−2.6	−2.9	−1.1	0.5	−2.0	−3.5	−1.8
1976	1.3	−1.0	1.2	0.6	−0.2	1.7	0.4	0.7
1977	0.2	−0.2	0.9	−0.4	1.7	1.1	−0.2	0.3
1978	0.3	−1.8	−0.4	−1.5	−2.1	−1.8	−0.7	−0.6
1979	0.3	0.6	−0.6	0.9	0.6	−0.6	1.3	0.3
1980	−0.5	0.2	−0.2	1.6	2.1	1.1	−0.1	0.1
1981	0.9	0.6	0.1	−1.0	2.9	−3.4	1.2	0.6
1982	−1.3	0.7	1.5	−0.4	1.5	0.0	−0.7	−0.3
1983	−0.5	0.6	1.4	−0.1	−1.7	2.3	−0.7	−0.1

Source: Price and Muller (1984).

rather than on the basis of specific supply and demand considerations. There is some evidence that the increase in movement trading was financed by traders switching funds out of equities into commodity markets.[3]

Following this sharp rise in commodity prices came the quadrupling of the price of internationally-traded oil in late 1973. In this inflationary environment of sharply rising non-oil commodity prices and then oil prices, the growth of wage settlements began to accelerate sharply in most countries, resulting in a marked increase in OECD-generated inflation – as measured by the growth of the GNP deflator, inflation accelerated in 1973 in every OECD country other than the United Kingdom, Switzerland and New Zealand. The most important development from the point of view of overall price stability was an acceleration of 1½ percentage points in the United States. And this acceleration continued in 1974 in nearly all OECD countries, with a further, particularly important, acceleration of nearly 3 percentage points in the United States. The rate of increase of the GNP deflator for the OECD area as a whole increased by 4 percentage points.

Thus 1974 was a very odd year. The OECD economy was in recession, yet at the onset of that recession non-oil commodity

Chart 3.1 Cyclical fluctuations in industrial production and commodity prices

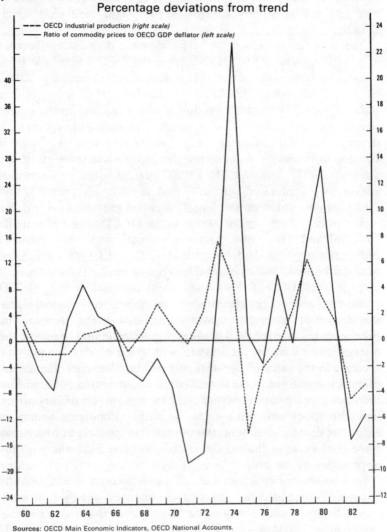

Percentage deviations from trend

Sources: OECD Main Economic Indicators, OECD National Accounts.

prices were rising very fast, and throughout oil prices and wage rates were rising sharply. Of itself the oil price rise probably directly raised the OECD general price level by 2 percentage points relative to what it would have been otherwise: and over the next few years the induced wage/price spiral was to multiply this figure several-fold. The overall OECD inflation rate that year, as measured by the growth of the consumer price index, was an astonishing 13.4 per cent, considerably higher even than during the Korean war period, and very much higher than anything that had been seen subsequently.

The oil price increase also had important demand and output effects. It transferred to OPEC, from the OECD area and from non-oil developing countries, an amount of real income equivalent to about 2 per cent of OECD GNP – about $150 billion per year in today's prices. This transfer reduced world demand to the extent that OPEC had, at first, a lower marginal propensity to spend than did the OECD consumers and companies, and the non-oil developing countries, from whom this income was transferred. By the end of 1977, however, the OPEC current surplus – but not of course its accumulated surplus – had virtually disappeared, and OPEC import volumes had largely stopped growing (Table 3.2).

The price of fuels produced within the OECD area – principally coal, oil and gas – also rose, in sympathy with the price of internationally-traded oil, but with a lag. The OECD area produced at that time about half of its total fuel needs, so that something over 1 per cent of OECD GNP was potentially transferable from OECD consumers and energy-consuming enterprises to the energy-producing part of the corporate sector, including public utilities. The precise magnitude for each country depended upon the size of the energy sector and on the degree and speed of this sympathetic increase in the price of domestically-produced energy. Hence the effect was much greater in some OECD countries than others. This increment to corporate income, like that of the OPEC countries, was also spent only with a lag, a further important source of short-run demand deflation, the potential magnitude of which may have been close to that of the OPEC surplus. This was not fully appreciated at the time.

In a number of countries the main policy concern was with the expected demand-deflationary consequences of this process. Accordingly a number of governments shifted the stance of fiscal policy in an expansionary direction – among the biggest OECD economies Germany (which had tightened its stance in 1973 in response to the boom conditions in that year) expanded in 1974, and the United States, Japan, France, Italy, Canada and several of the Scandinavian countries boosted demand in 1975. Taking the major seven countries as a group, the discretionary shift of fiscal policy towards expansion in 1975 was nearly 2 per cent of their combined

Table 3.2 *OPEC import volume and current balance*

	1974	1975	1976	1977	1978
Import volume growth, per cent	40	36	15	14½	4
Current balance, $ billion	60	27	37	29	5

Source: OECD.

GNP. Monetary policy was accommodating, with even nominal interest rates falling over the 1974/75 period in some countries: monetary policy thus apparently broadly accommodated both the expansionary swing in fiscal policy and the increase in the general price level.

In the environment created by these forces, OECD GNP fell slightly through 1974, at annual rates of ½ per cent in the first half and about 1 per cent in the second, and then fell very sharply in the first half of 1975, at an annual rate of about 3 per cent. This was mainly the result of a sharp, and unpredicted, collapse in private non-residential investment and a dramatic, and also unexpected, reduction of inventories (Table 3.3).

Throughout this period consumers' expenditure too was volatile and difficult to forecast correctly; even after the event, some of the fluctuations in the proportion of income that was spent are hard to account for. While less volatile than investment and stockbuilding, consumption accounts for about 60 per cent of total expenditure in the OECD area as a whole, so that its fluctuations are quantitatively important. The most important effects of the numerous jumps in the personal saving ratio were to reduce OECD consumption by about 1¼ per cent in 1973 and about ½ a per cent in 1975.

Towards the end of 1975 the OECD economy came out of recession. The OPEC current surplus, though still large, was falling. Inflation was slowing, and the impact of budgetary changes was strongly expansionary. After a sharp fall in the first half of the year, OECD GNP grew 5 per cent at an annual rate in the second half of 1975 and at a 6½ per cent annual rate in the first half of 1976. This was led by a sharp rebuilding of stocks and was sustained by consumption which, as a result of a significant and unexpectedly large fall in the saving ratio, grew in 1976 about 2 percentage points faster than income. Ultimately, private fixed investment picked up

Table 3.3   *Arithmetic contributions[a] to change in real GNP in seven major OECD countries*
Seasonally-adjusted annual rates

	1974		1975
	I	II	I
Private non-residential investment[b]	−¾	−1¼	−1½
Change in stockbuilding[b]	1	−1½	−3½
Memorandum item: change in GNP	−½	−1	−3

[a]   Direct effects only, i.e. excluding multiplier effects.
[b]   Expressed as a percentage of GNP in the previous period, at annual rate.
Source: OECD.

also. Thereafter OECD spending behaviour became both more stable and more predictable. The rapid growth of early 1976 was not maintained, however, and GNP in Europe and Japan remained well short of potential.

Evaluating this policy response

Although the OECD economy started to recover in 1975, four main problems for policy persisted. First, the rate of recovery was never sufficient to reduce unemployment significantly in the majority of OECD countries. Taking the OECD area as a whole, unemployment rose from 3¼ per cent in 1973 to 5½ per cent in 1975 and was still 5½ per cent in 1978. Second, while the large combined current account deficit of the OECD area – in large part the counterpart of OPEC's substantial surplus – did decline reasonably quickly, it nevertheless became very unevenly distributed across OECD countries, partly as a result of differential rates of domestic demand growth, partly as a result of differential rates of inflation and hence international price competitiveness, and partly because of different rates of supply-side adaptation to changed patterns of demand. Third, the combination, in many countries, of a large oil-induced deficit on the current account of the balance of payments, and the large fall in private sector investment and stockbuilding, meant that activity could be sustained and expanded only if the public sector dis-saved – went into deficit – on a substantial scale. This the authorities in a number of countries were at the time willing to do (Table 3.4).

Table 3.4 *General government net lending*[a]
(Per cent of GNP/GDP)

	1971	1973	1975	1977	1979
United States	−1.7	0.5	−4.2	−0.9	0.6
Japan	1.4	0.5	−2.7	−3.8	−4.8
Germany	−0.2	1.2	−5.7	−2.4	−2.7
France	0.7	0.9	−2.2	−0.8	−0.7
United Kingdom	1.5	−2.7	−4.5	−3.1	−3.1
Italy	−7.1	−8.5	−11.7	−8.0	−9.3
Canada	0.1	1.0	−2.4	−2.6	−2.0
Average, seven countries[b]	−0.8	−0.1	−4.3	−2.2	−1.7

[a] A minus sign indicates dis-saving.
[b] 1981 GNP/GDP weights and exchange rates.
Source: OECD.

The fourth problem was inflation which, while declining substantially from its peak rate of some 13½ per cent for the OECD area in 1974 was, at nearly 10 per cent in 1979, still higher than it had been in any previous period since the Korean war. Concern over inflation had two dimensions: the apparent increasing proneness of the OECD economy to inflation, and concern over the declining share of national income accruing as profit.

For reasons that have not been completely satisfactorily explained, many firms in the period following the 1973/74 oil price rise, when capacity utilization rates were still quite high, did not pass their higher fuel and wage costs fully into prices. Profitability suffered considerably, and cash flow positions deteriorated, these being important factors behind the dramatic decline of investment and stockbuilding in 1974 and 1975. The extent of this phenomenon can be indicated by the so-called 'real labour cost gap', a measure which is obtained by taking the changes in the ratio of real total compensation per head of dependent employment to real national income per person employed. The individual figures shown in Table 3.5, being ratios of index numbers, have no absolute significance: but changes over the period illustrate the extent to which profits suffered after 1973. In retrospect, most observers seem to agree that the failure to ensure that the increase in energy prices was fully passed on to consumers, with the result that profit shares were eroded, was a regrettable feature of the period following the first large oil price rise.

Table 3.5   *Real labour costs[a] relative to real national income*
(indices, 1972 = 100)

	1973	1974	1975	1976
United States	99.7	100.8	100.1	100.1
Japan	103.9	110.4	113.2	111.7
Germany	101.5	105.2	104.1	101.7
France	101.3	105.0	109.5	109.8
United Kingdom	101.1	107.0	112.0	106.7
Italy	101.5	102.4	107.2	104.9
Canada	98.4	100.5	105.2	106.7
Average, seven countries[b]	100.9	103.9	105.1	104.2

[a]   Change in real total compensation per employee divided by real
     national income per employed person, national accounts basis.
[b]   1981 GNP/GDP weights and exchange rates.
Source: OECD. For further information, and the basic data, see *OECD
     Economic Outlook* 32, December 1982, Table 21 page 45.

An incomplete recovery

Between 1975 and 1978 fiscal policy in the seven major countries
taken as a group was broadly neutral, although a number of
countries, generally those which earlier had supported demand,
tightened policy (Table 3.1) when downward pressures re-emerged
on exchange rates, threatening to boost inflation. In France, after a
dash for growth in 1975-76, the 'Barre Plan' imposed tighter
budgetary and monetary norms on the economy. In Italy and the
United Kingdom, runs on their currencies in 1976 prompted sharp
rises in interest rates, quantitative credit restrictions, and fiscal
tightening.

Overall, the growth rate in the 1975 to 1978 period looks, in
retrospect, reasonably satisfactory. At the time, however, many
considered it disappointing for a recovery period. Unemployment,
outside the United States, was hardly declining. Above all, the
recovery was uneven as between different countries. The United
States economy was growing relatively rapidly, and its current
account steadily deteriorating. Many of the medium and smaller-
sized European economies felt constrained in their desire to see
more rapid growth by their external positions. Hence there was a
widespread desire that Germany and Japan, two countries in

current surplus and with low inflation, should adopt an actively expansionary policy. An international package of measures was finally put together at the 1978 Summit of Heads of State and Government in Bonn, an episode discussed in chapter 12. But before there was a chance to see whether recovery would ultimately become self-sustaining, the OECD economy was hit by the second oil shock.

The 1979/80 oil price rise – direct effects and policy responses

The second oil price rise, equivalent, like its predecessor, to some 2 per cent of OECD GNP, struck before OECD economies had fully recovered from the first. Inflation re-accelerated, current account deficits increased, public sector deficits swelled, and unemployment rose yet further. Taken together, these presented a greater problem for policy in nearly all economies than in any previous post-war cycle – see the 'diamonds' in Chart 3.2, which show, for each of the three or four post-war cycles, average values for each of the twelve countries for which comparable data are available. The larger the diamond, the greater the values of these variables and hence the greater the overall policy problem.

Faced with these four major problems, the policy imperatives this second time round were judged rather differently. Rather than seeking to support demand in the short run, the over-riding concern, felt by virtually all OECD governments, was to contain the inflationary impulse and to prevent, through a rapid adjustment of real wages, the price shock becoming built into the domestic wage/price spiral. Part of the concern was over inflation *per se*, but perhaps the more important part of the concern was to prevent wages rising at the expense of profits. It was hoped to maintain and, if possible, increase profitability, in order to lay the foundations for a high and sustained level of investment, needed if the upswing (when it came) was to prove self-sustaining.

There was also considerable concern over budget deficits, partly because of their perceived large and growing structural elements, partly because of a fear that their financing might crowd out productive investment, and partly because the composition of public expenditure, and the growing share of the public sector in general, were considered to be obstacles to future growth.

Chart 3.2 Macroeconomic imbalances
Percentages, annual averages

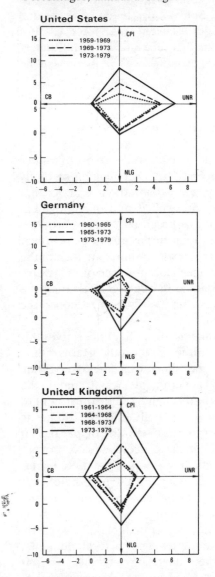

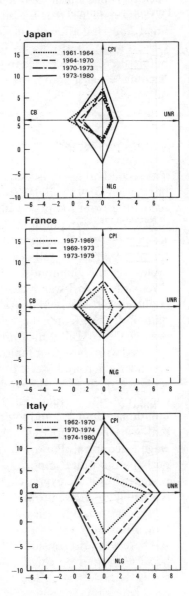

Note: The four axes represent:
CPI: Percentage increase in consumer prices, annual rate;
NLG: Net lending of general government, expressed as a percentage of GNP/GDP;
CB: Current external balance expressed as a percentage of GNP/GDP;
UNR: Rate of unemployment.

Macroeconomic imbalances (cont.)
Percentages, annual averages

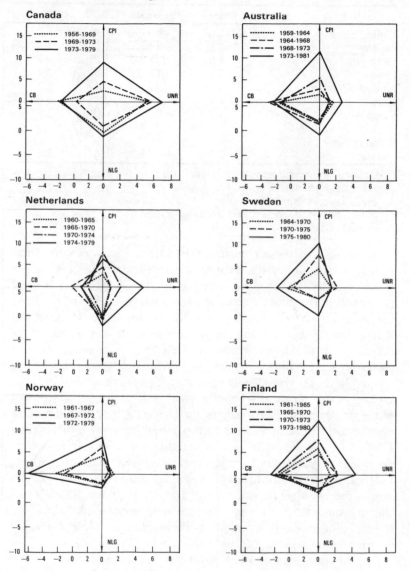

Note: The four axes represent:
CPI: Percentage increase in consumer prices, annual rate;
NLG: Net lending of general government, expressed as a percentage of GNP/GDP;
CB: Current external balance expressed as a percentage of GNP/GDP;
UNR: Rate of unemployment.

Table 3.6   *Real interest rates* [a]
Averages of monthly data

	1965–72	1973–75	1976–79	1980–82[b]
United States	1.6	−2.0	−0.2	2.0
Japan	2.6	−6.1	1.5	3.3
Germany	4.0	2.8	3.0	3.7
France	3.1	−0.8	1.0	2.4
United Kingdom	3.4	−1.9	0.1	1.7
Italy	4.1	−5.7	−1.4	0.9
Canada	3.0	−1.3	0.9	2.8
Average, seven counties[c]	2.5	−2.3	0.6	2.4

[a]   Defined as average long term interest rates minus the average annual percentage change in consumer prices.
[b]   1982, January-November only.
[c]   1981 GNP/GDP weights and exchange rates.
Source: OECD.

In the light of these concerns OECD governments shifted the stance of fiscal policy significantly towards restriction. Taking the three years to 1982 together, the cumulative swing towards fiscal restriction of the major 7 economies as a whole amounted to about ½ per cent of their combined GNP (Table 3.1). Thus to the deflationary impact of the oil price rise itself was added extra deflation by the fiscal action of OECD governments. But in addition, and in contrast to the post-1973 period, monetary policy was to play an important restrictive role. Toward the end of 1979 the United States changed its methods of monetary control and set more strictly-adhered-to targets for the growth of the monetary aggregates. Taken in relation to the prevailing growth of nominal GNP, this represented a significant tightening of monetary policy, resulting in volatile and, on average, high real rates of interest, defined, somewhat arbitrarily, as average long-term interest rates minus the average growth rate of consumer prices. These rates quickly spread to other countries which, concerned to prevent depreciation-induced inflation, swiftly tightened their monetary policies too in an effort to limit this effect (Table 3.6).

The oil price rise took place in several steps in the course of 1979, and may have exerted its main contractionary effect on OECD GNP in 1980. The effect was beginning to taper off in 1981, as the OECD's terms of trade stabilized and OPEC import volumes

Table 3.7 *Estimates of main forces acting on the OECD economy*
Per cent contribution to change in real GNP

	1978	1979	1980	1981	1982
Oil	0	−½	−2 ¼	−½	0
Fiscal policy	½	−½	−½	−1 ½	−½
Monetary policy	0	0	0	−½	−¾
Memorandum item:					
Change in GNP	4	3	1 ¼	1 ¼	−¼

Source: These figures, which include estimated multiplier effects, are
based on simulations carried out using the OECD's INTERLINK
model.

grew strongly. The effect of fiscal policy would seem to have been
mildly contractionary from 1979 to 1982. The effects of monetary
policy are much harder to quantify. On the basis of past evidence of
the effects of interest rate changes on expenditure the negative
impact would be assessed as having started to be felt in 1981,
reducing OECD GNP by around 1½ per cent relative to what
would have been the case under a neutral monetary policy. But the
general weakness of demand in 1982 suggests that the effects of tight
money continued to build up, with a somewhat greater negative
impact in that year than in 1981. These estimates purport to
quantify the effects on spending within OECD economies. To the
extent – which is difficult to quantify – that high interest rates also
caused highly indebted developing countries to contract their
imports, the assessment of the contractionary effect of monetary
policy in Table 3.7 is probably an underestimate.

The estimated deflationary effects of the oil price rise on OECD
domestic expenditure are slightly smaller than earlier seemed likely
to have been the case,[4] because it is now apparent that OPEC
import volumes grew somewhat faster (and hence OPEC countries'
current accounts approached balance somewhat sooner) than had
earlier been expected. Particular uncertainty attaches to the
estimated effects of monetary policy which, at least as represented
by real interest rates, was unusually tight, and for a comparatively
long period. The estimated effects have been derived from evidence
of earlier episodes, when real interest rates were, on average,
considerably lower. Perhaps the most notable feature of the period
after the second large oil price rise is that, despite the much

tighter fiscal policy stance than after the 1973/74 episode, OECD GNP continued to grow in both 1980 and 1981. In substantial part this was due to the steadier behaviour of inventories and, particularly, private non-residential investment, which held up better than many forecasters had expected. It was not until 1982 that OECD GNP was to fall, and this was almost certainly due much more to tight monetary policy than it was to the stance of fiscal policy.

Evaluating the second policy response

The most conspicuous success of policy over this period was the reduction of inflation (Table 3.8). The inflation outcome for 1983 was lower than for any year between the two oil shocks – indeed, the best performance for a decade. And the 7½ percentage point reduction from nearly 13 per cent in 1980 to about 5½ per cent in 1983 was about 2 percentage points greater than the reduction in the two years following the 1974 peak. On the other hand, the record is not one of complete success. First, OECD inflation still remained above the rate of the late 1960s and early 1970s. Second, probably a third or more of the decline in inflation may be attributed to the weakness of primary product prices, which could be expected to recover in the event of a pick-up of activity. Third, international disparities were still wide; eight OECD countries still had inflation rates above 10 per cent.

In line with this better inflation picture has been a greater degree of nominal and real wage flexibility, promoting the adjustment of factor shares and, to a lesser extent, profit positions. For example, the growth in hourly earnings in manufacturing for the seven largest economies in 1982 was barely ½ percentage point above the average rate of increase over the 1962-72 period and real wages in most countries did not move significantly out of line in the way that they had after the 1973/74 shock (Table 3.9).

Nevertheless the sharp reduction in productivity growth that occurred during the recession meant that progress in reducing unit labour costs, and in improving corporate balance sheet positions, was more limited. For example, had productivity gains after 1979 been merely half those experienced during the 1960-72 period (2 per cent rather than 4 per cent annually), factor shares both in the

Table 3.8 *Consumer prices*
per cent

	Peak annual increase[a] (1)	1983 (2)	Change (1)–(2)
United States	13.5	3.7	9.8
Japan	8.0	1.6	6.4
Germany	5.9	2.9	3.0
France	13.6	9.6	4.0
United Kingdom	18.0	5.1	12.9
Italy	21.2	14.9	6.3
Canada	12.5	5.9	6.6
Total OECD	12.9	5.3	7.6

[a] 1980, except for Germany and Canada (1981).
Source: OECD.

Table 3.9 *Real labour costs relative to real national income*[a]
(indices, 1979 = 100)

	1980	1981	1982
United States	100.3	99.8	101.3
Japan	99.1	99.4	100.4
Germany	101.2	100.9	98.5
France	101.5	103.5	102.3
United Kingdom	102.7	101.6	98.5
Italy	99.1	103.4	104.2
Canada	100.4	100.9	103.6
Average, seven countries[b]	100.4	100.6	101.0

[a] Real total compensation per employee divided by real national income per employed person, national accounts basis.
[b] 1981 GNP/GDP weights and exchange rates.
Source: OECD. For further information, and the basic data, see
OECD Economic Outlook 32, December 1982, Table 21 page 45.

total OECD economy and in manufacturing would have been approximately back to the levels prevailing in the early 1970s. Furthermore, factor shares are not the whole story: profitability is also important as a determinant of investment. Although comparable cross-country data are somewhat fragmentary, it is clear that in a number of countries profitability fell quite sharply after the second oil shock also, partly as a result of the exceptionally high real interest rates.

Current account deficits evolved somewhat better than after the 1973/74 oil price shock: while the total OECD deficit was about the same size in relation to GNP as in the earlier episode, the distribution was somewhat less uneven across OECD countries, partly because Germany and Japan had relatively weak positions at the outset, following the expansionary action taken in the context of the Bonn Summit. However, while the recycling experience gained over the earlier period ensured, for three years, the relatively smooth financing of current account deficits within the OECD, the growing debt burden of some non-oil developing countries threatened to become unsustainable.

In the reduction of budget deficits, however, policy was less successful, in part because with most countries deflating simultaneously, the recession made for sharply increased public sector deficits as a result of reduced tax receipts and payments to an increased number of unemployed. (This question of the international linkage aspects of public sector deficit reduction is taken up in chapter 4.)

Lastly unemployment, the fourth of the major policy concerns, continued to increase, and in Europe the rise seemed inexorable. The OECD average rate moved up from 5¼ per cent in 1978 to over 8½ per cent at the end of 1982, with all countries apart from Japan and a few of the smaller European countries experiencing big increases. The main factor behind the rise was probably the virtual stagnation of demand, although cost and structural factors were also important, notably in Europe.

Difficulties in evaluating the effectiveness of policy in the 1970s

In contrast to the 1950s and 1960s, when many countries set the stabilization of the level of activity as their main, if not their sole, policy goal, no country was in a position to do this for any significant length of time over the decade of the 1970s. The goal of stabilizing the level of activity had to be subordinated to other aims, even in those countries where in earlier decades the stabilization of activity had been given a high priority. Important policy objectives in addition to the stabilization of output included variously the reduction of inflation and improving profitability, trimming the size of public sector deficits, avoiding unwanted currency movements and eliminating large current account deficits on the balance of payments.

Hence, assessing how effective policy was in achieving its various ends is not easy. For the decade of the 1960s it was possible – just – to assume that stabilization of output was a major aim of policy, and to estimate the stability of output relative to what calculations suggested that it might have been had policy been neutral, in some sense. But in the 1970s the policy aims of governments were not always clearly stated; nor can they readily be assumed. On the contrary, they differed from country to country, and varied from period to period. Moreover, even when a country clearly stated that reducing inflation, for example, was its overriding aim, this did not necessarily mean that this objective was pursued to the complete exclusion of other considerations. Nor do governments normally state a target for the rate to which they wish to see inflation reduced.

In an even less rigorous way, however, than the analysis in chapter 2 of the effectiveness of stabilization policy in the 1950s and 1960s, some tentative conclusions do suggest themselves from the policy experience of the 1970s:

– when the OECD economy as a whole is hit by a large shock, and particularly a novel one such as the first oil shock early in the decade, analysis may not be solid enough, and forecasts not accurate enough, to permit the customary sort of economic policy-making;
– when OECD economies are afflicted by a number of serious problems simultaneously, policy-makers are likely to be short of sufficient policy instruments to achieve even their most basic economic goals: for example, the experience of two oil-inflation episodes is that although pursuit of traditional policies of restraint does enable progress to be made in reducing inflation, in the majority of countries this cannot be achieved without also incurring a substantial reduction in the rate of growth of activity;
– in the face of a sharp inflationary shock, a single country may fare best by tightening policy early, preventing the shock from being embedded in the domestic price/wage spiral, thereby

gaining either increased international competitiveness, or a further reduction of inflation through appreciation of its currency, or some combination of the two. But all countries cannot simultaneously achieve inflation relief through currency appreciation;

- if all countries do tighten policy simultaneously to control inflation, the overall reduction in activity may be greater, because of the size of the OECD multiplier, than each separately had bargained for, resulting in a sharp contraction of world trade and hence a slower than hoped-for recovery in activity generally. At the same time, the reduction in inflation may be larger than individual countries had expected, partly because of the effect on OECD traded goods prices of the lower level of demand in OECD countries and partly because of the effect of weak demand worldwide on commodity prices.

Parenthetically, it seems also that when simultaneous tightening leads to a sharp reduction in activity, protectionist pressures and indeed protectionist measures may intensify, jeopardizing, after the very short run, at least some of the reduction in inflation.

While such general conclusions can perhaps be drawn, the number of firm lessons that it is possible to draw from the decade of the 1970s is unavoidably limited. In essence the period consisted of two inflationary shocks separated by an incomplete recovery. Although the policy responses to the two episodes were different, this diversity was by no means sufficient to provide clear guidance as to the best way to make policy should such events recur. It is not possible to re-run the OECD economy under alternative policy responses to see what would have happened.

Although the number of firmly-based lessons for policy may be relatively limited, quite a lot was learned about the ways in which policies and performance in a single country interact with those of other countries, as well as about ways in which the behaviour of the economy of the OECD countries as a group differs from that of individual economies. Indeed, the tentative conclusions put forward immediately above have a distinctly international flavour. The chapter which follows looks in more detail at the implications of increased international interdependence.

4 The influence of international linkages

Summary

The OECD economies have become much more open to international trade and financial movements in the post-war period. The process of liberalization was undoubtedly an important factor making for rapid growth in the period up to the early 1970s, and the present degree of international specialization goes far in supporting current living standards. At the same time, increased openness can bring to policy-making an additional set of considerations, which may be regarded as increased opportunities in some circumstances and problems in others. The tendency towards international synchronization of individual countries' business cycles has been strengthened; and the scope for pursuing policies out of line with those in a country's trading partners has generally been limited, even for the largest countries. The OECD economy as a whole is relatively closed, and has properties markedly different from those of the typical national economy; if policies are set in the same direction, whether expansionary or restrictive, in a large number of countries, their combined effect can be surprisingly great.

Introduction

The problems afflicting OECD economies have increasingly appeared, from the perspective of the individual economy, to come from abroad. For example, over the last five years:

- the typical OECD country has seen its exports to other OECD countries decelerate from 9 per cent growth in 1979 to falls in 1981 and 1982;
- meanwhile export markets in the non-OECD area, which

account for almost one-third of OECD countries' total exports, were expanding increasingly rapidly, with a peak of 9 per cent growth in 1981, but then they too showed an absolute fall in 1982;
- at times, many countries have perceived their monetary policies as largely dictated by the stance of policies elsewhere;
- attempts by individual countries to reduce budget deficits have been made more difficult by similar attempts elsewhere, though this is less widely perceived than monetary inter-dependence;
- a number of developing countries, faced by low export prices and volumes, the strong dollar and high real interest rates, have been in financial straits that could threaten bank solvency and, hence, the stability of the world's financial system;
- with depressed growth of total sales, and unemployment high and rising almost everywhere, countries have increasingly been facing protectionist measures in their traditional export markets;
- protectionist pressures have been reinforced in some countries by misaligned exchange rates.

The perception of most countries singly that many of their problems flow from abroad is correct: but for the OECD countries as a group it is *not* true that most problems originate abroad. Many originate *within* the OECD area, and are transmitted from one country to another by strong international economic linkages. And others, which appear to emanate from outside the OECD area, are in fact often traceable back to earlier developments within the OECD area.

Ultimate causes of economic success in earlier years, and of disappointing performance more recently, are to be found *within* individual OECD economies. To take just one example, important rigidities persist in many, probably most, OECD countries, making for stickiness in the pattern of relative wages and prices as well as an insufficiently quick adaptation of production to changing patterns of costs and demand. And there are many other factors of essentially domestic origin that prevent economic performance from being as good as it might be. In concentrating on the part played by international economic linkages, the focus of this chapter is on the way economic impulses, which may be the manifestation of problems within individual economies, are transmitted from one economy to another.

The openness of individual OECD economies

Much of the increase in the openness of individual OECD economies over the last thirty years has come about through an increase in trade in manufactures and services. Each OECD country has penetrated the markets of its partners.

This tighter linking of OECD economies through international trade came about as the result of deliberate policy and the desire, in the early post-war period, to reverse the protectionist approach of the inter-war years and return to the sort of open trading conditions prevailing before the First World War. The progressive liberalization of foreign trade, current invisibles and capital movements, initiated in the OEEC and sustained by the Bretton Woods financial institutions, spread to all OECD countries and a number of non-Member countries. In conditions of rapid growth of the world economy, the system of international economic relations became freer and increasingly multilateral. Under the auspices of the General Agreement on Tariffs and Trade (GATT), which came into force with 23 Member countries in 1948, seven major rounds of tariff reduction have taken place. With 88 countries (representing four-fifths of world trade) now signatories, the average weighted tariff on industrial products is now less than 5 per cent. Non-tariff barriers, on the other hand, have always been important in some markets, and in recent years have become even more so.

In addition to deliberate action to reduce restrictions and tariffs, communication has improved, and transport has become relatively cheaper and better organized. In this environment the trend growth of international trade has been about twice that of OECD GNP. The share of exports (of goods and services) in GNP has about doubled over the last thirty years in six OECD countries, including the United States, and has increased by one half or more in another five OECD countries. On average, OECD countries today export about 30 per cent of their GNP (on an unweighted basis), but with considerable differences between countries. The smaller countries

Table 4.1   *External assets and liabilities of six OECD countries*[a]
Stocks at end–1981

	$ billion	As per cent of 1981:	
		GNP	Exports
Total external assets	1980	35	250
of which:			
Banks	985	17	125
Non-bank private sector	705	12	90
Total external liabilities	1735	31	220
of which:			
Banks	940	17	120
Non-bank private sector	510	9	65

[a]   United States, Japan, Germany, United Kingdom, Italy and Belgium.
Source: OECD.

are generally the most open – in Belgium, for example, exports amount to more than 60 per cent of GNP, whereas the United States figure is about 12 per cent.

This increasing openness of OECD countries to trade has been matched on the investment and financial side (Table 4.1). There is of course nothing new about international investment: the United Kingdom for example was investing abroad some 5 per cent of GDP in the 1870s and 1880s. But in the 1950s and 1960s there was a particularly rapid growth of direct investment flows, which differed from those in earlier periods; they went to a large extent from one developed country to another, and tended to be in manufacturing facilities rather than primary production and extraction. More recently, direct investment flows have been relatively smaller, but the proportion of world industrial production accounted for by multinational enterprises continues to grow, now amounting to some 15-20 per cent.

The process of financial integration has perhaps been most remarkable of all. The revolutions in information and communication technology, coupled with the liberalization of capital movements by countries in which the main financial centres are situated, have led to financial markets becoming truly international, with new information being instantly processed and acted upon worldwide. The most impressive indication of financial integration is perhaps the growth of international banking: over the last two decades, Eurocurrency markets have grown by about 30 per cent a year, twice as fast as the value of world trade and nearly three times as fast as the OECD's nominal GNP. Perhaps one sixth of total commercial bank claims are now on non-residents.

The various consequences of increased openness have important implications for the making of economic policy. This point is of course not new. Early attempts to formalize key international transmission mechanisms have been made by Metzler (1942, 1950), Neisser and Modigliani (1953), Polak (1954), and Machlup (1961). These involved allowing for the incidence of international trade flows among countries on the calculation of policy multipliers for a given country. An early attempt to give empirical content to this discussion was made by Beckerman (1956). With economies becoming increasingly open over the last three decades or more, this aspect of the economic environment has become even more important.

The OECD economy as a whole

The 'external sector' of the OECD economy as a whole is smaller in relation to GNP than that of any of its constituent economies, trade in goods and services with the rest of the world amounting to perhaps 7 per cent of the area's GNP. At the same time, however, the OECD economy as a whole is so large in the world system that even its limited degree of openness to the rest of the world is of enormous significance to the latter. While OECD countries account for only 19 per cent of the world's population, and 24 per cent of its land area, they account for over 65 per cent of its production and absorb about 60 per cent of non-OECD countries' exports.

Seen from the standpoint of the individual OECD economy, imports of other OECD countries taken together represent the major part – on average some two-thirds – of the total export market, and imports of non-OECD countries the remainder. While any one country can, if it has a favourable competitive position or a favourable commodity composition, experience a growth of exports *in excess* of the combined growth of its markets in OECD and non-OECD countries, this can only be at the expense of other countries suffering a loss of market share.

In the short term, non-OECD markets can occasionally grow buoyantly and somewhat independently of general world conditions. The most notable recent cases are the years immediately following each of the two large oil price rises, when OPEC countries adjusted expenditure to newly-acquired revenue fairly rapidly and, in 1978 and from 1981, even ran down reserves; at the same time, demand from non-oil developing countries was supported by sizeable borrowing through international markets. But such a boost to OECD activity from outside the area comes to an end as the non-OECD countries reach the limit of what can be sustainably financed, whether out of reserves or by increasing indebtedness: over a run of years, non-OECD imports are constrained by their export proceeds.

Furthermore the growth of the value of non-OECD exports is determined in substantial part by the growth of the value of the relevant imports of OECD countries, largely primary commodities, though increasingly manufactures in recent years. As a first approximation, OECD import volumes of primary commodities rise and fall broadly in proportion with OECD GNP. The prices of these primary commodities also fluctuate with OECD activity. Over the last two decades or so a growth of OECD GNP of about 4 per cent was, on average, sufficient to keep the prices of non-oil primary commodities broadly in line with those of OECD manufactures; depressed investment in raw material production in recent years may now have lowered this 'break-even' rate of growth. Relative to this trend, each 1 per cent acceleration or deceleration in OECD GNP growth has apparently tended to change the prices of non-oil primary commodities by some 2 percentage points.

Oil prices, too, are influenced importantly by the level of OECD activity. Variations in supply and OECD stockbuilding, and in the power of OPEC to affect the price, have also been considerable, making it difficult to provide a short-run rule of thumb for the relationship between OECD activity and world oil prices. There is little doubt, however, that the weakening of oil prices in the early 1980s has been related to the several years of weakness of OECD demand.

Taking intra-OECD trade and trade with non-OECD countries together, the growth of the exports of OECD economies is therefore determined in large part, directly or indirectly, by the growth of the imports of OECD countries. When the growth of the

Table 4.2 *Peak-to-peak output growth*
(compound annual rates)

	1962–66	1966–69	1969–73	1973–79	1980	1981	1982
OECD	5.4	4.8	4.6	1.9	1.2	1.5	−0.3
Oil exporting countries	7.5	8.2	8.9	5.9	−2.0	−4.0	−4.3
Non-oil developing countries	5.2	6.2	6.0	5.0	4.1	2.3[a]	1.5[a]
USSR[b]	7.0	7.0	6.8	3.8	4.0	3.5	2.0[a]

[a] Provisional estimate
[b] Net material product.
Sources: OECD and United Nations Statistical Year Books.

OECD economies slows down, these powerful trade linkages ensure that no OECD economy, and no major non-OECD region, is able to avoid a significant contractionary influence (Table 4.2).

The combination of open individual OECD economies with their relatively closed aggregate means that the OECD area's economic policy multipliers are larger than those for most countries considered individually, possibly as much as double in some circumstances. This means that it is easy to underestimate the consequences for the OECD area of a change in policy that is occurring in a number of countries simultaneously. When demand expands in a single country, a significant proportion leaks abroad. The reverse holds true for a contraction; the net effect, either way, is to reduce the size of the country's multiplier relative to what it would be if the economy were closed, or even just moderately open, like the OECD economy as a whole. This is not to say that the impact on activity is lost: a part simply flows abroad. A representative estimate is that a $1 stimulus to a typical economy may, when the effect is at its peak, raise output in that country by $1½ and activity abroad by another $1 to 1½. The precise magnitude will depend upon a number of factors, including any induced exchange rate movement. But in the short term the income effect is likely to be the dominant one, whether under fixed exchange rates or floating rates, because relative price effects on trade volumes tend to work through slowly. Thus total OECD output expands by $2½ to 3, but the initiating country sees only $1½ of that. If a number of major countries are experiencing demand expansion at the same time, however, and the full implications are not carefully allowed for, the total effect can be unexpectedly large.[1] Each country finds, in addition to the expected expansion of its domestic demand components, that its exports too are growing sharply. Excess demand can then arise in the world economy. The equivalent effect – a greater than expected downturn – can just as readily occur in times of synchronized deflation.

Similarly, inflationary and disinflationary effects can be unexpectedly large when business cycles are coincident. When a country is experiencing an acceleration of inflation relative to its partners under a regime of fixed exchange rates, perhaps (but not necessarily) as a result of excess demand, part of the acceleration shows up domestically, but part leaks abroad in the form of higher export prices. Meanwhile, import prices damp inflation. But if all countries are experiencing an acceleration of inflation, their export prices will all be accelerating; hence all countries' import prices are accelerating too. If exchange rates are free to float they could in principle move so as precisely to offset inflation differences between countries. In practice, however, exchange rates have seldom moved in this way, and the transmission of inflation between countries remains a feature under flexible exchange rates.

A further point relates to inflation in the OECD economy as a whole. When countries are experiencing a synchronized expansion, the overall level of demand is likely to be rising so fast that it causes a powerful increase in the prices of primary commodities determined in international markets. Overall, inflation can be markedly greater than expected. Equivalently, synchronized deflation can result in a greater than expected disinflation.

Constraints on individual performance

The openness of individual OECD economies to the rest of the OECD economy, and to the highly dependent non-OECD economy, is such that the performance of the overall OECD economy goes far towards determining the limits to the performance of each economy individually.

Depending upon the policy regime, this external constraint can manifest itself either through the balance of payments and foreign indebtedness, or the exchange rate. A few numbers illustrate the forces at work, and hence the potential complications for policy-making. Imports are equivalent on average to about 20 per cent of GNP (on a weighted basis) in OECD countries, and the typical elasticity of import volume growth with respect to GNP has for many years been around 1½ to 2. This means that a country initially in current account balance would, if it were to experience an increase in the growth of its domestic demand of 3 percentage points relative to its partners, move into current account deficit of around 1 per cent of GNP. Equivalently, if a country were initially in current account balance, and the growth of the domestic demand of its trading partners were to slow relatively by 3 percentage points, the country would also find its current account tending to worsen by about 1 per cent of GNP.

The size of current account deficit that can be tolerated differs from country to country, depending upon the country's willingness to incur international debt and a variety of factors that influence the willingness of other countries to lend. Depending upon the balance of these factors some countries can be in current account deficit for many years, while others may be in persistent surplus. But for most a *change* in the current account position equivalent to 1 per cent of GNP over one or two years would, depending on the starting point, be considered significant, and could well be sufficient to set in train a process of adjustment.

Pressure to respond to a change in current account position generally comes when a country moves into, or further into, deficit; surplus countries are often not put under equivalent pressure to adjust. With a deficit, there will tend to be downward pressure on the exchange rate. If the rate is allowed to move down, this will in due course increase exports and reduce imports, thereby reducing the current account implications of the country's faster-than-average rate of domestic demand expansion, or slower-than-average rate of domestic demand decline. But export and import volumes tend to respond only slowly, the mean lag for a typical OECD country being between one and two years, with the maximum adjustment apparently occurring after two to three years. This might well not be sufficiently quick to prevent a serious loss of foreign currency reserves, or an unnecessary degree of depreciation, or both – especially as depreciation frequently causes a terms-of-trade deterioration well in advance of any volume response, so that the current balance worsens in the short run. Furthermore, the high weight of imports in total expenditure would cause the depreciating country to experience an immediate and significant increment to inflation, and a typical wage response could well magnify this several-fold. If this were thought unacceptable, a country would have little option but to take policy action to deflate domestic demand.

These considerations do not mean that all countries individually will be constrained to have the *same* performance. Tendencies for some countries to grow faster than others, and for some countries to be more inflation-prone than others, are evident. Indeed, although average growth rates in recent years have been much lower, and average inflation rates much higher, than in the 1960s, the broad relative positions of individual countries have in many cases not changed significantly, despite marked changes in structure and policy regime. (One exception to this generalization is that Japan has become a 'low-inflation' country.) The fact that different countries can have such differences in secular trends is attributable to two factors in particular. First, differing industrial specialization and supply-side responsiveness mean that income elasticities of both imports and exports differ significantly between countries. Second, there is some tendency for inflation differentials to be offset over time by exchange rate changes. But this last factor is tempered by a growing awareness that the inflation differential that can be successfully offset through recurrent adjustments of the exchange rate, while impossible to determine with any precision, may not be very large, and the possibility of inflation and exchange rate depreciation inter-acting in an accelerating spiral is often seen as a danger. Similarly, because of feedbacks on inflation, changes in nominal and real exchange rates to offset a current account deficit resulting from a speeding-up of economic growth relative to partner countries may generally be used only sparingly. Hence, as illustrated below, international linkages, real and financial, work powerfully to limit the degree of divergence that is possible for individual countries. In particular, there is a marked tendency towards international coincidence of both business cycles and policy stance.

Hence for reasons that begin with the balance of payments and end with inflation, a country has little scope, in the great majority of cases, to allow its domestic demand to grow significantly faster than its traditional relativity with demand in its trading partners.

In today's conditions, with speeds of response far faster in financial markets than in goods and labour markets, it is possible that attempts to pursue more expansionary policies than partner countries, particularly on the monetary side, would lead to depreciation – with associated inflationary pressure – long before there are perceptible signs of the current account worsening. Moreover, the exchange rate may well go beyond ('overshoot') its new equilibrium level. Concern at this risk can act as a powerful inhibitor of moves towards policy easing.

More generally, the exchange rate, and hence the external constraint, has been increasingly affected over the last few years by financial linkages – the international movement of capital. Conceptually, financial linkages could offset real linkages, compound them, or play an independent role. Following the breakdown of the fixed rate system in 1973 it was hoped that floating would permit countries to pursue more independent domestic objectives than had hitherto been the case, insulating them from the monetary policies of dominant partners. In part, this view rested on the assumption that capital movements would tend to offset temporary current account disequilibria and play a stabilizing role. These hopes proved too optimistic, however: the exchange rate has remained a constraint, and financial linkages have often compounded real linkages. Moreover, exchange rates are, at times, affected by incipient capital movements induced by foreign financial disturbances or international political considerations.

The ability of financial markets to generate very large movements of capital between countries has meant that exchange rates have been subject to much stronger and more erratic movements than had been foreseen at the outset of floating. Typically, interest rates adjust to maintain domestic money market equilibrium, and the yield differentials that open up between countries tend to be mirrored in movements in expected appreciation or depreciation and premiums associated with market perceptions of risk. Given expectations about the future level of exchange rates, actual spot rates tend to move relatively sharply in response to differential monetary policies between countries, shifts in portfolio preferences, and changes in supplies of non-monetary assets denominated in different currencies. Because the latter are influenced by bond-financed fiscal deficits and current account imbalances, factors other than differential short-run monetary policies can also influence international financial linkages.

Exchange rate movements induced by financial disturbances can constrain domestic policies. Expansionary monetary policies have often resulted in depreciation and rising import prices, which quickly lead to higher domestic inflation. On the other hand, the tightening of domestic policies to control inflation may cause the exchange rate to appreciate to levels which substantially reduce competitiveness. While contributing to a reduction in inflation, such tightening particularly affects industries most exposed to international competition. This may lead not only to a short-run misallocation of resources but, by affecting investment in these industries – and even their financial viability – risks longer-run structural effects which may persist after the real exchange rate has returned to a sustainable level.

Implications of individual action for the OECD as a group

Just as individual countries are typically constrained by the performance of the OECD economy as a whole, so too is the performance of OECD countries as a group constrained in several ways not necessarily applicable to any country individually. Some of the policy objectives that can be pursued successfully by an individual OECD country may prove largely or wholly self-defeating when pursued by many countries simultaneously.

Reducing real unit labour costs/improving competitiveness. Attempts to increase employment and profits by reducing real labour costs relative to productivity (or nominal wages relative to output prices) can be one such case in point. A typical open economy that succeeds in improving its competitiveness in this way, or by depreciating its exchange rate, is likely to experience a rise in demand and output from an increase in its net exports via a combination of price-induced demand effects and profit-induced supply side effects. But this gain in demand and output will be achieved, at least in part, at the expense of lower demand and output abroad: demand and output in the OECD economy as a whole may be broadly unaffected. This is not to say that reducing unit labour costs may not be important in its own right in some countries, or in a number of countries, at one time or another; if this increases profit shares and the rate of capital accumulation, it can increase output and employment without 'beggaring' trading partners. But any policy action which enables one country to gain largely *at the expense of others* will not generalize into a successful policy for all countries simultaneously.

Reducing public sector deficits. Another case of successful single-country policies which do not generalize, at least not fully, is the discretionary reduction of public sector deficits. When the typical OECD country reduces government expenditure, or raises taxes, the effect will generally, in the near term at least, be to reduce overall demand and output. In most countries resulting lower tax receipts and payments to an increased number of unemployed will mean that the budget deficit is reduced by less than the initial reduction. For the typical OECD country, it is nevertheless likely that the deficit will be reduced, perhaps by around half the amount of the *ex ante* change in the relatively near term.

The figures work out in this way for the typical OECD country because, while some of the reduction in demand represents a reduction in demand for the country's own output, the other part of the reduction is for output produced abroad. The effect of this part of the demand reduction is to increase budget deficits abroad, as payments to their unemployed increase, and tax receipts fall. At the level of the OECD economy as a whole, therefore, the reduction in public sector deficits is markedly smaller than appears from a consideration only of developments in the budget-cutting country. Indeed, when full account is taken of the effects in *all* countries, the fact that the region as a whole is relatively closed implies a very much smaller reduction in public sector deficits overall.

Important linkage episodes

There have been numerous occasions over the last decade or so when what may be termed 'linkage episodes' have significantly affected the economic performance of individual economies. And virtually all economies have been affected, at one time or another, from the smallest to the largest.

'Bucking the trend'

There have been various instances when countries have come up against powerful linkage constraints when seeking to accelerate their growth relative to that of their trading partners. A striking example was the policy reaction in the period following the 1973 oil price increase. Some countries (in particular larger OECD countries) placed greater weight on controlling inflation while others (in particular smaller countries) concentrated more on offsetting the demand-deflationary and thereby employment-reducing consequences of the oil price increases. While the distinction between small and large countries is somewhat stylized, it is nonetheless instructive to examine the relative fortunes of these two groupings. Reflecting the differences in policy stance, total domestic demand in the smaller countries (taken to be all OECD countries other than the seven biggest) increased by 1¾ per cent on average in 1974 and 1975 while domestic demand in the larger countries fell by more than 1 per cent per year. In consequence the current balance position of smaller countries as a group deteriorated by more than 3 per cent of GNP between 1973 and 1975, while that of larger countries actually improved.

The increased current account deficits of smaller countries did not, in general, result in substantial exchange-rate pressures – deficits were on the whole financed relatively smoothly through both private and official capital inflows. However, the resulting build-up of indebtedness was generally unwelcome and sometimes unsustainable. This factor, along with growing fiscal deficits and slow progress in reducing inflation (particularly in relation to the larger countries), put increasing strain on the supportive demand-management policies of the smaller countries. Between 1975 and 1978 the policy stance shifted towards restriction in many of these countries. In a number of cases, the competitive position had moved markedly out of line, triggering exchange rate depreciation. Between 1975 and 1978 domestic demand in the smaller countries grew at about 2½ per cent per year, compared with 4½ per cent in the larger countries. The implications of these experiences of international linkages were, in general, not lost: as observed in the previous chapter, there was much greater uniformity of policies across countries following the second oil shock .

Among larger countries, each has experienced at least one

episode, in the period since floating began, when the effects of divergent policies, acting through international linkages, significantly influenced subsequent policy, forcing it to move more closely into line with policy elsewhere.

Following the 1974-75 recession, the United States grew faster than most other countries. Inflation in the United States accelerated from below 6 per cent in 1976 to close to 8 per cent in 1978, while it decelerated very sharply in Japan and significantly in Germany. The U.S. current account deteriorated by nearly $35 billion between 1975 and 1978, while the current positions of Japan and Germany improved by over $15 billion and some $5 billion respectively. The effective exchange rate of the dollar changed relatively little during 1976 and the first part in 1977, but depreciated steadily from the fourth quarter of 1977: between September 1977 and October 1978 the dollar fell some 20 per cent in effective terms.

Initially the United States authorities appeared to feel that exchange rate movements could be absorbed without driving policy off course. As external pressures persisted, however, the effects on inflation became increasingly difficult to ignore – especially when they combined with a general weakening of confidence in the ability of policy to achieve longer-run goals. In October 1978 domestic measures were taken to strengthen the counter-inflationary programme. These changes were not, however, sufficient to avoid a serious loss of confidence in the dollar, culminating in a speculative run at the end of October 1978. These movements were reversed by a significant tightening of U.S. monetary policy in November 1978, together with various measures taken in cooperation with partner countries directly to counter dollar weakness.

This episode suggested that even the largest OECD economy, with a relatively small share of trade in GNP, is not immune to the pressures of international linkages. In 1982-83, however, an expansion got under way in the United States that was even more rapid in relation to the growth of activity elsewhere, leading to a deficit on current external account of a size unprecedented this century. With this evolution being accompanied by an *appreciating* currency, it was tempting to think that the United States could indeed pursue the policies of its choice without paying heed to the situation in other countries. Aspects of this episode, which was still incomplete at the time of writing, are discussed in chapter 11.[2]

In the United Kingdom the effective value of sterling fell by 12 to 13 per cent between early March and early June 1976 and, after a short period of relative stability, fell a further 9 per cent between early-September and mid-November. The proximate causes of this pressure were continuing weakness of the current account, sharp declines in officially-held sterling balances and strong short-term private outflows during the first half of the year. While the first factor may have reflected a longer-term structural weakness in the economy, as well as some short-term elements including a slight deterioration of competitiveness, the other two were probably due to perceptions of the general stance of economic policy in relation to other countries – and notably hesitant adjustments of monetary management to external requirements. During the first three quarters of 1976 the authorities aimed to prevent a rise in interest rates in order not to jeopardize an expected increase in investment. As a result, the growth of monetary aggregates accelerated very sharply, both in relation to targets and to monetary growth in other countries. The ensuing downward pressure on the exchange rate forced a sharp adjustment of policy, the authorities adopting a major stabilization package: the minimum lending rate was raised to 15 per cent in October (compared with 9 per cent in April), and it was agreed with the IMF that domestic credit expansion would be limited and the budget deficit lowered.

In 1980-81, Italy was faced with a similar manifestation of the workings of international linkages. From the second half of 1978 through to the early part of 1980, the Italian economy went through a phase of very substantial growth, appreciably higher than the average recorded in the main OECD countries. As in previous comparable phases of the cycle, the expansion triggered strong pressure on prices and the foreign balance, which were compounded by the effects of the second oil shock. The annual rate of increase in consumer prices was more than 20 per cent in 1980. The current account balance swung from a surplus of $5 billion in 1979 to a deficit of $10 billion in 1980 (2½ per cent of GDP). The central rate for the lira within the European Monetary System was lowered by 6 per cent in March 1981. In response to these imbalances, and for the third time in eight years, the Italian authorities introduced restrictive policies. Monetary policy was progressively tightened with a further squeeze on credit and higher interest rates, the discount rate reaching an all-time high of 19 per cent in March 1981, interest rates in Italy then following the trend seen in the majority of OECD countries. Fiscal policy was considerably more restrictive in 1980 than originally planned, as a result of inflation-induced fiscal drag and higher indirect taxation as well as the advance payment of certain taxes. Consequently, the general government borrowing requirement, expressed as a percentage of GDP, fell from 9.4 per cent in 1979 to 7.8 per cent in 1980.

More recently, action by the French authorities to stimulate the economy was frustrated by the workings of international linkages. In mid-1981 macroeconomic policy in France was directed at supporting demand to combat unemployment. The process was envisaged as involving: (i) increased income transfers to stimulate the demand for output of consumer goods; (ii) a general world recovery in 1982, which would stimulate exports and reduce the growth differential between France and its trading partners; and (iii) improved financial results and more optimistic expectations in the business sector, inducing an upturn in investment. The task was made particularly difficult by the fact that the package adopted threatened to boost wage costs directly; and it was enacted by a new government thought by many to be hostile to private enterprise. While France did succeed in growing more rapidly than partner countries, the recovery was limited to private consumption, much of which 'leaked' abroad and was not matched by recovery in partner countries – in 1982 the real foreign balance deteriorated by an amount equivalent to 2¼ per cent of GDP. The corresponding current account deterioration was from a deficit of some $4¾ billion in 1981 to $12 billion in 1982. Given this, the continuance of a substantially higher rate of inflation in France than in the country's main trading partners and steady downward pressure on the franc, the authorities set economic policy on a more restrictive course in June 1982, adjusted the exchange rate of the franc in the EMS and took specific measures aimed at reducing inflation. In March 1983 there was a further EMS realignment and a strongly restrictive demand package was introduced.

Monetary and financial linkages

In the early 1980s incipient capital movements and exchange rates have often been driven more by financial and special factors than by the current account and 'real' economic considerations. This has been notably the case of the dollar, on one side, and the yen and, to a lesser extent, European currencies, on the other. In the United States an expansionary fiscal policy in combination with a tight monetary policy resulted in high nominal and real interest rates which, in the framework of credible monetary policy and expectations of continuing large deficits in the federal budget translated into favourable expected yields on dollar assets and massive incipient capital inflows. The external debt crisis, fears for the stability of the international banking system and political problems in a number of countries further enhanced the attraction of dollar assets and increased the risk premium on other currencies. The virtual elimination of controls on capital outflows in Japan may have led to an important once-and-for-all adjustment of portfolios and accentuated the pressure on the yen. Hence, the dollar and the yen moved in ways largely unrelated to their current account positions.

The importance of the dollar internationally is such that the counterpart downward pressure on many other OECD currencies resulting from the strong dollar, with the implied incipient boost to inflation from higher import prices, was a factor – perceived in some countries as the overriding factor – leading to increases, or delaying declines, in their interest rates.

In Germany in 1980 and early 1981 the combination of weakening demand, a current external deficit and high international interest rates created a dilemma for monetary policy. On the one hand, a relaxation of monetary policy to moderate or reverse the weakening of domestic demand would have risked escalating capital outflows, downward pressure on the Deutschemark, higher import prices and further short-run deterioration of the current account. On the other hand, adherence to the official objective of financing the current deficit by autonomous capital inflows, thereby keeping the exchange rate stable, would have implied higher interest rates, with further depressive effects on output and employment. During 1980 and into early 1981 the authorities chose a middle path of keeping monetary policy restrictive enough to avoid excessive depreciation, while intervening in the markets to smooth erratic fluctuations in the exchange rate and trying to limit the impact of policy on the domestic economy. But faced with continuing downward pressure on the exchange rate and capital outflows in early 1981, external factors became more important in the setting of monetary policy, entailing a sharp rise in short-term interest rates in February.

In Japan, inflation as measured by the CPI was reduced from 10 per cent at an annual rate in the first half of 1980 to around 3 per cent in 1982. In relation to this good inflation performance and the relative sluggishness of the economy, long-term interest rates were considered too high. However, the monetary authorities felt obliged to exercise considerable caution because of a conflicting concern to support the yen rate in order to contain protectionist pressures abroad (thereby reducing the need for the plethora of voluntary export restraints and associated structural distortions).

One of the specific problems noted above concerns potential difficulties arising from the combination of international linkages and the different reaction speeds of financial and goods markets. One school of thought suggests that this phenomenon is illustrated by 'vicious' and 'virtuous' circles. These would seem to have been exemplified by the experience in the mid-1970s of the United Kingdom and Italy on the one hand, and Germany and other 'strong currency' countries on the other. Another school suggests that such 'circles' could have been avoided had monetary policy been better coordinated across countries.

The examples of Germany and Switzerland provide evidence of a further kind of financial linkage. In the period up to 1978, when these two countries pursued relatively stable anti-inflationary monetary policies, growing weakness of the dollar was associated with substantial portfolio diversification on the part of the dollar holders. Germany and Switzerland, whose currencies were perceived as being particularly strong, received substantial capital inflows. Moreover, both the Deutschemark and the Swiss franc began increasingly to play the role of substitute reserve currencies. Both currencies appreciated substantially in real terms, and beyond a certain point the potential costs of this were considered to be particularly high. In both cases the authorities were led to abandon the previous stance of policy, substantially expanding the supply of their respective currencies in order to alleviate pressures and overshooting their monetary targets.

Synchronized policy episodes

Difficulty in judging the overall consequences of major bunching of expansionary moves in a number of individual countries or, what is the same thing, the large size of OECD area multipliers, would appear to be part of the explanation for the undesired strength of demand in the OECD booms of 1968 and 1972-73. The same phenomenon may well have been at work in reverse in the recent recession.

The 1968 overheating was caused substantially by simultaneous expansionary policies in the United States, Japan and a number of European countries. Considering first the United States, the long expansion which began in 1961 was still proceeding strongly in 1965. Demand pressure, as indicated by the GNP gap, became excessive in the second half of 1965, and remained heavy until mid-1969. Unemployment in 1966 dipped below the 4 per cent level then thought to represent a state of full employment, and reached a low of 3.5 per cent in 1969. Inflation accelerated, from around 2 per cent in the early 1960s to 5½ per cent in 1969. Fiscal policy was tightened only in June 1968, with a temporary tax surcharge, and monetary policy actually turned expansionary after 1966. Meanwhile fiscal policy turned strongly expansionary in Japan, in Germany after its first significant post-War recession in 1967, and in several other European countries. Taking the nine largest economies together, the fiscal impulse in 1967 was the largest in any year from 1965 to 1976. There was a general acceleration of inflation in most countries, the OECD inflation rate reaching 4 per cent in 1968 and increasing in each of the next two years. This episode is considered in greater detail in chapter 6, in which it is suggested that failure to make sufficient allowance for the strong linkages between countries, and hence for the size of the multiplier of the OECD area as a whole, was a main reason for the widespread under-prediction of activity in 1968 and 1969.

The 1972–73 overheating. After a mild recession in 1970-71 the OECD economy began another cyclical upswing. Fiscal policy in the United States was expansionary in 1970, although this was progressively reduced by fiscal drag in the following years. In other countries, however, there was an important stimulus; Germany, the United Kingdom and Japan all moved in the direction of expansion. For the OECD area as a whole, the swing towards expansion from

1970 to 1973 was 1 per cent of GNP. Monetary policy too was expansionary. Taking the largest OECD countries, M1 started to accelerate at the beginning of 1970, and in 1971 expanded by 12 per cent; M2 grew by 14 per cent. Rates of increase in 1972 were slightly higher. Average short-term interest rates, having reached a peak in early 1970, declined to 4 per cent by early 1972, about the same as the rate of inflation. Given these stimuli, the OECD economy grew over the 1972-73 period at its most rapid rate since the 1950s. All major countries were taking up slack simultaneously, as had happened in 1968. The *levels* of resource utilization reached in 1972-73 may also have been similar to those of 1968. What was exceptional was the *speed* of the expansion. The result was an inflationary outburst as early as the second half of 1972. OECD inflation rose to 5½ per cent, with a further increase to 7½ per cent in the first half of 1973. Although at that point more than half of this acceleration derived from food prices, and was not therefore directly traceable to the rate of economic activity, there followed the more generalized commodity price boom discussed in chapter 3 and the oil price explosion at the end of 1973. Thus the 1972-73 inflation outburst, like its milder predecessor in 1968, was attributable in substantial part to the synchronization, whether deliberate or unwitting, of policies in major countries.

The 1980–82 recession. This recession began with the strong deflationary force on OECD economies exerted by the 1979-80 oil price rise, which may have depressed OECD GNP by 2 to 3 per cent in 1980. Subsequently output was supported by strong growth of exports to OPEC – more rapidly, indeed, than expected beforehand. For a time, too, OECD growth was also supported by the strong increase of imports by non-oil developing countries. But these positive influences on demand from outside the OECD area were outweighed by the effects of macroeconomic policy inside. Fiscal policy became somewhat tighter in 1979 and 1980, and may have had its most important depressive effect on output growth in 1981. Monetary conditions tightened generally during 1979 and 1980 as much higher inflation was met by approximately unchanged rates of monetary growth. In Europe, monetary policy was tightened further in 1981 in an effort to stave off additional depreciation-induced inflation. The unusually high interest rates – both nominal and real – of 1980 and 1981 may have had a large effect on spending in 1981 and perhaps even more in 1982, at a time when fiscal changes seem to have been broadly neutral. Subsequently, trade with the non-OECD area on balance depressed OECD activity. Over the three years as a whole, OECD output rose by only about 2 per cent. Inflation came down sharply in most countries, from a peak OECD rate of 12.9 per cent in 1980 to 5 per cent over the twelve months to July 1983.

Reducing public sector deficits. A central aim of most governments since about 1979 has been the reduction of budget deficits. Over the three years from 1979 the effect of action taken by the seven largest countries in respect of expenditure and tax rate changes might, taken by itself, have been such as to reduce their combined deficit by 1 to 1½ per cent of GNP; only in the United States was there a move, on this basis, towards greater ease, and that only small (until fiscal 1983). But governments' efforts in many countries have been frustrated by two factors in particular. First, in the general deflationary climate, itself in part due to the fact that many countries were simultaneously adopting tight policies, all deficits were swollen by the 'automatic stabilizers' – reduced tax yields and increased payments to the unemployed – on average by perhaps 2½ to 3 per cent of GNP. Second, increased interest payments, resulting both from higher interest rates and increased indebtedness, may have pushed deficits up by between 1/2 and 1 per cent of GNP. Overall, then, actual deficits widened on average by nearly 2½ per cent of GNP (Table 4.3). The only countries among the seven to achieve reductions were Japan, where the cyclical effect on the public finances was relatively small, due largely to a strong boost to activity from the external sector, and the United Kingdom, where the apparent *ex ante* change in the budget position was exceptionally large.

The international debt problem. A further feature of that episode was the negative effect of the protracted OECD recession and high interest rates on the non-OECD world, and the induced impact of the worsening of the latter group's fortunes on the OECD countries themselves. These effects were in fact somewhat stronger than might have been expected on the basis of the trade linkages alone. The exacerbating factor was the deterioration in the debt position of a number of the largest non-OECD borrowers, whose development plans had been predicated on assumptions about the global economic environment that turned out to be too optimistic.

Table 4.3 *Changes in budget balances[a], 1979 to 1982*
per cent of GDP/GNP,
a '−' sign indicates a movement towards deficit

	Actual change	Effect of changes in economic activity	Effect of increased interest payments[b]	Apparent 'ex ante' change[c]
United Kingdom	1.6	−4.5	−0.5	6.6
Canada	−3.5	−5.7	−1.3	3.5
Japan	1.0	−0.4	−1.2	2.6
Germany	−1.1	−2.7	−0.7	2.3
Italy	−3.0	−2.3	−1.8	1.1
France	−2.2	−1.9	−0.9	0.6
United States	−4.4	−3.2	−0.6	−0.6
Average, seven countries[d]	−2.4	−2.9	−0.8	1.3

[a] General government financial balances.
[b] On public debt, assuming one-third of interest payments is returned to the government in taxes.
[c] i.e., excluding effects of changes in economic activity and increased interest payments.
[d] 1981 GNP/GDP weights and exchange rates.
Source: OECD

Some lessons

The fact that individual economies are generally unlikely to be able to depart in any fundamental way from what is dictated by the performance of the OECD economy as a whole may have appeared over the last decade or so as an important restriction imposed by international economic linkage. Indeed this is the aspect of linkage that is likely to be dwelt upon when, as at present, economic performance is widely considered unsatisfactory. But there is the important corollary that when the overall OECD economy is performing well, as it generally was over much of the 1950s and 1960s, any individual economy is likely to find that a number of constraints on policy are eased. This is not to say, for example, that a higher level of activity in the OECD economy as a whole will guarantee the same for every individual OECD economy. Domestic policies and responses will still be critically important. But the typical economy will tend to have higher exports, a better balance of payments, at a given level of domestic demand, and a better public sector balance; on the other hand there will tend to be a boost to its inflation from the world economy.

Perhaps the second main linkage lesson is that when the policies of a number of major OECD countries become synchronized, whether in the direction of expansion or contraction, the effect on the OECD economy risks being markedly greater than policy-makers might expect on the basis of single-country properties. Countries typically find the effect of their own policies on domestic demand being powerfully reinforced by the development of their export markets and import prices, these effects coming both from within the OECD area and from outside. The events of 1968 and 1972-73 illustrate this in one direction, those of 1980 to 1982 in the other.

The third main linkage lesson is that, while floating exchange rates may have served somewhat to enable economies to avoid the full force of economic shocks coming from abroad, they have by no means conferred full domestic policy autonomy on any individual OECD economy.

Hence international linkages, in transmitting fundamental economic forces, tend to limit the scope for countries to diverge very far or for very long from the performance dictated by overall OECD behaviour. A country's performance is powerfully affected by what happens abroad. And sooner or later policy generally has to respond to bring the diverging economy or economies more closely into line.

Yet into line with what? If policy in most countries is set on the basis of expectations of non-cooperative policy-making elsewhere, international linkages can easily lead to convergence on policies whose global effects are different from what countries individually might have desired or expected. A satisfactory overall economic performance therefore requires two main ingredients. First, it is necessary for policy-makers individually and collectively to have as accurate an idea as possible of the developments they are likely to face, at home and abroad, on the basis of present policies. Then they have to make national policies which are in broad harmony, which add up to neither too-rapid nor too-slow a growth of world demand, and which avoid creating significant shocks.

The first step in achieving this is in carefully and accurately monitoring and projecting the behaviour of economies collectively and individually. This matter is taken up in the next chapter.

5 The need for monitoring and forecasting

Summary

Economic policy-making requires good and timely information. Reliable statistics are unavoidably out of date. Policy takes time to make, in part for institutional reasons, and there is a further interval before policy decisions take effect. For all these reasons policy-makers have to take decisions on the basis not of actual data but of a forecast of current and future events. But a forecast is unlikely to be entirely accurate. Economic behaviour may be changing and, increasingly in recent years, the forecast is likely to have been blown off course by developments transmitted from abroad. To be of use to the policy-maker, forecasts need to be continually monitored against incoming data, with more detailed post-mortems conducted periodically. This can help ensure that changes in economic behaviour are identified in sufficient time for an appropriate policy response to be devised.

Introduction

Any policy decision needs, if it is not to be arbitrary or capricious, to be based on a solid understanding of how the economy works, its present state and its future course. This is obviously true for a government which is going to attempt counter-cyclical policy. It is less obviously the case, though true none the less, for a government seeking to operate with some of the simple policy rules of thumb like 'balancing the budget' – a more difficult operation than might intuitively be supposed, because of the complicated dependence of both receipts and expenditures on the level of economic activity.

Satisfying these requirements is difficult – and significantly more so than in the physical sciences. In contrast with meteorology, for example, the data on the current state of the economy are less comprehensive, and much less immediately available; the policy-maker is considerably less certain than his weather forecasting colleague about the state of the world at the time the forecast is being made. A second contrast with the physical sciences is that in economics there are no fundamentals like Newton's Laws of Motion and the Laws of Thermodynamics. There are numerous empirical relationships, and these may hold for quite long periods, but they are typically neither as stable nor as universal.

Thus, compared with the physical scientist, the economic policy-maker starts from a less certain base, and seeks to influence a system which is less stable and less well understood. This chapter examines first the nature of the data that are available to the economic policy-maker on the state of the economy. It then considers the importance of the lags in the system, and hence the unavoidable importance of forecasts in the policy-making process. It concludes by considering ways in which monitoring, and more detailed post-mortems of forecasts, can help the policy-maker by giving early warning of changing economic behaviour.

Information on the current state of the economy

It is often supposed that there is available, in most industrial countries, a comprehensive and timely body of macroeconomic data that gives an accurate picture of the current state of the economy. This is however not so, even though considerable advances have been made over the last two or three decades, in part as a consequence of the post-war decision by a number of governments to apply Keynesian theory to practical policy-making.

Before the Second World War, regular macroeconomic statistics were largely confined to those for foreign trade, gold reserves, interest rates, registered unemployment, government expenditure and the labour force. There was naturally a good deal of more partial information available which could help in building up a picture of the state of the economy, relating for example to steel production, freight carried by rail, housebuilding activity, shipping movements and crop production. But there was no overall integrating framework.

The first comprehensive national accounts were produced in the early 1940s by the United Kingdom and the United States. Pioneering work in developing the national accounting concepts and in encouraging countries to follow standardized approaches was carried out in the late 1940s and early 1950s by the OEEC, which began collecting standardized national accounts statistics from its member countries in 1953. By 1955, nearly 100 countries were producing at least annual accounts. A number of industrial countries also felt it useful, and feasible, to produce quarterly accounts too. The United States had started doing so in 1942, and Canada, Japan and the United Kingdom followed suit in the mid-1950s. But it was not until 1968 that quarterly national accounts were available for the seven major countries. Following active encouragment by the OECD in the 1970s, sixteen countries were producing quarterly national accounts by 1983.

Vital though national accounts data are, they are insufficiently timely for policy advisers. Depending upon the country, reasonably firm national accounts data become available anywhere between three months and a year after the period to which they relate. This is too slow to inform policy-makers how the economic situation is currently developing. It is not necessary to go to the other extreme of monitoring the economy on a day-to-day basis, in the way, for example, that has become the practice over recent years where figures for the U.S. money supply are concerned. But it is always necessary and appropriate to have an up-to-date notion of how the economy is behaving in all major respects. This involves piecing together diverse, often seemingly contradictory, indicators of short-term economic movements.

Even the most assiduous monitoring, however, can of itself give only a somewhat out-of-date picture of the economy. The only instantaneously-available data are those for interest rates, exchange rates and various market-determined prices. Figures for money, retail prices, unemployment and the value of foreign trade are typically available with a lag of a month, and those for retail sales, industrial production and the volume of foreign trade with a lag of perhaps two months. Allowing for the erratic nature of most monthly series, it may not be possible to put together a satisfactorily coherent overall picture of the economy that is less than four to six months out of date. For the policy-maker this is generally not good enough – it is necessary to know where the economy is 'now'. Hence, considerable effort is typically devoted in most national administrations, as well as in the international organizations and private forecasting institutions, to the activity of 'bringing the story up to the present' (there seems to be no word in English which captures it), an activity which is normally thought of as 'estimating', but which is, in a statistical sense, 'forecasting'. Perhaps the most noteworthy example in the public domain is the 'flash' estimate of GNP and its deflator, produced in the United States before the end of the quarter to which the estimate relates.

This type of very short-term analysis is greatly helped by the availability of seasonally-adjusted statistics. These are another post-war development now taken largely for granted. Here too the United States was in the vanguard, with other countries adopting the practice partly as a result of its active propagation by international organizations, and in the first place generally by means of the statistical techniques developed at the U.S. Bureau of the Census. But some countries seem to have been hesitant to make much use of seasonally adjusted data, preferring to base comparisons on the corresponding period in the previous year. For some purposes this may indeed provide a solid basis for analysis, but it is of limited use if the focus of interest is the course of the economy over the most recent few months.

Thus the state of the economy at any given time is less than perfectly recorded by the available data. Furthermore, even if the data were thoroughly timely and comprehensive, they would be insufficient for the policy-maker's purpose; the policy-maker also usually needs a forecast of the likely future course of the economy, on the assumption of a continuation of present policies. The reasons for this are considered in the next section.

Policy lags and the need for a forecast

The policy-maker's need for an economic forecast derives not only from the delays in gathering, processing and disseminating data. Additional reasons are that policy takes time to formulate and implement, and further time to take effect upon an economy. While monetary instruments can be adjusted quickly, on the initiative of the central bank, fiscal action to change government expenditure or tax rates often requires enabling legislation, which can take months, and sometimes a year or more, to enact. Further, the maximum impact of fiscal policy is generally believed (on the evidence embodied in major ·macroeconomic models) to be reached only after a year or more. The evidence about monetary policy is less clear-cut, but most empirical studies represent monetary policy as exerting a rather spread-out effect, over a period of several years – for model evidence for a range of countries, see Chan-Lee and Kato (1984).

Hence, the sum of the time that it takes to enact policy measures (often called the 'inside' lag) and the further time before significant effects are felt on the economy (often called the 'outside' lag) typically amounts to a year or more. For these reasons policy settings have to be made in response to expected, rather than actual, economic circumstances. And to give policy-makers the best chance of getting their decisions acceptably correct requires that the forecast of future events on which they base these decisions be as accurate as possible.

The notion that economic policy has to be made in response not to an actual situation, but rather in response to a forecast of what might happen in the future, can be unsettling to the policy-maker. Not surprisingly, many balk at the idea – although, interestingly enough, the notion typically seems to trouble businessmen much less. In part policy-makers feel uncomfortable because it is not possible to make completely accurate forecasts, whether of the cause and effects of domestic developments or, even more difficult for the national forecaster, of the impulses that will come from abroad. But once it has been accepted that assessment of where the economy currently stands itself requires an important degree of 'forecasting the present', the intellectual jump required to embrace a 'forecast of the future' is perhaps less formidable.

The perception that forecasts are seldom wholly accurate is of course correct. But it is an unavoidable fact that economic policy and business decisions have to be made on the basis of predicted, rather than actual, developments. Hence the relevant matter to establish is how accurate these forecasts are likely to be, this accuracy being one of the key factors determining what sort of economic policy it is technically feasible to make.

Faith in the accuracy of forecasts, and the ability of policy-makers to make satisfactory policy on the basis of them, seems to differ from country to country and to vary over time. In the 1960s there was widespread optimism. But over the last few years in particular there has been a tendency to go to the other extreme, and reject the notion that forecasts can be accurate enough for *any* active policymaking. This has led to a belief, sometimes strongly expressed, that the possibility of active policymaking should be rejected; that it should be replaced by something more simple, and less ambitious, taking the form for example of a passive policy rule, such as a constant rate of growth of the money supply. But that sort of proposition does not really represent a way out of the dilemma, whether at the philosophic or the practical level.

Indeed, there is now a significant theoretical and applied literature which suggests that rigid adherence to a rule for any single policy variable cannot be optimal in the face of all the various sorts of shocks to which economies are typically subject.[1] Given that events have a habit of unfolding in unexpected and novel ways, faith in the ability of any one simple policy rule to perform best in all circumstances, which would imply that all types of future event can be envisaged, and would deny in advance the ability of analysis to devise any better practice, would seem unnecessarily restrictive.

In other words, there is no way of avoiding the fact that what should be aimed at in every circumstance is the *best* policy, and that while on some occasions this may well involve continued adherence to existing policy rules, on other occasions a change in policy settings might be preferable. And in turn that choice depends, unavoidably, on an assessment of the way that events are likely to unfold. Hence an important determinant of the type of policy that should be made in each circumstance is the accuracy of economic forecasts, a matter which is taken up in chapter 6.

The need for review and post-mortems

The economic policy-maker typically has to contend not only with uncertainty about how the economy is likely to evolve, but also with data on the current state of the economy that are neither fully comprehensive nor wholly reliable. In addition he has the problem that economic structure and behaviour, unlike many phenomena in the physical sciences, are typically not invariant.[2] This is particularly likely to be the case when the economy, and hence economic agents, are subjected to new types of economic impulses.

It is therefore important that the policy-maker should know as soon as possible that such change is occurring. To achieve this, it is necessary that a forecast, rather than being regarded as set in stone from the moment it is completed, should be continually reviewed and modified in the light of new incoming information. There are two main purposes to this. The simpler, and the more obvious, is to establish whether events are evolving as forecast. This information is interesting, and important in its own right. But to the policy-maker it is of itself of only limited usefulness. Much more useful is to go further, and set up some form of positive interaction between the forecast and incoming data, whereby the policy-maker is informed not only that events are not evolving as forecast, but also that the economy may not be *working* in the way that was expected or presumed when the forecast was constructed and the associated policy made.

Perhaps the simplest form of review is to check on the rate at which an expected development is taking place, so as continually to update its predicted time of arrival. There is a close analogue here with weather forecasting. Until the advent of satellite monitoring, weather forecasters in sparsely-monitored areas, such as the South Pacific, typically knew from reports from isolated weather stations what broad weather developments were in prospect, but could not plot accurately how fast these weather patterns were moving. Hence while they were able to make reasonably accurate predictions of the *type* of weather that was to come, they were unable to predict accurately *when* these changes would occur. With the development of various types of remote information-gathering devices, it is now possible to monitor rather better the rate of progress of major weather patterns, thereby increasing the accuracy of forecasts of when weather conditions will change.

The monitoring of economic events can similarly convey information of considerable significance to the policy-maker. There are many examples. A recent case involving the monitoring of OPEC imports serves to make the point. In early 1974 it was clear that the quadrupling of the oil price represented a transfer to OPEC of some 2 per cent of OECD GNP. For the OPEC countries this was so large an increase in their income that they would take time to spend it; and the precise rate of their spending would do much to determine the path of OECD exports and hence OECD GNP – for a sensitivity analysis, see Fabritius and Petersen (1981). But the likely rate of OPEC spending could only be guessed at, there being no precedent. When the 1978/79 oil price rise occurred, again transferring about 2 per cent of OECD GNP to OPEC, it was considered that it should prove possible, by drawing on the experience of the earlier episode, to make rather more accurate forecasts than had been achieved the first time. As is shown in chapter 6, this was so. But it was nevertheless recognized that there was no guarantee that OPEC's spending rate would be exactly the same on the second occasion as it had been on the first. OPEC countries had had a number of intervening years in which to design projects that waited only on the requisite finance, and they had made considerable improvement to the harbours, airports and the general transport infrastructure which had been important bottlenecks in 1974 and 1975.

While it was possible and indeed appropriate to speculate about the effects that these developments might have on the rate at which OPEC would spend their newly-acquired income, the most practicable course for the forecaster was to make an initial projection of the likely volume of OPEC imports, based broadly upon experience after the 1973/74 oil price rise, and then attempt to monitor how imports were actually moving as compared with the projections.

This poses problems, however, in part because the first data to become available relate to aggregate trade flows; they do not disaggregate trade by regions. As these data came in through 1981 it became apparent that world trade growth was relatively buoyant, by the standards of the period. Taken at face value, this buoyancy of world trade might have been taken as suggestive of reasonably buoyant general economic conditions. Indeed some observers interpreted it as such. But an examination of disaggregated trade data as they became available suggested that this buoyancy was in fact due not so much to buoyant trade amongst OECD countries, which *would* have been indicative of buoyant overall demand conditions, but rather to OPEC's spending at a very high rate, a phenomenon which could not continue for long. Indeed, the higher the rate at which OPEC spent, the sooner would they reach the point where they would be financially constrained to curtail the high rate of spending. Hence in mid-1982 the OECD Secretariat warned of the likely declining demand influence of 'OPEC imports, whose growth, after being a significant source of demand strength over the last year or two, is expected to decelerate as the OPEC current surplus shrinks'.[3]

And indeed that happened. As the data for the second quarter became available (in the third quarter), it became apparent that there had been a substantial fall.[4] The mid-year warning that the rate of OPEC importing, and hence the growth of OECD export markets, would be as markedly below trend as the preceding quarters had been above, proved to be correct. It was an important element in drawing the correct conclusion about buoyant first-half trade growth. For some countries at least, this had policy significance. Over the three years to the first half of 1982, the Japanese economy had been receiving a strong stimulus from the foreign sector, which had contributed an average of 3 percentage points per year to total demand growth. This came to a rather abrupt end because of the slowdown in OPEC import growth, which particularly affects Japan, and also because of growth restrictions on Japanese exports in OECD markets. Within six months the Japanese authorities had taken fiscal policy action to support domestic demand. It was largely the monitoring of world trade, and the drawing of the correct conclusions from those data, that permitted the Japanese authorities to take such timely action.

Once a deviation of performance from the expected path is identified, the main task is to establish whether this is due to a phenomenon that is likely to be essentially random, such as an involuntary change in stockbuilding or a fluctuation in the personal saving ratio that is likely to reverse itself before very long, or whether the deviation heralds a change in behaviour which is likely to make performance deviate persistently from the previously-projected path.

It is therefore important that the forecasting and review process be set up wherever possible in such a way that all the main elements in the forecast, and more importantly the behavioural processes underpinning its construction, can be tested continuously against new incoming information, thereby increasing the likelihood that changes in behaviour and circumstances will be recognized early. Such early knowledge spurs the critical examination of the parts of the forecasting system which are performing badly because of unexpected changes in behaviour. This in turn can give the policy-maker early warning that the basis upon which the current policy stance was predicated is wrong, possibly in turn warranting some change in that policy.

The possible implications of changing behaviour or structure for economic prediction and more especially policy-making have been explored recently by the so-called 'rational expectations' school, led by Lucas and others. These matters are discussed in chapter 7, where it is argued that while the rational expectations argument is conceptually important, its tactical significance for economic forecasting and policy-making may have been implicitly overstated by some writers.

Practical aspects of reviewing a forecast

A major problem in subjecting an economic forecast to continuing test against incoming data, particularly in the case of an international forecast involving many countries simultaneously, is the sheer volume of data involved. OECD forecasts for individual countries are inevitably less disaggregated than those typically produced by national administrations, reflecting OECD's emphasis on the analysis and forecasting of international trade and financial flows, and hence the transmission of economic impulses among countries. Even so, some 7,000-odd data series are involved, and these have to be reviewed if the forecast is to be continually confronted with incoming data. Thus, even with parsimonious disaggregation, the data-handling task is enormous if it is to be undertaken properly.

The only practicable way in which such quantities of incoming data can be handled, and thereafter analysed, is by computer. Prior to the widespread use of computers, and the dissemination of data in machine-readable form, it was not feasible to examine the quantity of data needed to keep other than the most basic tabs on an international forecast. It was necessary to rely instead on a series-by-series scanning of incoming statistics by the experienced forecaster, who had to assess each piece of data for its potential information. A few people possess the extraordinary gift of being able to do this in their heads, of being able to scan column after column of data, picking out with an apparently unerring accuracy those figures which look odd. The process involved is not well understood, but it seems to involve the checking of data against the predictions and workings of a mental model of how the economy works. The disadvantage of such a method is that the number of people truly gifted in this way is small, and the technique is difficult to explain and transmit to others.

If instead the requisite data scanning can be undertaken, or at least assisted, by computer, the process can be made more readily and more widely available. But it is important that the examination of the large quantities of incoming data be done in such a way as to allow people individually to retain an overall comprehension of how the forecast as a whole was constructed and how events are unfolding in relation to that forecast. If the procedure is only partially developed, so that different people each assume responsibility for only part of the forecast, with none having an overall grip on it, the result is likely to be less successful than when one or two have complete control, albeit at the cost of examining fewer data. It is vital that, to the extent that disaggregation and increased frequency of data add to the quantity of information that has to be analysed, ways be found to enable a limited number of minds to come to appreciate the entirety of the situation, so that they can think in a related way about the various problems involved.

In the OECD Secretariat the desk officers, responsible for individual OECD countries, are able, as are their counterparts in national and other international organizations, to keep a reasonably close watch on the evolving situation through studying the data flow from their countries. Hence they are able, to the extent the quality of these data permits, to modify their perception of what has been happening or is likely to happen as events and policies unfold. Obviously this technique is at its most refined in the case of the larger countries, where the range, timeliness and quality of data tend to be greater.

However, the area in which the OECD has a comparative advantage, and hence particularly seeks to analyse, forecast, review and refine its projections, is the transmission of economic impulses from one country to another through international trade and financial flows. Here the problem of monitoring all the data as they become available, assessing their quality (which can be extremely variable) and working out the most likely implications for the overall forecast, is a large task that requires both the technical mastery of a large quantity of data and subtlety of interpretation. The task can be aided considerably by computer-based methods but has to be supplemented by the exercise of that elusive phenomenon 'judgement'.

The tendency towards internationally-synchronous business cycle developments noted in the previous two chapters means that there can sometimes be a particularly high pay-off to monitoring carried out on a cross-country basis. Monthly trade figures, for example, tend in most countries to be erratic; turning points in a single country's time series may not be clear until well after the event. But if an apparent 'blip' in one country's figures is found to have a parallel in other countries' figures the probability that it is 'just a blip' is less: turning points may be detected sooner. The same can also be true of industrial production. According to oral tradition at the OECD, it was only when (apparently fortuitously) a staff statistician calculated a combined European industrial production index for the first time that there was confirmation that the 1958 recession had reached Europe. Evidence which still appeared ambiguous for each European country in isolation became convincing when aggregated internationally.

The need for fully-detailed post-mortems

Thus monitoring of the sort described above in connection with OPEC importing behaviour in 1981 can be extremely important, giving early warning of new or unexpected developments in economic behaviour. But such successes are relatively rare. While there is scope for improving the range of monitoring somewhat further, the underlying problem is likely to remain for many years yet; the full range of data needed to undertake such monitoring is simply not available until well after the events they describe have occurred.

This means that some changes in behaviour, particularly rather fundamental ones affecting the behaviour of the economic system as a whole, cannot be discovered and fully analysed until well after the event. Nevertheless it is important that they should indeed be discovered, and as soon as possible. To this end forecasters need to conduct full 'post-mortems' of the performance of their forecasts once all the data are in.

In principle the first step in a full post-mortem – the measurement of forecast accuracy – would seem straightforward; simply compare what was forecast with what actually happened. But the issue is rather more complicated than that.

First, all forecasts rest on assumptions, which in practice may or may not be ratified. Hence there is an immediate distinction to be made between a 'technical' test of forecast accuracy and a 'practical' test. As a *technical* test of forecast accuracy, it is appropriate to 'adjust a forecast for its assumptions', i.e. establish what would have been forecast had the elements exogenous to the forecast been as they actually were, rather than as they were assumed to be. However, while this test may be the fairest to the forecaster, it may not impress the user, who has to take decisions on the basis of the forecasts as they actually were. It is of no practical comfort to a businessman or policy-maker to be told that the forecasts he was using would have been correct if only certain key assumptions had been made correctly. At the limit, he may retort that he has to take decisions on the basis of forecasts, and when he pays a forecaster to produce them he is paying him to get *everything* right. Care therefore has to be taken in setting up the appropriate test of forecast accuracy. Sometimes it will be the technical test, sometimes the practical test and sometimes, unavoidably, a mixture of the two.

The two areas in which the assumptions cause particular problems for the assessment of the accuracy of single-country macroeconomic forecasts are government policy and developments abroad. Government policy affects the *ex post* accuracy of a projection in at least two ways. First, it is often not certain, even when policy statements give the appearance of being quite clear, what the stance of policy actually is. For example it is not at all uncommon to find the underlying stance of fiscal policy, as measured by the cyclically-adjusted budget position, ultimately differing by at least 1 per cent of GNP from what governments project and, indeed, intend it to be. Allowing for the effects of multipliers, the total effect on the forecast will be rather greater, perhaps by a factor of around 2. And the stance of monetary policy is even harder to define; various measures are available, but none on its own is sufficient. Second, fiscal and monetary policy can be changed after a projection has been made, affecting the outcome. For forecasts looking only one or two quarters ahead, the consequences are in most cases relatively minor, because policy changes typically take several quarters to take effect. But for forecasts with a twelve to eighteen month horizon, the policy assumption can be a quantitatively important reason for divergence between forecast and outcome.

Forecasters in the public sector who make the sort of forecasts that, as an input into the policy-making process, are the main concern of this chapter, are in general not keen to accept responsibility for errors that arise because the government cannot quantify its own policy accurately. While on occasion this can be merely a convenient excuse, they have a case when, by the rules of the game, they are *instructed* to forecast on the basis of the policy stance as stated by government. Forecasters serving private sector clients, on the other hand, customarily forecast on a 'most likely outcome' basis, which typically encompasses the stance of policy not as the government says it will be, but as the forecaster expects it to be. If the forecaster has any reason to expect that policy will be different from what the government says it will be, an attempt is made to allow for this in the projection. Thus the forecaster's skill here includes the ability to establish what the stance of policy *is*, and to anticipate changes in the stance of policy. Hence as far as policy assumptions are concerned, the appropriate test of forecast accuracy for the government forecaster may often be the technical, or policy-adjusted, test, whereas that for the business forecaster might more often be the practical, or unadjusted, test.

The consequences of developments abroad also enter into any assessment of forecast accuracy. The forecaster whose responsibility is limited to making a projection for a single economy is likely, when conducting a post-mortem, to wish to adjust his projection, after the event, to establish what he would have projected had he assumed that the rest of the world would evolve as it actually did, rather than as he assumed it would. He does this because, typically, he does not regard it as legitimate to be blamed for errors that derive from an area of the forecast for which he is not responsible. On the other hand the user of the forecast, whether in the government or the private sector, is again unlikely to be mollified by the argument that the forecast would have been better, if only better assumptions had been made about developments abroad. Policy-makers and private sector users need, for most purposes, an assessment of what is actually expected to happen abroad. Hence in respect of developments abroad the practical assessment, with no adjustment for unforeseen developments abroad, would probably be the better test, both for national government forecasts and for business forecasts.

But a third dimension enters when the forecast being assessed has been constructed to assist policy-making at the international level. This is essentially the international counterpart of the domestic policy-making process. Like national policy discussions, international consultations, such as those which take place in the Economic Policy Committee of the OECD, need as a starting point for their discussions internationally-consistent country-by-country projections of what is most likely to happen if countries, individually and collectively, continue with present policies. Given such projections, discussion can then proceed to consider how developments might look instead if a country or group of countries were to change policies.

In assessing the accuracy of the single-country forecasts produced for this purpose by the international organizations it is legitimate, as with the forecasts produced by national administrations, to adjust them for the effects of post-forecast changes in policy, because these were explicitly excluded from the forecast at the express request of the policy-makers. And it is appropriate to take the consequences of such changes in policy into *all* the country forecasts, by making due allowances for the transmission of policy effects from one country to another through trade and financial linkages. But it is not appropriate to adjust for other errors transmitted via the trade and financial linkages because, unlike the case with the national forecast, trade and financial flows are *endogenous* to the forecasts of the international organizations.

These considerations suggest that, in assessing the accuracy of forecasts made to assist economic policy-making, it is appropriate, regardless of whether the forecast was made by a national administration or an international organization, to adjust the forecast for its policy assumptions. But it is in general not appropriate, for either type of forecast, to make any other adjustment.

Post-mortems of this kind are unavoidably restricted to a consideration of quantitative forecasts, the main reason being that they are the only ones about which it is possible to form a reasonably objective assessment. As McNees (1979), for many years now the quasi-official scorekeeper of all the major U.S. forecasters, has observed, 'Some of the most highly regarded macroeonomic forecasters do not issue numerical forecasts. Qualitative, verbal forecasts can be extremely valuable either by themselves or as supplements to numerical forecasts. Such forecasts are, however, virtually impossible to evaluate. For example, a forecast that 'things are going to get worse' (or 'going to get better') will almost always ring true to someone who subsequently fares poorly (or well). The difficulty is that words have different quantitative implications to different persons and at different times. The word 'slowdown' for example, has recently been applied to economic growth rates ranging from 5.5 to −3.5 percent'.[5]

That being said, however, it is unfortunate that post-mortems have to be limited to quantitative forecasts, because it is also the case that the verbal, non-quantitative assessment can be an important adjunct to a quantitative forecast, to the extent that on occasions of extreme uncertainty it can even be the more important part. Again to quote McNees '... the inherent uncertainty or randomness associated with different forecast periods seems to vary widely over time. On some occasions, such as 1974-75, even a fairly sizeable deviation between a forecast and the actual outcome would represent a comparatively brilliant forecast. On others, such as 1972 and 1976-77, even the least gifted forecasters anticipated the future course of the economy almost perfectly. Accordingly, it is meaningless to label a forecast "good" or "bad" on the basis of the absolute magnitude of its error. Forecast evaluation must be *relative* rather than *absolute* because no reasonable absolute standard exists'.[6]

The balanced approach is to assess objectively the accuracy of quantitative forecasts, but to recognize also the importance of a good supplementary qualitative assessment: a good forecaster writes informative explanatory text around his forecasts, just as a good policy-maker takes note of such information when making policy.

Practical problems in assessing forecast accuracy

While the broad principles by which a post-mortem on forecast performance should be conducted are fairly straight forward, in practice detailed comprehensive post-mortems are not carried out particularly often. There are various reasons for this, one being that the exercise is technically more difficult than might be supposed.

The first technical problem in conducting a post-mortem is in establishing what figures ought to be selected as the representation of what actually happened, for economic data in most OECD countries are typically subject to frequent and sometimes considerable revision. In the United States, for example, the so-called 'flash' estimate of real quarterly GNP is released just prior to the end of the quarter itself. This estimate is calculated from partial data, and is revised, often considerably, a month or so later, when the preliminary estimates are published. These first revisions typically do not change the sign of the estimated change, but they commonly result in a change in the estimated rate of growth or decline by 2 percentage points or more at an annual rate.

Other OECD countries do not publish 'flash' estimates of GDP, in part because of the typical size of the revisions to these initial estimates. Statistics Canada produces a monthly series of total domestic product, which has a significantly wider coverage than just industrial output. But even in the majority of countries which do not produce such early estimates, the differences between the first, full, estimates of real GDP and the subsequent revisions are also typically large. For the larger OECD economies, revisions of 1 or 2 percentage points in the rate of change at an annual rate are the rule rather than the exception. There is a general tendency for first estimates to understate quarterly changes in GDP, possibly because they tend to omit information from the small enterprise sector, where output changes are likely to be particularly volatile. Furthermore, countries that compile quarterly national accounts generally take the opportunity of the production of the annual figure – which itself may be subject to revision in later years – to revise the year's quarterly numbers. This revision often changes the GDP growth rates of the constituent quarters quite substantially, sometimes by as much as 3 per cent at an annual rate. Changes to the growth rates for the expenditure components are even larger, and revisions of 4 or 5 percentage points are common for gross fixed capital formation and the trade balance. Clearly, changes of this magnitude will often reverse the sign of the original growth estimates – particularly when the underlying rates of growth or decline are only 1 or 2 per cent per year.

In addition to revisions which result from the processing and re-processing of more complete and wider data, revisions also get made from time to time because of a change of base year, with attendant changes to the weighting given the various components, and even the coverage of the overall series. These changes sometimes result in large changes to the measured rate of change of such series as real GNP.[7] The 1973/74 oil price rise markedly changed relative prices and, with a lag, relative quantities of major components of the series. Energy consumption itself fell per unit of GNP, with the fall in oil consumption being particularly marked, and in due course the relative prices of energy-intensive products also rose, bringing about a relative decline in their consumption too. Correspondingly the relative prices of non-energy-intensive products fell, and their weight in total expenditure rose. Some of the major OECD countries are still using a pre-oil-price-rise base-year for their constant price estimates, and their estimated growth rates for the period since 1973 are likely to undergo substantial revisions when eventually the accounts are rebased to reflect the changes in relative prices. For example, when Japan rebased its national accounts from 1970 to 1975 prices, the figure for the average growth rate over the period 1975 to 1978 fell from 6 per cent per year to just over 5 per cent. And the 1976 growth figure for U.S. GNP was reduced from 5.6 per cent using 1970 prices to 4.9 per cent at 1975 prices.

Statistics are also periodically revised to increase their coverage. The invention and production of changed or completely new products goes on continually, and they have to be incorporated in the relevant output indicators if these are not to become progressively less representative. But often national statistical authorities pay less attention than economists feel they should to providing an overlap of old and new series: typically statisticians are more concerned about getting the *level* right than about continuity. Economists on the other hand are often less concerned about whether the absolute level of a series is correct than about having a long run of data – which may well be several series of data linked together – that have no discontinuities and therefore are amenable to time series analysis.

Given the number and scale of the revisions to the data which economic forecasters have to project, it is by no means straightforward to select, or lay down a rule for selecting, the value that should be used as the actual when conducting a post-mortem. Indeed this question has occasioned much debate. The practice adopted by most forecasters when assessing the accuracy of forecasts is to take as the actual the first full GNP figure that is available – that is on the one hand to ignore a 'flash' or other initial partial estimate, but also to ignore a late figure that incorporates significant composition changes or changes in base. There is a logic to this. The most appropriate, as well perhaps as the most legitimate, test of forecasting accuracy is take as the actual the series that most closely measures what the forecaster purported to be forecasting.

The second problem in conducting a proper post-mortem lies in adjusting a forecast for its assumptions about policy. To begin with, it is virtually impossible for anyone other than the original forecaster to establish what would have been projected had it been assumed that policy would be as it actually turned out to be. Clearly this problem is at its most acute when the forecast in question was made many years previously. But even in the case of recent forecasts, generally only the forecaster can assess the extent to which a different policy assumption would have affected the forecast.

The task is becoming easier – and more replicable – to the extent that forecasters increasingly use formal macroeconomic models in which the impact of monetary and fiscal stance is explicitly quantified. (This question is taken up in chapter 7.) But even this development does not fully solve the problem. Few forecasters would accept uncritically a pure model-constructed baseline projection, just as few would accept uncritically a model-based simulation of an alternative projection. Virtually all forecasters would seek to supplement the information embodied formally in their model with other information external to the model. To do this they may take into account information or relationships which are moderately well-attested but not yet incorporated in the model; at the limit they may make changes purely on the basis of 'hunch' or 'feeling'. But establishing after the event the contribution of such judgement to a forecast requires that very careful records be kept.

The problem is more demanding still at the level of a set of internationally-consistent projections. Until relatively recently the resource implications of simultaneously adjusting a set of projections for all their policy assumptions for a large number of countries represented too demanding a task. Constructing even the baseline 'no policy change' projection is a large exercise. Such work began, in the OECD, only in the early 1960s. To date nearly all of the resources available have been absorbed in constructing the basic projections and ensuring that they are internationally coherent – an essential criterion which, if not met, guarantees that jointly the forecasts must be incorrect.

When the internationally-consistent projection has been made it is then, in principle, possible after the event to establish what the forecast would have been had it been constructed on the basis of policy as it actually was, rather than as it was assumed that it would be. But in practice the task of doing this is complex, and significant resources are needed. Work in this area is proceeding at OECD, but it seems unlikely that it will be possible to carry out full post-mortems for the period before the 1980s.

For the years before 1980, therefore, judgement on the accuracy of international forecasts has to be based on a much simpler analysis. This necessitates considerable caution in interpretation. With these caveats in mind, nevertheless it is the case that several striking conclusions result from a study of forecasting accuracy over the last thirty years. The next chapter considers the evidence on the accuracy of single-country forecasts and those for the OECD economy as a whole, so as to establish what sort of forecasting accuracy it would seem reasonable for the policy-maker to expect. Particular emphasis is placed on the apparent 'transmission' of forecasting error from one country to another. This information is a necessary input into deciding what sort of policy it is appropriate and feasible to attempt to make.

6 The dependability of economic forecasts

Summary

The accuracy of the forecasts which underpin economic policy-making has been somewhat changeable. On the basis of a simple comparison of forecast with out-turn, forecasts of real year-ahead GNP were poor (by modern standards) immediately after World War II, soon got better, fared badly during the 1973/74 oil shock, but have been relatively accurate since. Year-ahead forecasts for OECD area real GNP and inflation for each of the first three years following the second oil shock have, but for one year, been within a percentage point or so of the outcome. For individual countries errors are, understandably, somewhat larger, but even so half of the single-country year-ahead real GNP forecasts have been accurate to within 1 percentage point. Forecasts of inflation have had a broadly similar record although, unlike forecasts of activity, there seems to have been some systematic underprediction, at least in the 1960s. This sort of forecasting accuracy should generally be maintainable in the future, and quite possibly even improved upon. Further, the experience of the last twenty years suggests that, in future, the circumstances when relatively large mistakes are liable to be made should be recognizable in advance; if so, policy-makers could be warned accordingly.

Introduction

Economic forecasting is not, generally, an end in itself. It is, rather, an input – an aid to those who make economic decisions, whether in the private or public sector. The value and usefulness of a forecast therefore depends fundamentally on the extent to which it contributes constructively to that end. It is natural to wish to evaluate this contribution. In practice, however, this is not easy to do, if only because it is almost impossible to establish precisely what role a forecast has played in any given policy decision. In assessing forecasts, therefore, it is common to attempt an apparently simpler task, which is to find out how accurate – or rather how inaccurate – forecasts actually have been. From the results, it might be hoped that it would prove possible to infer what sort of assistance they can or do provide to the policy-maker.

In fact even this apparently straightforward task raises considerable conceptual and practical problems, described in the previous chapter. In short, it is surprisingly difficult to specify precisely what constitutes a 'good' or 'right' forecast. Nevertheless the task is important. Policy-makers need to know how dependable forecasts are – what degree of reliance it is appropriate to place upon them. Furthermore, it is necessary for forecasters to know how much weight they should place on the accuracy of various forecast components when advising policy-makers.

The purpose of this chapter therefore is to look, in a broad way, at the accuracy of the sort of economic forecasts made available to, and used by, OECD governments in the process of making economic policy. To do this, data are examined for as many countries as possible over as long a period as possible, relating to projections by national forecasters, both public and private, as well as by the OECD. Particular attention is paid to the reasons for the largest errors, especially when there appears to be an international dimension to them.[1]

The forecasts of most concern to policy makers

Policy-advisers in virtually all OECD countries, who assist in the setting of monetary policy or the construction of their countries' annual budgets, typically have been most interested in:

- a forecast of the likely economic conditions over the coming year or two;
- an assessment of the sensitivity of this forecast to the more uncertain elements underlying its construction;

- perhaps also a projection of possible economic conditions further ahead than the twelve months or so of the basic frecast.

Over the last few years, policy-makers have given somewhat more weight in their policy statements, and to some extent in their policy-making also, to events over the slightly longer term. This shift of emphasis is discussed in chapter 11. But so far few comprehensive forecasts have been made with a horizon of more than two years. Medium or long-term projections, where they exist, are generally quite explicitly 'not forecasts'. Hence it is difficult to assess with any confidence how well forecasting might be able to assist policy-makers who have this longer time perspective.

While most national forecasters project many economic variables, this chapter focusses on two of those of most concern to the policy-maker – real GNP and the price level, whether measured by the GNP deflator or an index of consumer prices. This is not to say, of course, that forecasts of other variables, such as the balance of payments or the money supply, have not been extremely important on some occasions.

There have been various examinations of forecasting accuracy for individual countries over the years, conducted with a variety of purposes in mind. Some studies seek to compare the predictions of 'serious' economic forecasts with those of 'naive' models, in order to see if 'serious' forecasts are worth the attention accorded them. Other studies are concerned more with comparing the forecasts of different forecasters in order to find out which have the better track record. Some studies seek to establish which variables tend to be forecast relatively well, and which relatively badly. And sometimes the main concern is with the accuracy of the levels of the variables being forecast, whereas others are concerned more with the accuracy with which the dates of turning points are predicted.[2]

Various summary statistics of forecasting accuracy are typically calculated. These include the average error of the variable being forecast; the root-mean-square error, which gives greater weight to large forecasting errors; and the standardized root-mean-square error, which gives greater weight to forecasting error for variables that vary little. These measures frequently appear in post-mortems in the academic literature, which often is concerned with summary measures to permit comparison of a large number of forecasts over different time periods. The concern in this chapter, however, is with the usefulness of forecasts to the policy-maker, who is not only likely to be concerned with forecasting error *on average*, but also with the maximum size of error that he is liable to be faced with. Hence, the main emphasis is on the overall *range* of forecast error. Within this basic concern, particular attention is paid to the factors which seem to have caused relatively large forecasting errors to be made from time to time, and to establishing whether the circumstances that caused them are such that it is possible to warn the policy-maker in advance when there is a risk of unusually large error.[3]

Early forecasting performance – the transition from war to peace

Serious macroeconomic forecasting started only after the second World War, and then initially in only a few countries. The outgrowth of the acceptance of Keynesian views on the potential for economic control and management required two main elements – national economic accounts, to measure what had recently been going on in the economy considered in its entirety, and macroeconomic forecasts, to provide a rational basis from which to make policy.

It is not surprising, given their particular interest in and commitment to securing a better economic performance with high levels of employment, that serious economic forecasting got under way first in the Nordic countries, with detailed forecasts being produced annually from 1948 in Finland, 1949 in Sweden, and 1952 in Norway.

In the United States some forecasts were made in the early post-War years too, but the early commitment to stabilization policy there was less strong, and systematic macroeconomic forecasting largely stopped during the period of the Eisenhower administration.

These early forecasts were in general highly inaccurate, when judged by the standards of later years. This may have been because events at that time were particularly difficult to forecast (growth rates were high and variable), and forecasters were inexperienced. But an additional reason, important for the smaller,more open economies, is likely to have been incorrect assumptions about developments in the rest of the world, leading to incorrect projections of export volumes, import prices and financial influences emanating from abroad. Certainly, some of the early forecasts for smaller open economies were rather inaccurate. The official GDP forecasts for Sweden in 1949 and 1950, for example, were wrong by 5 percentage points and 4.4 points respectively. Errors of such size were seldom made again, except in 1953 and 1959, when it is clear that unexpected international developments helped blow the forecasts off course, a point which is taken up later in this chapter. An early Finnish GDP forecast, for 1949, was off by 4.2 points, inexperience again being a likely important reason.[4]

In the United States, too, the early post-war period saw many of the largest forecasting errors on record,[5] although here it seems that the main difficulty was in forecasting domestic developments. Systematic data on forecasts and their accuracy are not available in the way they are for Sweden and Finland. But Zarnowitz (1979) records that whereas nominal GNP grew by about 11 per cent in 1948 and again in 1949, one reputable group of forecasters projected a 6 per cent *decline* for the first of the years, and a further slight fall for the second. As Zarnowitz notes, 'The developments of the time simply could not be predicted well with estimates based on data and relationships for the 1930s and false analogies with the early post-World War I period'.[6] Large underpredictions of industrial production were also made for 1950, largely because of the unexpected outbreak of the war in Korea, with its associated military build-up.

Over the remainder of the decade, however, and into the 1960s, economies settled down into a somewhat more stable peacetime pattern of demand and production. The commitment to full employment, and policies to achieve it, became more widespread, forecasting techniques developed, experience was gained, and forecasting performance in the increasing (but still by present day standards limited) number of countries that were making systematic predictions generally improved – see McMahon (1965). In line with improved techniques and better performance, ambition also increased. The forecast for GNP was more systematically split into its price and volume components, and an increasing number of components of demand were distinguished and separately forecast.

It was only by the mid-1960s that serious macroeconomic forecasting got under way in the majority of OECD countries. It was at that time, too, that the OECD, which had been making forecasts since the beginning of the decade, started to publish them. There the aim from the outset was to produce an integrated set of internationally consistent country forecasts, taking due account of the linkages between economies. From the outset these year-ahead GNP forecasts formed the basis for discussion at many international policy discussions, as well as providing the international part of many countries' economic projections.

As an overall indication of the accuracy of the economic forecasts available to policy-makers, it is therefore instructive to consider first the forecasting record for the OECD economy considered as a whole. The OECD's own forecasts are used for this purpose.

The accuracy of global forecasts

Since the mid-1960s, the year-ahead forecasts of real OECD GNP have generally been within a percentage point of the outcome (Table 6.1). The exceptions during the last seventeen years were:

(i)   the 4 percentage points over-prediction for 1974, the price of internationally-traded oil having quadrupled at the end of 1973 (an increase of only about 50 per cent was incorporated in the forecasts, which were finalized just before the December 1973 increases took effect);

(ii) the under-predictions of 1968 ($-1\frac{1}{4}$ percentage points) and of 1976 (also $-1\frac{1}{4}$ points);

(iii) the over-predictions of 1971 ($1\frac{1}{2}$ percentage points), 1975 ($1\frac{3}{4}$ points) and 1982 ($1\frac{1}{2}$ points).

The data on forecasts and actuals are plotted in the upper panel of Chart 6.1; the forecasts broadly tracked the year-to-year changes in real GDP growth, as well as picking up the general downward trend since the mid-1960s. Also apparent is a tendency to mis-predict many of the years of maximum change, although 1973 was an honourable exception.

To examine the issue of systematic bias further, the data on forecasts and actuals are plotted in Chart 6.2. The various points, which represent forecasts for individual years, should each be considered in relation to the 45° line AA´. Any forecast lying on this line is correct; forecasts to the left are under-predictions, and

Table 6.1 *Forecast and actual OECD real GNP growth*

	Forecast	Actual	Error
	(1)	(2)	(1)–(2)
1966	4¾*	5.4*	−¾
1967	4¼*	4.0*	¼
1968	4½*	5.8*	−1¼
1969	3¾*	4.8*	−1
1970	3¼*	2.4*	¾
1971	4¾*	3.3*	1½
1972	5*	5.8*	−¾
1973	6½*	6.5*	0
1974	3¾	−0.1	4
1975	½	−1.2	1¾
1976	4	5.2	−1¼
1977	3¾	3.7	0
1978	3½	3.9	−½
1979	3	3.3	−¼
1980	1	1.2	−¼
1981	1	1.2	−¼
1982	1¼	−0.2	1½

| Mean absolute error | | | 1 |

* Seven largest countries.

Note: Forecast values for year t are taken from the December OECD *Economic Outlook* of year $t-1$, and actual values from the December OECD *Economic Outlook* of year $t+1$. The 1967 forecast was taken from the November 1966 edition of the OECD Observer, and the 1966 forecast from the March 1966 edition of the OECD Observer. Where forecasts were expressed as ranges, the mid-point was taken. Exceptionally, the December 1971 OECD *Economic Outlook* did not present a year-ahead forecast because of uncertainty about exchange rates just before the Smithsonian realignment; accordingly the 1972 forecast and the 1970 actual shown in the table are the figures published in the July 1972 OECD *Economic Outlook*. The 1966 and 1967 actuals, and the 1966, 1967, 1968 and 1969 forecasts were obtained by weighting together the individual-country forecasts, using the weights published with the forecasts. The 1982 actual was adjusted for exceptionally large data revisions to the U.K. national accounts, and differs slightly from the figure published in the December 1983 OECD *Economic Outlook*.

The correlation coefficient (r^2) between the forecast growth rates and the actual growth rates is 0.7. If the observations for 1974 and 1975 are excluded, the coefficient (as referred to in the text) is 0.8.

forecasts to the right are over-predictions. It can be seen that, discounting 1974 and 1975, which as discussed later in this chapter were highly special years, the forecasts for most years lie close to the 45° line. That having been said, there is some evidence of modest systematic bias. The dotted regression line was fitted to the data excluding the observations for 1974 and 1975. The equation of the line (with the standard errors in brackets) is

$$\text{Actual} = -0.3 + 1.1*\text{Forecast} \qquad r^2 = 0.8$$
$$(0.59) \quad (0.15)$$

The fact that the slope coefficient is slightly greater than unity suggests some tendency towards proportionate under-prediction of the growth rate when this is above 3 per cent, and the fact that the constant is less than zero suggests that there is a tendency to over-predict when growth is slower than 3 per cent. However, these conclusions are not statistically significant, given the size of the standard errors of estimate; the constant term is insignificantly different at the 5 per cent level from zero, and similarly the slope coefficient is insignificantly different from unity. Further, the effects of the adjustments which would be implied, at least *ex post*, to the projections are rather small. For example, taking the regression coefficients at face value, the following 'adjustments' might be implied:

Forecast	Adjusted Forecast
0	$-\frac{1}{4}$
3	3
5	$5\frac{1}{4}$

This forecasting performance, which is consistent with a broad understanding of the forces acting on the OECD economy, is a better performance than that offered by conventional naive models, which take as their prediction for each year either the growth rate of the previous year (Column (i) below), or the average of some previous run of years – three in the example shown in Column (ii). The projections produced by a more sophisticated ARIMA (Auto-Regressive Integrated Moving Average) model also prove inferior to those produced by methods founded in structural economic relationships (Column (iii))[7]. These naive models would have yielded the following errors:

	(i)	(ii)	(iii)
1967	1.4	1.7	1.1
1968	−1.8	−0.9	−2.6
1969	1.0	0.3	1.0
1970	2.4	2.5	0.9
1971	−0.9	1.0	−0.2
1972	−2.5	−2.3	−2.3
1973	−0.7	−2.7	−1.4
1974	6.6	5.3	4.9
1975	1.1	5.3	1.2
1976	−6.4	−3.5	−3.6
1977	1.5	−2.4	1.0
1978	−0.2	−1.3	−2.1
1979	0.6	1.0	0.9
1980	2.1	2.4	0.9
1981	0	1.6	0.7
1982	1.4	2.1	1.9
Mean absolute error	1.9	2.3	1.7

Many of these errors are greater than 1 percentage point, and some are very large. The mean absolute error is on average twice as large as for the OECD Secretariat's forecasts.

It is not clear what qualitative interpretation should be placed upon the OECD's forecasting performance, for in part how impressive or unimpressive it is considered to be depends upon how difficult the forecasting task is assessed as being, and what sort of accuracy had been expected. But it is probably fair to say that such accuracy is somewhat less than many forecasters once had hoped would prove possible, but better than some present-day detractors would suggest.

To some extent, such forecasts for the OECD area as a whole might, on *a priori* grounds, be expected to benefit from a law-of-large-numbers type of compensation of errors, with positive errors for some countries being offset by negative errors for others. On the other hand, international linkage effects – and the express requirement that OECD forecasts take these into account – might suggest a tendency on occasions for area-wide forecast errors to be magnified relative to individual country errors. Stronger or weaker than expected GNP growth in one country will lead, through allowance for the trade linkage effects, to stronger or weaker than expected growth in other countries. The effect will be quantitatively the most important in respect of the United States, for which a 1 per

Chart 6.1 Forecast and actual OECD real GNP growth, and errors

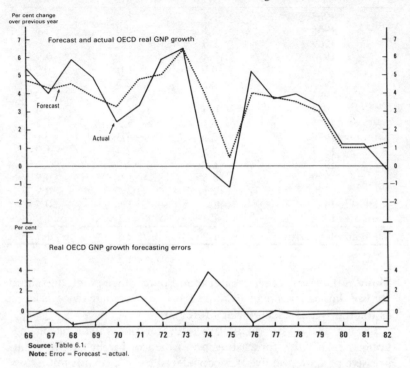

Per cent change
over previous year

Forecast and actual OECD real GNP growth

Forecast

Actual

Per cent

Real OECD GNP growth forecasting errors

Source: Table 6.1.
Note: Error = Forecast – actual.

cent change in GNP probably changes the GNP of the rest of the OECD area by about ¼ of a percentage point, and for Germany, where a 1 percentage point change in GNP changes GNP in the rest of Europe (but not North America or Japan) also by perhaps ¼ of a percentage point.

In fact single-country forecasts do appear to be somewhat less accurate than forecasts for the OECD area, although whether this is for the reason considered above, or due to some other factor, such as the impact of unexpected exchange rate movements, is hard to establish. The evidence on the accuracy of single-country forecasts is based upon a sample of 33 sets of forecasts for 14 OECD countries – the data and sources are given in Llewellyn and Araí (1984). Nineteen of the sets of forecasts were made by national forecasters, whether official or private, and the rest were made by the OECD Secretariat. For the period from the mid-1960s to 1982, about half of these forecasts for individual countries were within 1 percentage

Chart 6.2 Scatter diagram of forecast and actual OECD real GNP growth

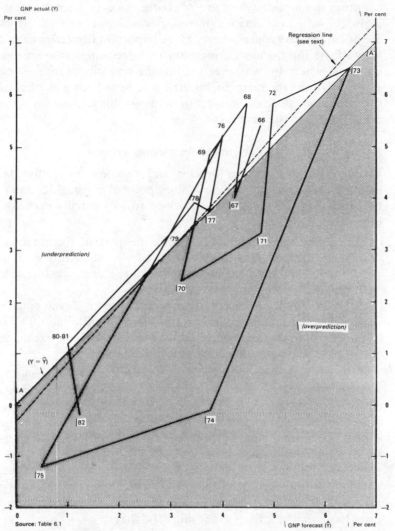

Source: Table 6.1

point of the outcome, with a further one-fourth of the forecasts within 2 percentage points of the outcome (Chart 6.3). On the other hand, there were some extremely large errors, much larger than for the OECD area as a whole, even when taken in relation to the 10 per cent-odd growth rates of real GNP that some countries were experiencing at the time.

When large errors in any given year are made for just one or two countries, the reasons are often largely specific to the country or countries in question. They are of course important and, increasingly, the subject of detailed post-mortems. However, such errors are not of primary concern here. More important from the point of view of the international dimension to forecasting error are the occasions when, for whatever reason, the majority of forecasting errors all run in the same direction. There have been a number of such occasions since the mid-1960s, and possible reasons for them are taken up in the next section.

Domestic and foreign origins of forecasting error

The differences between forecast and outcome for individual country forecasts can, from the vantage point of any single country, be divided (at least conceptually) into two essentially exclusive categories:

(i)   errors originating in the domestic part of the forecast, whether because of a post-forecast policy change, or error in one or more of the components of the domestic forecast; and

(ii) error in the forecast of, or assumption about, developments in other countries, whether inside or outside the OECD. Error in the assumption about, or forecast of, the exchange rate implicitly also falls into this category.

If, in any given year, the forces acting on the OECD economy were broadly neutral, and if each single-country forecast were made essentially in isolation, with little contact between and discussion among those making forecasts for other countries, it might be expected that some country forecasters would over-predict domestic developments, while others would under-predict. Likewise, some would over-predict, or make too strong an assumption about, developments in the rest of the world, while others would do the reverse. Hence in a broadly normal year without significant discussion among forecasters it might be that

(i)   the balance between the number of positive forecasting errors and the number of negative forecasting errors would be fairly close to zero; and

(ii) the various single-country errors would approximately cancel one another, so that a forecast for the total OECD, made up from component country forecasts, would turn out to be relatively close to the actual outcome.

Chart 6.3 Single-country GNP forecasting errors
OECD and National Forecasts

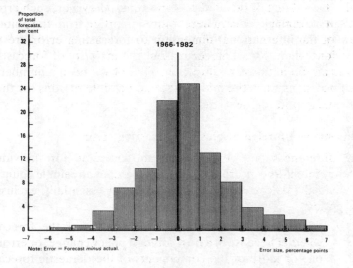

Of course this is somewhat of a stylization. Seldom is a year perfectly normal for any country, and in some years the OECD economy as a whole is markedly affected by a non-neutral force or set of forces. Furthermore, national forecasters do in fact talk to OECD forecasters, and to one another, each trying to form a view of likely developments abroad. Hence neither proposition (i) nor proposition (ii) could be expected to hold in a strict sense; there will probably be random fluctuation in the balance of pluses over minuses, so that the balance would be unlikely to be exactly zero except by chance.

However, in addition to the years – which over the last decade and a half have represented the majority – when the balance between positive and negative country errors has been fairly close to zero, there have also been certain special atypical years when the single-country errors are rather far from randomly distributed. This can arise in any one of a variety of ways. It can be that the entire OECD economy is affected by an external shock. If the shock is unexpected, or the likely effects are fairly generally misunderstood, the result is likely to be a significant forecasting error for the OECD area as a whole and therefore for most countries individually. The first oil shock, in 1973/74, is a case in point. Or it may be that something rather general happens and is misforecast *within* the

Table 6.2   *Analysis of single-country forecasting errors: year-ahead real*
GNP

| | Balance of single country errors (OECD plus national forecasts) (B) | Memorandum Items | |
		GNP-weighted sum of single country errors [a] (National forecasts)	Error of OECD forecasts for OECD area
	(1)	(2)	(3)
1966	−0.13	−0.6[b]	−3/4
1967	0.22	−0.2[b]	1/4
1968	−0.58	−1.7[c]	−1 1/4
1969	−0.40	−0.4[c]	−1
1970	−0.10	0.6[d]	3/4
1971	0.38	1.3[d]	1 1/2
1972	−0.52	−0.8[d]	−3/4
1973	0.33	0.8[d]	0
1974	0.94	2.2	4
1975	0.69	1.7	1 3/4
1976	−0.52	−0.4	−1 1/4
1977	0.39	0.5	0
1978	0.03	0.2	−1/2
1979	−0.39	0.2	−1/4
1980	0.09	−0.3	−1/4
1981	0.39	0.5	−1/4
1982	0.52	2.3	1 1/2

[a]   United States, Japan, Germany, France, United Kingdom, Italy,
     Austria, Denmark, Finland, Netherlands, Norway, Sweden and Swit-
     zerland.
[b]   Excluding France, Italy, Denmark and Switzerland.
[c]   Excluding Italy, Denmark and Switzerland.
[d]   Excluding Denmark.

Notes
1.   The balance, B, was computed as the sum of the number of
     over-predictions minus the sum of the number of the under-predi-
     citions, divided by the total number of forecasts. Hence the Statistic B
     lies in the range -1 < B < 1.
2.   This column gives the error for OECD-area GNP implicit in the
     single-country forecasts. It is computed as the GNP-weighted sum of
     the single-country errors: the errors of the various national forecasts
     for each country (see the Annex to Llewellyn and Arai 1984) were first
     averaged, to give an overall figure for each country.
3.   These are the same figures as in Table 6.1.

The correlation coefficient (r^2) between the columns of figures (all
correlations are positive) are:
$r^2_{1,2} = 0.87$ $r^2_{1,3} = 0.83$ $r^2_{2,3} = 0.88$

OECD area, leading to errors for most countries individually and thereby for the OECD area as a whole. The widespread shift in the personal savings ratio following a sharp change in inflation worldwide is a recent example, and a slightly earlier example is an underestimation of the (linkage) effects of a significant swing in the stance of aggregate demand policy in a number of countries simultaneously. The obverse can also occur, with individual-country forecasters, as a result of talking together, convincing themselves that something important is going to happen but which in the event does not. This however is a much harder type of error to pinpoint.

The evidence

In order to look systematically at the sources and causes of forecasting error from this international transmission standpoint, it is useful to consider the balance statistic B, being the total number of positive forecasting errors (from the data used to plot Chart 6.3) minus the total number of negative errors, the whole divided by the total number of forecasts. Hence B is bounded by the values ± 1, a value of +1 indicating that all 33 forecasters over-predicted, a value of -1 that all 33 under-predicted, and a value of 0 that as many over-predicted as under-predicted. The results are shown in the first column of Table 6.2.

Since the mid-1960s almost half the years were basically 'normal' from the forecasting point of view, in that in those years the number of over-predictions was approximately balanced by the number of under-predictions. But there were also five years in which a significant majority of country forecasters underestimated growth – 1968, 1969, 1972, 1976 and 1979, and four years when a significantly large number overestimated growth – 1971, 1974, 1975 and 1982.

By and large these years in which single-country forecasts exhibited systematic error were indeed also the years in which the largest forecasting errors were made for the OECD as a whole, whether by national forecasters or by the OECD. For the single-country national forecasts, 1968 was the year of largest under-prediction for the OECD area as a whole when all their forecasts are taken together, and 1971, 1974, 1975 and 1982 were the years of greatest over-prediction. For the OECD forecasts, 1968, 1969 and 1976 were years of significant under-prediction of OECD GNP, and

again 1971, 1974, 1975 and 1982 were years of significant over-prediction.

The equivalence is thus not perfect: 1979 does not fit, for
example. Inspection of the errors here reveals that while in 1979 a
large proportion of forecasters (nearly half of the total of single-
country forecasts) underestimated growth, the errors for the
OECD economy as a whole were typically small, amounting to only
¼ of a percentage point for the OECD Secretariat's forecast and an
overestimation of about the same size for national forecasts. And
there are other examples too. But overall there is a high and
significant positive correlation between each column in Table 6.2
and each of the other two, indicating that there is a strong tendency
for the largest errors for the OECD area as a whole to be made on
the *occasions* when the majority of single-country forecasters make
errors in the same direction (for correlation coefficients, see the
bottom of the table). And it is emphasized that there is no *necessary*
reason why there should be as high a correlation between columns
(1) and (2), and (1) and (3), as there is between (2) and (3).

The fact that the years in which single-country forecasts exhibited
systematic error were generally also the years in which the largest
forecasting errors were made for the OECD as a whole suggests two
possible explanations:

- a misunderstanding, a misquantification (for instance due to
  policy changes), or both, of some force or group of forces that
  affected the OECD economy as a whole; or
- a misunderstanding or misquantification of a force or group of
  forces that affected just a few economies (or maybe even just
  one) with the effects then being transmitted to the others. The
  main 'transmission' channels would have been, presumably,
  the international trade and financial linkages, although on
  occasion less tangible effects such as the international transmission of a loss of confidence may also have been important.

Both explanations appeal to international linkage phenomena.
While the importance of international linkage effects in the
forecasting errors of individual countries should not be pushed too
hard, nevertheless it is noticeable that:

(i)   the largest forecasting errors for year-ahead real OECD
       GNP were each typically made following a year or two in
       which there had been an atypical and relatively large shock
       to the OECD economy – generally from policy or (on the

first of the two occasions) a large change in the price of
internationally-traded oil;

(ii) at the level of the OECD economy as a whole, this suggests
either that the direct impact of these shocks was under-predicted, or that the forecasting processes did not allow for a
full tracing-through of the multiplier effects, or both. This
error in predicting OECD domestic demand will have
resulted in a (generally larger than proportionate) error of
the same sign in predicting intra-OECD imports. Hence at
the level of the individual economy not only will the direct
impact of the shock on the domestic economy have been
mis-projected, but there will also tend to have been a
mis-projection, with the same sign, of the rate of growth of
the individual countries' imports, and hence exports.

These points are considered in the section below, which looks at
the largest forecasting errors in chronological order.

The major forecasting errors since the mid 1960s

The 1968 under-prediction. One possible cause that stands out for
the widespread under-prediction of 1968, and which continued into
1969, is failure to estimate accurately the strength of the impulse to
growth provided by the very large fiscal expansion over the previous
three years and the pronounced easing of the stance of monetary
policy. Certainly, the stance of policy *was* expansionary. Consider
first the United States. The McCracken Report[8] observes that
'... the long expansion which began in 1961 was proceeding strongly
as it entered 1965. Fiscal policy was expansionary ... reflecting the
tax cuts of 1964 and the inability to finance by taxes the Vietnam war
build-up and the social programmes stemming from the civil rights
thrust and the "great society" goals of the Johnson administration.
Demand pressures, as indicated by the GNP gap, became excessive
in the second half of 1965, and remained heavy until mid-1969. ...
The Administration did not seek a temporary tax surcharge until
1967, and it was not enacted until June 1968. ... Monetary policy,
after a contractionary phase (when the Federal Reserve Board may
have attempted to compensate for excessive fiscal stimulus), eased
and turned expansionary. ... By the time of the election in 1968, the
impact of budgetary changes was turning negative, and the Federal
Reserve Board was about to enter a period of severe restraint and
rising interest rates that would persist through 1969.'

Table 6.3   *Fiscal impact measure, nine OECD countries*[a]
Weighted sum of total budgetary changes,
excluding multiplier effects

A positive number indicates a stimulus to aggregate demand

	Per cent of GNP/GDP
1965	0.2
1966	0.9
1967	2.2
1968	−0.4
1969	−1.9
1970	0.0
1971	−0.2
1972	−0.7
1973	−1.5
1974	−0.9
1975	1.9
1976	−0.9

[a] The United States, Japan, Germany, France, United Kingdom, Italy, Canada, Netherlands, and Sweden. The figures are taken from McCracken et al. (1977), pp. 339-340, which also describes how they were compiled. They are by no means ideal, because they do not allow for the effects that fluctuations in the economy had upon the budget. It would be preferable to have a measure of the change in the cyclically-adjusted budget balance, of the sort quoted in Table 3.1. However figures on this basis are not available for the period before 1971.

In Japan too, aggregate demand policy was expansionary, adding to the strong demand boost coming from exports, particularly to the United States. Again quoting McCracken 'The economy was coming out of a mild recession in 1965. Supported by expansionary monetary policy and a government budget which was both expansionary and strongly oriented towards government and private investment, the economy entered upon a long period of strong economic growth, real GNP increasing by 55 per cent in the four years to 1969.' (p. 48).

Lastly, aggregate demand policy was expansionary in Europe also. McCracken again: 'A major expansionary budget in 1967, Germany's first recourse to deficit financing, contributed to an unprecedented boom in 1968-70. ... In France, 1966-67 was a period of relatively sluggish demand expansion, but following the *événements de mai* in 1968 strongly expansionary policies were followed, subsequently moderated in conjunction with the 1969 devaluation...' (pp. 48-49).

Thus in the years leading up to 1968 there was a synchronized expansion in the three largest OECD countries, and then policy swung in the fourth too. The size of the impact of the fiscal part of this expansion was quantified in the McCracken Report (op. cit. pp. 278-281) (Table 6.3).

These figures are not ideal, in that they measure only the first round impact of fiscal policy, but they are the best available for the period. They indicate that, in terms of the size of the initial impact, the years 1965 to 1968 witnessed one of the two biggest swings in the stance of fiscal policy over the twelve-year period for which those data were calculated (the other, equally large, swing was the movement towards contraction over the three years 1972 to 1974, but in this case monetary policy tended to counteract, rather than reinforce, the fiscal influence).

As discussed in chapter 4, a synchronization of policy across countries, particularly the major countries, risks leading to an under-prediction of the consequences. There is no necessary reason why this should be so: it ought to be possible to capture the international linkage effects fully. But the risk is that while the typical single-country forecast may capture broadly correctly the domestic consequences of its own policy, insufficient allowance may be made for the effects on its exports, and hence its GNP, of the consequences of the expansionary policies in other countries. One area where miscalculation of this sort was almost certainly important for a number of single-country forecasts in 1968 was the error in predicting U.S. imports, which grew much faster than import functions at that time were predicting.[9]

If policy-related linkage errors were important then, taking into account the lags with which fiscal policy is generally considered to operate, it would seem likely that the peak effect, and hence also perhaps the major underestimation, would have been in 1968. Further, it would have manifested itself, for some countries at least, as a significant under-prediction of the growth of world trade. An explanation of this sort seems to have been offered at the time, although somewhat hesitantly. Under the heading 'The Unexpected strength of Demand in 1968', the OECD Secretariat pointed in 1968 to faster than expected domestic demand growth in the United States, Germany, France and the United Kingdom. This spread through international trade to the other OECD countries: 'The sharp upturn in import demand in the major OECD countries brought about a significant change in the business conditions of the smaller industrial countries in Europe, all of whom are highly dependent on international trade'; and 'In Canada and Japan, the export boom had an immediate effect on activity, both through its domestic impact and by sustaining productive investment'.[10]

Not only was the boom somewhat stronger than expected, but it also surprised many commentators by the time it took to tail off – also an indication that the lagged effects of policy stimulus were being underestimated. The OECD noted in July 1969 that 'In the second half of last year output was expanding strongly in nearly all OECD countries. The United States was responding only slowly to disinflationary policies and in Europe demand was building up rapidly, with general reflation continuing in Germany and a resurgence of demand in France...Only in the United Kingdom has pressure eased so far this year as much as expected.'[11]

Thus while all such situations have a 'chicken and egg' element to them, it would seem likely that an important reason for the 1968 underestimation was a failure to allow fully for the effects of international linkage. At the level of the individual country forecast, this failure manifested itself as unexpectedly strong exports. At the level of the OECD area as a whole the failure would have manifested itself – if the exercise were indeed performed at that time at that level of aggregation – as the application of too low an OECD area multiplier to the change in the combined fiscal stance.

The over-prediction of 1971. Although 1971 is singled out by the arbitrarily-taken 1-point criterion, it is probably more appropriate to consider the years 1970 and 1971 together; the year-ahead GNP forecasting error made by the OECD Secretariat was an over-prediction on both occasions, ¾ point for 1970 and 1½ points for 1971, just as 1968 and 1969 were both years of under-prediction. Similarly, the years 1974 and 1975, both years of over-prediction, are considered together below.

It is rather hard to disentangle the various reasons for the 1970/71 over-prediction. In July 1971 the OECD noted that 'The deceleration in the growth of OECD output in 1970 was greater than foreseen', but the only suggested reason was special factors, '...in particular the General Motors strike in the United States and the continuing social unrest in Italy'.[12] Then, writing in November 1971 about the year which was then nearly over, the OECD noted that 'Growth has strengthened less than was expected a year ago', but again does not really establish why this was so.[13]

However, it seems suggestive at least that the years 1970 and 1971 immediately followed a substantial restrictive policy swing. The McCracken Report notes that 'Between 1968 and 1969, the stance of both fiscal and monetary policies moved strongly towards restriction...'.[14] And on the basis of the fiscal impact calculations cited in Table 6.3, the size of the swing of fiscal policy towards restriction in 1968 and 1969 together was measured as over 2 percentage points of the combined GNP of the nine biggest economies. This was the second-largest fiscal policy swing in the twelve years from 1965 to 1976.

The over-predictions of 1974 and 1975, and the under-prediction of 1976. These three errors occurred in sequence, and are best examined in that way. The 1974 over-prediction followed the 1972-73 boom which, at the level of the OECD economy as a whole, had been accurately forecast (a point returned to below). Unravelling the reasons for the over-predictions of 1974 and 1975 is one of the most complex tasks for the whole post-war period. The basic elements of the story have however been written about.[15] It is generally considered that quantitatively the most important factors shaping the level of aggregate demand at that time were the rapid build up of the OPEC current surplus (deflationary), a fiscal swing towards restriction (impact measure -1.5 per cent in 1973, and -0.9 per cent in 1974 (Table 6.3), monetary policy which, according to McCracken, moved 'markedly' towards restriction in 1973 (op, cit. p.65) and a sharp deterioration in consumer and business confidence (also deflationary).

The very large (4 percentage point) over-prediction for 1974 made by the OECD in November 1973 and published in December 1973 can be largely discounted because, although the policy stance was known, that forecast did not take account of the substantial end-1973 hike in the price of internationally-traded oil. Comfort might be taken from the fact that the July 1974 OECD *Economic Outlook*, containing forecasts made *after* the oil price rise had taken place, predicted 1 per cent OECD GNP growth for that year; the outcome was a marginal decline, of 0.1 per cent, so this forecast might appear to have represented a reasonable forecast in the light of the new circumstances. However the December 1974 OECD *Economic Outlook* predicted growth of ½ per cent for 1975, whereas the outcome was a decline of 1.2 per cent – an over-prediction of 1¾ per cent. Hence, while it would appear, on the basis of the *analysis* published at the time, that the basic economic forces then operating on the OECD economy were broadly understood, it cannot be claimed that their impact or, perhaps more importantly, their timing was at all well predicted.

Furthermore, there was reluctance at a number of levels to believe that the oil situation could and would markedly affect macroeconomic performance. Hence for reasons that relate to the novelty of the shock (simultaneously demand-deflationary and price-inflationary), its size, and its pervasiveness, large forecasting errors were made. To have forecast those events correctly would have required, at a minimum, an international analytic framework and a quantified set of relationships that was not available at the time. It is interesting that back-of-the-envelope calculations made for the OECD area as a whole proved, on that occasion, to be more pertinent than what resulted from summing (much more detailed) single-country forecasts.

The two years of declining GNP in 1974 and 1975 were followed by a year of very rapid (5.2 per cent) OECD growth in 1976. Creditably an upturn, of 4 per cent, was predicted by the OECD. However this was 1¼ points less than the outcome, and hence qualifies as a 'large error'. The main forces acting on the OECD economy at that time were the expansionary effect of rapidly-increasing OPEC spending, a large fiscal swing towards expansion, equivalent to nearly 2 per cent of the GNP of the seven largest economies (chapter 3, Table 3.1), and a return of private and business confidence which resulted in a stockbuilding and investment boom. Pinpointing the precise cause of the under-prediction when there were so many influences at work is probably impossible, although it seems fair to observe that the strength of the reversal of the previous downward trend in stockbuilding was, while it lasted, tremendous.

The 1982 over-prediction. The economic conditions prevailing in 1982 have already been described in chapter 4. The principal reason for the 1½ percentage point over-prediction made by the OECD Secretariat for OECD real GNP would seem to have been a failure to appreciate the cumulative effect of tight monetary policy. Not only were monetary conditions tight – as measured by the height of nominal and real short and long-term interest rates – but this was so for a sustained period and in virtually all OECD countries simultaneously. Little empirical evidence was available at the time about what exactly the effects would be on spending within the OECD countries. In fact these turned out to be rather greater than expected, and it seems likely that, as with the simultaneous fiscal expansions and contractions already described, the linkage effects across the OECD countries were also under-estimated. Furthermore, the effect of these high interest rates on the debt burdens of heavily-indebted developing countries led to an unprecedented, and unexpectedly sharp, contraction in the imports of those countries, thereby lowering the exports and activity of the OECD countries as a group.

The forecasting record for inflation

Since the mid-1960s, the forecasting record for inflation, as measured by the errors in the forecasts for year-ahead GNP deflators, has in a number of respects been broadly similar to that for real GNP. For the 33 sets of forecasts for 14 individual countries, almost half of the forecasts were accurate to within a percentage point of the outcome, and a further quarter had errors between 1 and 2 per cent. Also, as was the case with real GDP, a minority of forecasts were very inaccurate, with a few errors as large as 7 percentage points (Chart 6.4). Some of the largest of these errors, although not all of them, are attributable substantially to the effects of each of the two major increases in the price of internationally-traded oil, first in 1973/74 and then in 1978/79.

At the level of the OECD area as a whole too there are parallels with the forecasting record for real GNP. Single-country inflation forecasting errors have had a tendency to offset one another, so that the forecasting errors for OECD inflation have been smaller. A GNP-weighted average of single-country errors made by national forecasters, which can be taken as representing the forecast for OECD inflation implicit in the sum total of single-country forecasts, exceeded 2 percentage points only in 1973 and 1974, when errors of 3½ to 4 percentage points were made. In the latter year, the apparent error was attributable to the oil price rise at end-1973, which happened too late to be incorporated in the forecasts. But the large error in 1973 seems to have been substantially due to under-prediction of the various effects of the strong world boom, reinforced by

Chart 6.4 Single-country inflation forecasting errors
(OECD and National Forecasts)

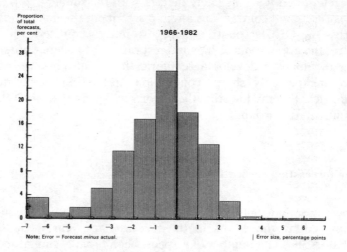

Note: Error = Forecast *minus* actual. | Error size, percentage points

speculative influences, on non-oil commodity prices. OECD forecasts for inflation in the OECD area show a broadly similar pattern (Table 6.4), although exact comparison cannot be made for the whole of the period since the mid 1960s because the OECD did not publish inflation forecasts in some of the earlier years.

An interesting and important difference however is that, unlike the forecasts of real activity, those for inflation appear to have exhibited a distinct bias – downwards – at least in the earlier years. From 1966 to 1972 the rate of OECD inflation implicit in individual country forecasts was systematically under-predicted. Forecasters were apparently slow to take full account of the fact that inflation was accelerating: while they forecast an acceleration, they did not appreciate its full extent, perhaps because of a failure, in a number of countries, to allow fully for the effects of increasingly-widespread indexation, *de facto* or *de jure*, of wage rates to the cost of living.

More recently, on the other hand, inflation errors have been smaller. They have almost always been less than 1 percentage point, the one exception being the 1978 OECD forecast for 1979, and much of that is attributable to the technical assumption of no change in the price of internationally-traded oil. Most recently of

Table 6.4 *Forecasting errors for OECD area GNP deflator*

	GNP-weighted sum of single-country errors[a]	Error of OECD forecast
1966	−1.1(b)	..
1967	−0.2(b)	..
1968	−0.5(c)	−1/4
1969	−1.5(d)	..
1970	−1.3(e)	−1 3/4
1971	−1.0(f)	..
1972	−0.8(f)	0
1973	−3.4(f)	−3
1974	−3.9	−4 3/4
1975	0.5	3/4
1976	−0.2	1/2
1977	−0.1	0
1978	−0.9	−1/2
1979	−1.0	−1 1/4
1980	−0.8	−1/2
1981	0.2	−1
1982	1.3	1 1/4

[a] Weighted average of national forecasts for United States, Japan, Germany, France, United Kingdom, Italy, Austria, Denmark, Finland, Netherlands, Norway, Sweden and Switzerland.
[b] Excluding France, Italy, Denmark, Finland, Norway and Switzerland.
[c] Excluding Italy, Denmark, Finland, Norway and Switzerland.
[d] Excluding Italy, Denmark, Norway and Switzerland.
[e] Excluding Denmark and Norway.
[f] Excluding Denmark.

all, in 1982, the rate of OECD inflation was over-predicted, in large part related to the over-prediction of worldwide activity and because of an unexpectedly widespread de-linking of wage settlements from the cost of living, itself probably a consequence (discussed in chapter 11) of the depth and length of the recession in OECD countries.

Having considered separately the forecasting errors for real GNP and inflation, it is natural to consider whether there is any tendency for the errors to cancel, that is to say for nominal GNP to be forecast better, on average, than its two components (Chart 6.5). Offsetting errors would reveal themselves as a tendency for the forecasting errors to lie along the negatively-sloped 45° line BB'. In fact no such tendency is apparent for the OECD forecasts, if 1974 is excluded

Chart 6.5 Forecasting errors for OECD real GNP and inflation

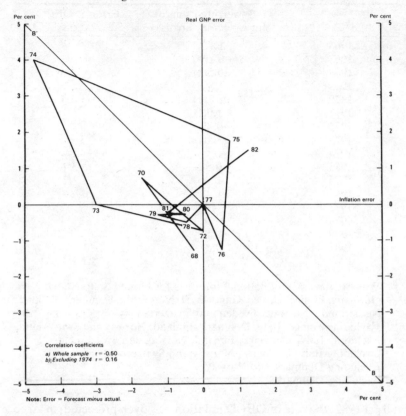

from the sample. For that year, the year of the largest-ever mistake in forecasting OECD real GNP, *nominal* GNP was forecast almost exactly.

Conclusions

Any catalogue of forecasting errors and the possible reasons for them is bound to engender the feeling that mistakes were being made perpetually. It is therefore worth reiterating that this was not so. Of seventeen year-ahead forecasts for real OECD GNP, only 5 show errors greater than 1 percentage point and if, on account of the specal circumstances surrounding it, the 4 point error of the

December 1973 pre-oil-price rise forecast is discounted, no error was as large as 2 percentage points. Furthermore not all of the years in which the smaller forecast errors were made were easy ones to forecast. For example, the years of the 1972-73 boom were well forecast (a ¾ point underestimation of 1972, and no error at all for 1973, despite that being one of the years of fastest GNP growth ever achieved by the OECD economy).[16] Secondly, the five-year period from 1977 to 1981, which saw the second major oil price rise, a shock that was proportionately as large as the first, produced no forecasting error larger than ½ a percentage point.

Overall, however, the evidence suggests that a major part of the process of improving the quality of individual-country forecasts, and thereby the analysis upon which national policy-making unavoidably has to be based, is likely to have to involve improving the analysis of internationally-transmitted impulses, and the dependability of international forecasts. While considerable advances have been made in the last fifteen to twenty years, to the extent that forecasting errors have if anything decreased even though the turbulence of the international environment has increased, it would seem that there is scope for further improvement.

Part II of this book therefore considers how international forecasts are made, and how it might prove possible to improve them in the future.

Part II
International economic forecasting

7 Approaches to economic forecasting

Summary

Economic forecasts can be made in many ways. Macroeconomic models supplemented by judgement seem the best available means for forecasting and establishing a subsequent basis for policy-making. The origins of macroeconomic modelling may be traced back to the 1930s, and the pioneering work of Tinbergen and Klein. It is only since the 1960s that increases in computing capacity, availability of data in machine-readable form, advances in statistical techniques and the development of 'user-friendly' software for purposes of model management have made regular and widespread application of macroeconomic models not only possible, but also common.

By providing a simplified, but coherent, representation of the major forces at work shaping the course of the economy, macroeconomic models help provide quantitative forecasts. In the case of international forecasting and monitoring, the problem of data acquisition, handling, sifting and dissemination is particularly large.

Introduction

There are many ways to make a forecast. The simplest is to guess, which in its purest form would be a random process. But even those who guess usually inform the process by their memory of what has happpened in the past, and they also usually constrain their prediction to lie within limits that are considered plausible. Most forecasting processes embody, either implicitly or explicitly, these twin characteristics: learning from the past, and constraining the prediction. Only a few do not, and they are of little use.

Perhaps the simplest expression of a forecasting process involving, if only implicitly, these twin characteristics is the 'judgemental' forecast. Typically, this is an informal assessment based on the experience and/or intuition of the forecaster. This assessment may, to a large extent, rely on the results of survey data. For example, survey data on household consumption plans (particularly for consumer durables) and of the investment, production, and hiring plans of business would be of particular importance to the purely judgemental forecaster. The relative importance of these and other factors, and their contribution to the building of the overall forecast picture, are to the judgemental forecaster largely a matter of subjective appreciation. This is a major limitation of the purely judgemental forecast; it is generally not clear what factors have, or have not, been taken into account in producing it. Nor is it clear what weight various factors have been given, and why.

The purely judgemental forecast therefore fails an essential test, that of replicability: given the same information on a different day, the judgemental forecaster might well come up with a different forecast. A judgemental forecast, unsupported by a clearly-specified analytic framework, and unaccompanied by its quantitative expression, cannot provide a useful basis for discussion with others involved in forecasting or policy-making. There is no basis for reasoned, quantitative consideration of forecast alternatives, nor of policy alternatives. Further, for want of an analytic framework to support his arguments, the purely judgemental forecaster may, on occasion, find it difficult to persuade others of his views. Judgement is, of course, an essential complement to formal quantitative analysis, but it is seldom an adequate substitute. A systematic, quantitative approach to economic forecasting is a necessary pre-condition for business decision-making and rational economic policy formulation.

Alternative methods of quantitative forecasting

Four classifications of quantitative forecasting technique can be distinguished: methods based on time series analysis, statistical indicators, single-equation econometric models, and multi-equation models of the whole economy.

Time series analysis. Time series analysis is the simplest of the quantitative approaches to forecasting. It is based on the underlying assumption of regular and repeating patterns of movement in components – whether trend, seasonal, or cyclical – of economic time series. Forecasting using time series analysis involves identifying these components on the basis of past movements in a given series, projecting them, and then aggregating them to obtain a projection for the series in question. To produce a projection by this method, nothing need be known about causal factors, or indeed economic theory.

Frequently-used methods of time series analysis are extrapolative forecasting (in which a variable is projected to continue growing or declining at its previous trend rate), regressive forecasting (in which a variable is projected to return towards a value observed in a preceding period), and adaptive forecasting (in which projections are revised upwards or downwards in light of the most recent forecast error). Box-Jenkins methods, or 'time series models', are a particularly elaborate expression of time series analysis, integrating elements of extrapolative, regressive, and adaptive aspects of time series analysis in a general framework (see, for example, Box and Jenkins, 1970).

Experience with forecasting on the basis of time series analysis is that while this process may, in some cases, predict well for relatively short periods ahead – say one month or one quarter – predictive accuracy falls off rapidly as the time horizon is lengthened. As McNees (1979) has observed, the prediction error of time series models over longer periods tends to accumulate, there being no exogenous data in the forecasting system after the first few periods. Hence over the longer horizon relevant for economic policy decisions the technical performance of time series models is unreliable.

A second problem with time series models – and which probably contributes to their poor forecasting ability – is that these methods eschew explanation of *how* the process being predicted actually works. The time series model does, it is true, give the appearance of 'learning' from the recent past, but this is purely mechanical, and will always be a lagging response to changing events. Hence, time series models are unlikely to do well in times of structural or behavioural change, or change in the general economic environment. And this is a serious limitation because it is at just such times that the need for reliable economic forecasts, or at least a reasoned consideration of the various factors likely to shape the future, becomes most pressing. Hence, because they provide little in the way of understanding the economic processes at work, projections obtained by time series analysis alone are of little use for policy-making. Furthermore, such methods do not provide a framework within which, for example, the sensitivity of the projected outcome to alternative policy assumptions can be assessed.

This is not to say that time series methods have no place in economic forecasting, but rather that their use must be conditioned by an appreciation, and an understanding, of the underlying economic structure. The forecaster should consider placing weight on the predictions of a time series model only when a consideration of the inherent characteristics of the system being projected suggests that simple extrapolation of past tendencies could be expected to hold reasonably satisfactorily in the future. Projections of technological influences on the trend of productivity, or the rate of population growth, provide such examples, at least in a short-term forecasting context.

Statistical Indicators. The use of statistical indicators as an approach to economic forecasting involves the study of the evolution of one or more statistical series found regularly to lead general movements in economic activity, with a view to inferring the probable direction of future macroeconomic trends on the basis of observed movements in the leading indicator(s). The use of statistical indicators in economic forecasting may be traced back to W.C. Mitchell's analysis of business cycle conditions.[1] What is involved is systematic processing and classification of hundreds of economic time series, with respect to their peaks, their troughs, the interval between peaks and troughs, and the relation of these peaks and troughs to generally-accepted data for peaks and troughs in aggregate economic activity. The emphasis is not on the level of economic activity, but rather on identifying changes in direction, or 'turning points', in economic activity. The series are subsequently classified into one of three groups: 'leading indicators', or series whose peaks and troughs regularly precede those in general business conditions; 'lagging indicators', or series whose peaks and troughs regularly lag behind those of general business conditions;

and 'coincident indicators', whose peaks and troughs regularly match those of general business conditions.

Examples of leading indicators of general trends in economic activity typically include such variables as hours worked, new orders, wholesale prices, construction contracts, new business formation, and business failures. These series may lead changes in overall economic activity by several months. In some countries, the money supply appears to be an important leading indicator of economic activity. Recently, a different kind of indicator, the diffusion index, has been devised. This provides a measure of the proportion of a given set of leading indicators that are, at any time, moving in the same direction. The pooling of indicators in the form of a diffusion index reduces the risk that false turning points in economic activity may be signalled. The presumption is that the greater the uniformity of direction of movement of various leading indicators, as revealed by the diffusion index, the greater the chances of the course of future economic activity being in the suggested direction.

A problem with the use of leading statistical indicators as a basis for economic forecasting is that the interval by which a given indicator leads economic cycles is usually irregular, ranging from a few months to a year or more. And, while some indicators do typically lead the cycle, economic upturns or downturns foreshadowed by a leading indicator often simply do not materialize. And because of data collection and publication delays, many leading indicators in effect can provide insights only as to where the economy currently is, rather than about where it is likely to be in the future. On balance, it would seem that the main use of statistical indicators is not so much in giving advance notice that a recession or recovery is likely to be getting underway, but rather in helping recognize that such a recession or recovery is, in fact, already occurring. In this respect, leading indicators can be of particular use in monitoring, as discussed in chapter 5.

The usefulness of statistical indicators as a basis for economic forecasting and policy-making is further limited by the relatively short forecast horizon they cover. Few have any reliability whatever more than six months ahead. Further, because statistical indicators, like time series models, lack an underlying economic rationale, they too can offer no insights about the causes which underlie a given recession or recovery, and to which policy-makers might wish to direct their policy.

For forecasts that look more than one or two quarters ahead, therefore, most forecasters seek to represent explicitly the basic features of the economic process which they wish to forecast. This typically involves the use of econometric models – mathematical equations which have been given empirical content through the application of econometric methods.

Econometric models. Mathematical equations have now become the principal means by which many theories of economic behaviour are expounded. Such models are simply the expression of economic theory in mathematical form, involving a set of formalized relationships among a set of economic variables. Marshall's supply and demand curve framework, which has proved so useful in understanding and analysing price changes, provides a classic example of a mathematical model, in this case in the microeconomic context. In a macroeconomic context, the Keynesian income-expenditure model is a classic example of a mathematical model. Indeed, it was the construction and analysis of mathematical models that contributed to an early understanding of the ideas of Keynes. (See, for example, Hicks (1937) and Hansen (1953).)

Mathematical models are theoretical constructs. To be useful in applied forecasting and policy analysis, they must be given empirical content. As discussed in chapter 5, this exercise is less solid than in the physical sciences, because the empirical regularities of behaviour observed in the social sciences are in general less robust than the major 'laws' in the physical sciences. Hence, it is important to identify and quantify the most important regularities, while always being on the lookout for signs of change. This is the role of econometric methods.

The use of econometric methods in analysing, explaining and forecasting economic developments, and guiding the policy-making process, is relatively recent. Early applications of econometric methods were essentially microeconomic in orientation, involving the estimation of demand and supply relationships. The development and use of econometric methods in a macroeconomic context became widespread in the 1950s, although their initial application was, for the most part, limited to the formal testing of hypotheses about the behaviour of economic agents. Examples were econometric studies of the determinants of consumption and investment behaviour, and of wage and price determination.

In contrast to time series and statistical indicator methods, econometric methods involve the explicit representation of the presumed causality between the variable to be projected and its determinants. The nature of the relationships involved is based on economic theory, or other logical bases, such as legislative or institutional arrangements. The parameter values of the equation, usually estimated by regression methods, are the quantitative expression of the way in which the variable whose behaviour is to be explained could be expected to respond to changes in each of its determinants. An important advantage of this approach to economic forecasting is that premises are made explicit, and lend themselves to generating forecasts which are conditional upon their assumptions.

While representing an improvement over forecasting methods based on time-series analysis or statistical indicators, single equation methods suffer from the limitation of being able to take into account only the direct influences on the variable being projected. Interactions and feedbacks of explanatory variables not explicitly represented in the equation are ignored. These considerations have led most, although by no means all, forecasters to use multi-equation macroeconomic models, as a basis not only for economic forecasting, but also for subsequent analysis of economic policy alternatives.

Multi-equation macroeconomic models. A macroeconomic model is a formal articulation, in explicit and quantitative terms, of the way in which a set of jointly-considered economic variables are interrelated. It consists of a set of simultaneous equations, each of which represents some important feature of the economy. The number of equations involved depends on the detail with which the behaviour of various groups of economic agents is to be represented. A macro model imposes, for example, the definitional and accounting relations that must be respected, and which an unstructured set of equations, or other forecasting methods, will in general not be able to satisfy. The various equations then interact with each other, because a variable explained by any one equation serves as an explanatory variable in other equations. This latter feature is the essence of the multiple-equation model.

Virtually anyone involved in economic forecasting or policy analysis today works with a model of some kind, whether implicit or explicit. The model is implicit when the behavioural phenomena and interactions among differing economic variables are taken into account in what might be called a 'judgemental' or 'intuitive' sense. The model is explicit when these relations are formally set out, for all to see. The model gains particular power when put on the computer, for this facilitates computation, and ensures that nothing is inadvertently overlooked in the causal chains involved. And the various accounting and definitional relations involved ensure the internal consistency of the results.

The development and regular use in economic forecasting and policy analysis of multi-equation macroeconomic models was essentially a phenomenon of the 1960s. The origins of multi-equation models for the study of behaviour of national economies go further back. Indeed, the first such macroeconomic model was that developed by Tinbergen in 1939, to study inter-war business cycles in the United States.

However, the real father of macroeconomic modelling, as practised today, is Lawrence Klein, who made the first of his pioneering attempts in the late 1930s, formulating a macroeconomic model of the United States. These efforts continued after the Second World War, resulting in a 12-equation model (which would be regarded as modest nowadays, even by textbook standards) of the United States (Klein, 1950), and a larger 20-equation model with Goldberger in 1955 (Klein and Goldberger, 1955).[2]

The 1960s were a period of rapid development of macro models. Commitment to social and economic goals in OECD countries increased the complexity of the task of economic management, as discussed in chapter 3. This led to increasing demand for the frequency, and the level of disaggregation, at which economic analysis, policy evaluation, and forecasting were carried out, and for the development of macroeconomic models to support these tasks. The task was made easier by enormous advances in computing power, the availability of economic data in machine-readable form, the development of 'user friendly' software for estimation, data management and manipulating models, and the writing of efficient model-solution algorithms. In most OECD countries, the use of econometric models became commonplace, with serious efforts to understand, forecast and control an economy being typically supported by such a formalized analytical framework.

The late 1960s and early 1970s also saw increased attention being paid to the external economic environment, reflecting the growing recognition of interdependence of national economies and the influence that policies in one country can have on another. This in turn led to the construction of world trade models and to attempts to link together two or more national models into a global model. A pioneering research effort in the former respect was the development in the late 1960s of the OECD's world trade model; Project LINK, under the intellectual leadership of Klein (Ball, 1973), represented the start of internationally-linked modelling.

Through the 1970s, various groups of economists, in private and governmental institutions throughout the world, were inspired to build their own international linkage models, tailored to specific operating requirements. These efforts were made feasible by continuing dramatic reductions in the cost of computing, together with increasing availability of worldwide economic data in machine-readable form. Building on the earlier models of world trade, the OECD Secretariat's INTERLINK, described in chapter 9, is an example of such a system.

Macroeconomic models: some general considerations

A number of simplifications are involved in the construction of a macroeconomic model. These are intended not only to make the model itself easier to manage and hence easier to bring to bear on problems, but also to enable the various interactions of key parts of the economy to be clearly visible and easily traced through. This simplification, by concentrating attention on the key interrelationships, facilitates analysis and discussion of the main issues in the forecasting and policy analytic process.

Following Tinbergen, it is customary to divide the equations of a macroeconomic model into two broad categories: *behavioural equations* and *definitions and identities* (Tinbergen, 1939). Behavioural equations are, in a sense, the 'heart' of a macroeconomic model. They are intended to represent, albeit in simplified form, the principal features of the behaviour of decision-making units in the economy (e.g., households and business). The consumption function is an example of a behavioural equation, in that it portrays the response of private consumption expenditure of households to changes in, for example, income, taxes, prices, and wealth.

Because their specification involves a measure of simplification, behavioural equations have a stochastic (or 'disturbance') term associated with them. That is, the determination of variables is not mathematically precise, but instead subject to random influences. Without the stochastic disturbance term, the consumption function would imply that consumption expenditure is precisely determined once its determinants are known. But this is unlikely to be so. Such precision could reasonably be expected to hold only with respect to certain physical phenomena. While changes in income and wealth are certainly main factors in determining private consumption expenditure, others are important too. Among these can be changes in tastes, the effects of various financial variables (such as interest rates), uncertainty about the economic outlook (the threat of inflation or unemployment), and so on. It would be impossible to include the full catalogue of variables for each and every equation and still be able to manage the overall model.

Behavioural equations may also represent technological relationships (such as a production function) and institutional relations (such as those for tax and transfer payments). Such equations too are typically stochastic, in that they almost inevitably represent a simplification of a set of complex laws and regulations. A final type of behavioural equation consists of disequilibrium or 'market clearing' relationships, such as wage and price adjustment mechanisms. Such equations describe how variables adjust to disequilibrium. Examples of this type of equation include the Philips-curve-type relationship (relating wage developments to labour market disequilibrium) and foreign trade equations (relating adjustments of imports and exports to changes in international competitiveness).

Identities and definitional equations, on the other hand, are non-stochastic. They hold exactly, in every time period. Examples include the accounting relations found in national income accounts, price-value-volume relationships, and definitions of concepts such as the savings ratio.

Exogenous and endogenous variables, and the structural form

The equations of a macroeconomic model are comprised of variables, parameters, and, for behavioural equations, disturbance terms. The variables of the model may be described as being either *endogenous* or *predetermined* (Koopmans, 1950). Endogenous variables are those whose values are determined explicitly within the system of equations comprising the model (e.g., consumption, investment, imports, interest rates, inflation rate, unemployment, etc.). It follows that there is one structural equation corresponding to each endogenous variable in the model. Predetermined variables are those whose values are determined outside the system of equations, but which nevertheless influence equations of the system. The set of predetermined variables consists of strictly *exogenous* variables, such as policy variables and other externally-given variables, as well as lagged values of endogenous variables.

The economic theory underlying a macroeconomic model is typically, for reasons of expository simplicity, couched in static terms. In such a static theoretical exposition, the endogenous variables are determined on the basis of given values of parameters and exogenous variables, with no attention as to how the variables adjust over time. Given fixed parameter values or 'structure', the endogenous variables take on unique equilibrium values for given fixed values of the exogenous variables. Any change in the exogenous variables produces a new set of equilibrium values for the endogenous variables. The method of comparative static anaysis involves analysis of the changes in the set of endogenous variables brought about by changes in one or more exogenous variables.

A static model implies that the adjustment of endogenous variables from one equilibrium state to another is rapid and smooth. But that is seldom the case. Economic phenomena are typically characterized by lagged adjustment processes, which must be captured if a model of the economy is to be realistic. There are many important examples. Consumption expenditure adjusts with a lag to changes in income; imports adjust with a lag to changes in relative prices; investment expenditure adjusts with a lag to its determinants; wages adjust with a lag to labour market conditions.

By taking account of such lagged adjustment processes, macroeconomic models are able to describe the time path of adjustment of endogenous variables to a change in one or more exogenous variables through difference equations which involve explicit time references (denoted by time subscripts). There is no guarantee that the adjustment paths implied by a set of simultaneous difference equations will be smooth, or even that new equilibrium values will ultimately be reached. The adjustment paths may oscillate, or cycle. Only if such fluctuations are damped will new equilibrium values eventually be reached.

For purposes of forecasting and policy formulation, the question of 'how long' can be as important as 'how much'. When considering alternative policies, for example, it makes a great deal of difference how long a recession is likely to last, or how long it typically is before a policy change takes effect. Indeed, if the timing is wrongly assessed, the thrust of policy can thereby be seriously adrift. It could, for example, turn out to be destabilizing rather than stabilizing.

Macroeconomic models thus provide a framework within which economic theory, institutional knowledge, historical evidence and judgement may be blended, and brought to bear systematically on the forecasting process. To the extent that parameter values are based on regression analysis, they embody historical evidence; to the extent that they depart from historical values, this will represent an explicit decision to modify model properties by embodying the judgement, or expert opinion, of the forecaster.

The simultaneity and complexity of the model resulting from the integration of the behavioural and other equations enrich analysis and increase realism. However, this integration makes it more difficult to determine intuitively the magnitude, or sometimes even the sign, of relationships among variables. A complete model may exhibit properties that the builders did not expect, on the basis of single equation relations, and to which they would not have been able to reason without the aid of a model.

If the user, faced with an unexpected result from the model, traces it through, finds out the reasons for it, and is then convinced, then the model has performed a useful function. If, on the other hand, the user were to take any result of the model on trust merely because each of the individual separate equations is believed in, he would be placing faith in a 'black box'. This could never be a sound basis for policy advice.

The scope and limitations of macroeconomic models

The late 1960s and early 1970s were a time of great optimism about the contribution macroeconomic models could make to understanding how economies operate, to the use of various policy instruments in the pursuit of stabilization, and in the projections and simulation results derived from them. Large macroeconomic models were in regular forecasting and policy analytic use in many OECD coun tries. Their structure conformed to generally-accepted economic theory of the day, and the estimated equations generally exhibited an acceptable degree of stability over time. The solution paths for the models generally tracked historical experience acceptably well, and simulation properties usually seemed reasonable. These models appeared to open new ways of assessing alternative economic policies, and modifying the course of economic events in line with policy-makers' intentions.

It is now clear, however, that that optimism and confidence was excessive. It coincided with the advent of widespread computing power, and the notion that 'computers don't make mistakes'. In a sense, the computer-based macroeconomic model had come to be revered as the oracle – the source of knowledge and truth – with the economist its priesthood. Models had become – at least to the uninitiated – an end in themselves, instead of being accepted merely for what they in fact are, a computational framework embodying various simplified representations of a complex economy, together with the discipline of various accounting relationships. There was insufficient appreciation of the limited range of application to which such models could properly be put.

The events of the 1970s ended the period of unreserved enthusiasm for macroeconomic models, and the approach to forecasting and policy analysis that they represented. The forecasting mistakes made at the time of the commodity price shocks of the early 1970s, and the oil price shock in particular, were highly significant in this. Economists, with their models and computers, were perceived by the public as having failed to foresee some of the most important developments of the decade, most notably rising inflation and the severity of the post-1973 recession. This undermined confidence in the ability of government and business to control the course of events, and in turn led policy-makers to be critical of forecasters and their models. The principal inadequacy of the models available at the time was that they simply were not capable of analysing the consequences of 'supply side' shocks. Later, in the latter half of the 1970s and the early 1980s, models failed again, though less badly, when many economies were subjected to unusually large financial disturbances, including volatile exchange rates and high interest rates. The available models generally lacked the equations needed to represent these phenomena. In the last analysis, of course, criticism should be directed not so much at the models as to those who used them uncritically in circumstances for which they were not designed. A large part of the skill of the forecaster lies in recognizing those circumstances where the tools at his disposal are inadequate, and making appropriate allowance for this in formulating policy advice.

Towards the end of the 1970s, the role of macroeconomic models in forecasting and policy analysis was also being called into question on theoretical grounds, by the so-called 'rational expectations' school. (See notably Lucas (1976).) The essence of their critique was that a change in government policy is likely systematically to change the expectations, and hence the behaviour, of households and businesses, tending to offset what policy was seeking to achieve. The extent of this offset, it is argued, is likely to be sufficient to invalidate model relationships which attempt to describe private sector behaviour.

The premises of the rational expectations critique have themselves been called into question, both on theoretical and empirical grounds. The assumptions on a theoretical plane that agents make systematic use of all information and that markets clear instantaneously have been challenged as unrealistic. It has also been pointed out that the critique confuses two issues, namely the inclusion (or lack thereof) of rational expectations variables in behavioural equations on the one hand, and the specification of the expectations process itself on the other (Wallis, 1980). Thus Klein has pointed out that, even if processes through which expectations are formed were changed, it is only the expectation variables in macroeconomic models that would have to be adjusted, and not other parts of the model (in Sims, 1982).

As to the empirical validity of the critique, Sims has argued that normal policy-making rarely involves regime shifts sufficiently drastic to induce fundamental changes in the behaviour of economic agents, pointing out that 'the rational expectation critique is only a special case of the more general cautionary note – statistical models are likely to become unreliable when extrapolated to make predictions for conditions far outside the range experienced in the sample' (Sims, 1982). Indeed, Eckstein, speaking of his experience with forecasting at DRI, had observed little in the way of empirical evidence to suggest that changes in government's policy stance as observed in recent years have altered the basic relationships among variables in macroeconomic models (Eckstein, 1979). Moreover, it now appears that some of the more striking theoretical findings of the rational expectations school (notably Lucas) result not from the assumption of rational expectations *per se* (which a wide range of economists could accept as useful), but from the assumption of instantaneous clearing of all markets (Begg, 1982).

The principal relevant thrust of the rational expectations critique may then be that, when appropriate, explicit representation of rational expectation terms is a necessary element in a correctly specified model. Expectational effects have, of course, long been recognized as important to households' consumption decisions, business investment decisions, to the wage-bargaining process, and to interest rate and exchange rate determination, to give just some examples. Yet while most macroeconomic models attempt to capture such expectational effects, it is clear that considerable scope exists for improving the modelling of the processes by which (rational) expectations are formed.

Model builders and academic theoreticians have, of course, undertaken repair work, taking into account supply side mechanisms, reexamining the channels through which financial variables influence the economy and the lags with which they operate, and addressing the question of both the formation and the role of expectations. Despite these improvements, an important lesson from the experience of the past ten years is that it is inappropriate for the practitioner to accept unquestioningly the validity and usefulness of the model-based approach to forecasting and analysis. It is by now generally recognized that a model should be used only by, or in conjunction with, those familiar with its construction, its properties, and its limitations. Confidence in the usefulness of a model can result only from a careful appreciation of what its analytic and forecasting capabilities – and limitations – are. Only then can the role to be played by a model in forecasting and policy analysis be established.

Care must be taken to note that the 'projections' of a macroeconomic model are only conditional projections – conditional on assumptions concerning the behaviour of the economy as embodied in the model's equations, assumptions concerning the paths of policy and other exogenous variables, and on judgemental 'add factor' adjustments, supplied to the model by the forecaster. The model does not predict; it is merely a 'logic' machine or 'information processor' for the economist using the model.

Incorporating judgement in predictions and analysis

Perhaps the most important advance conferred by econometric models is, paradoxically, the ability to incorporate the forecaster's judgement – an essentially non-econometric phenomenon. Indeed, for a given variable, judgemental information may on occasion completely override values predicted by the model relationships. The reason for exercising this judgement within the context of a model, however, is that the discipline imposed by the model as a whole ensures that this information is consistently carried through the entire set of projections.

Judgemental information is typically entered in the form of 'add-factor' or residual adjustments to an equation, as well as through alteration of exogenous variables. Such judgemental information can involve, for example, altering a given equation's projection on the basis of information available from preliminary data, or leading indicators. Add-factors are also often the most convenient way of incorporating information from surveys of business and household spending plans, and from various leading indicators. Allowance can also be made through the exercise of judgement for phenomena that may not be captured by equations alone, such as a strike, anticipatory buying in advance of a tax increase, or changes in import and export trading patterns in anticipation of exchange rate adjustments. Add-factors may also be used to keep equations of a model in line with recent experience, or to incorporate the view that a policy or other change may have altered the way expectations are formed.

The forecasting process has to be able regularly to accommodate various forms of structural change, such as changes in institutional setting or legislative action, together with changes in such variables as tax rates, transfer payment schemes, and so on. Data revisions and systematic tracking error also have to be accommodated: in the longer term this will be achieved by re-estimation of the relevant equations, but in the shorter term, when deadlines are tight, such allowance often has to be incorporated ad hoc. By allowing for the incorporation of judgemental information in this way, the model is interactive with the forecaster, in increasing the coherence, efficiency, and accuracy of the forecasting process.

Nevertheless, in a number of areas the appropriate criteria governing the proper exercise of judgement remain a vexed, but important, issue. Indeed, even the concept of judgement itself can at times be somewhat elusive, and gives rise to vigorous controversy. One such area concerns the weight that should, or should not, be placed on past evidence.

Most agree that any model ought to be firmly rooted in the evidence of the past. A welter of evidence has built up over the decades during which macroeconomic data have been collected and analysed on such matters as the relationship between costs and prices, income and expenditure, output and employment, employment and unemployment, expenditure and imports, incomes and tax revenues, the money supply and inflation. To disregard this evidence, or even some of it, and specify a model completely *a priori*, would be an arrogant and very likely unwarranted rejection of a large body of useful information.

Yet the forecasting process cannot always be immovably rooted in the past. One reason is that new events occur. For example, the first oil shock in 1973-74, which raised import prices substantially, gave OPEC a large surplus on the current account of the balance of payments, and deflated the level of world demand and hence output. These developments could not all be captured by most macroeconomic models in the form in which they stood in mid-1973. Furthermore, first attempts to specify and quantify the main channels of transmission of the major effects could not be rooted in historical evidence, for there was none. Instead, it was necessary to appeal to economic theory, to think through new channels of transmission, and then build these into the models. Initial parameter values could not be estimated; instead they had to be written down on the basis of partial information and informed guesswork. This was not ideal, but there was no alternative. The forecasts produced at that time were, therefore, a test more of the forecasters' analytical capabilities and judgement than of their models.

By the time of the second oil shock, of course, there was history to go by, and most macroeconomic models had been expanded to incorporate many of the appropriate channels of transmission, with an associated data base and more carefully-determined parameter values. Judgement, at least in this area, could once again play a more backseat role.

Vexed though the problem may be, judgement has to be exercised. Hence if its exercise is to confer any lasting benefit on the forecasting process, it is vital that it be made explicitly, in such a way that the forecaster is reminded, and the user made aware, that judgement has indeed been exercised. If that is done the user can consider whether judgement was exercised appropriately, and the validity of the judgement can be assessed later when the definitive data are available. It is an unavoidable fact that commonly some of the most important elements in a forecast are those on which the model is virtually silent, so that the forecaster's judgement plays the predominant role. Subsequently, when the forecast is confronted by the evidence, it is appropriate to take a slower, careful and data-informed view of the matter, and thereby to incorporate it formally in the model: today's matter of judgement becomes tomorrow's subject for empirical examination.

Conclusions

Macroeconomic models are by no means perfect, and mistakes can be and are made using them. But they have one overriding point in their favour, which should commend them to all who have to make policy and hence have to have a forecast. This is that they make the forecast process explicit: the steps are laid out for all to see, so that the appropriateness of each part can be discussed, evaluated, and, if desired, changed. A macroeconomic model, and its associated data bank, provide a convenient record of the forecast process, that can be drawn upon to help analyse the reasons for successes and failures in a given forecast. A clear statement of the policy assumptions and other economic variables is contained in the data bank, together with the add-factor adjustments applied to selected equations.

With this information, together with the formal structure of the model, it is easier to track down the causes of any significant forecast error, and to take any necessary remedial action. Forecasting error can have many causes, including unrealized assumptions, unexpected shocks, shifts in behaviour, and the inappropriate exercise of the forecaster's judgement. In some cases it may be found necessary, in the light of continuing evidence of poor predictive ability, to reformulate an equation, or set of equations. In this way, the model becomes not only an explicit representation of the forecaster's beliefs as to the key relationships among economic variables, but also a source of feedback which, in light of experience acquired, may result in a rethinking of those relationships.

The next chapter considers the particular issues that arise in the construction and maintenance of a system for making international economic forecasts, an area where the number and complexity of the channels of transmission, and the sheer number of data involved, make a macroeconomic model the only practicable mechanism for evaluating many of the problems of interest.

8 Developing a system for international forecasting

Summary

The construction of an international forecasting system involves four distinct phases: specification of equations, assembly of data, estimation and initial evaluation of the equations, and validation of the full system. Specification is guided by the purposes to be served by the system, and relevant economic theory. Many practical considerations, particularly as regards data, also influence specification of the linked system of country models.

Economic theory is confronted with empirical reality at the model estimation phase. Each equation is evaluated individually, to ensure not only that historical experience is captured satisfactorily, but also that coefficient estimates are consistent with economic theory, and that they are of of plausible sign and magnitude. Then, full system simulation and tracking properties are carefully reviewed. This involves carrying out a number of validation exercises with the complete system, including historical tracking tests of forecasting performance and analysis of multiplier properties.

Introduction

The construction and revision of a model of the world economy involves four distinct phases: *specification* of the equations of the model, *assembly of data* necessary to estimate and then operate the model, *estimation* of equations and initial evaluation of each equation's properties, and *validation* of the complete system. This chapter discusses these issues at a general level; the following chapter describes an actual system – OECD's INTERLINK.

Specifying the model

Specification of the model involves translating propositions about relationships among economic variables, suggested by economic theory, into explicit mathematical relationships. The specification process is governed, first and foremost, by the purposes to be served by the model. This involves consideration of what variables are to be projected, what policy questions are to be evaluated, establishing the observation interval and time horizon to be used, setting out simplifying assumptions to be made, choosing the functional form of equations as well as the length and shape of lag distributions, and ensuring the availability of suitable data.

Economic theory is an important guide in the initial specification of the model's equations, as is knowledge of relevant institutional relationships. Relying on economic theory in the specification of equations helps ensure that variables are not erroneously included in an equation on the basis of chance correlation with the dependent variable in the sample period, but for which there is in fact no underlying rationale. Such an equation, while perhaps 'fitting' the historical data, may well track poorly outside the sample period. Further, the interaction of such an equation with other equations in a simultaneous equations model may cause the model as a whole to track badly and simulate implausibly.

Often, however, theoretical considerations alone provide only an imperfect guide as to the nature of association among variables, and hence to the appropriate specification of the model's equations. Indeed, in some cases, there will be opposing forces at work. For example, it is generally accepted on both theoretical and empirical grounds that private consumption expenditure tends to increase when real disposable income increases, and to decrease when real disposable income decreases. But theoretical considerations do not, on the other hand, provide any clear guidance as to what the effects on consumption behaviour of, say, an increase in the inflation rate might be. On the one hand, consumption expenditure will tend to increase to the extent that households accelerate their purchases of goods and services in anticipation of further price increases. On the other hand, to the extent that over time households attempt to maintain real target savings, they will tend to reduce expenditure. One of the important aspects of the modelling process is, therefore, to assess the empirical significance of the various forces at work, and thereby to test the validity of theories of behaviour. If a theory, when confronted with the reality of historical data, leads to statistically insignificant results, the practical relevance of that theory is cast into doubt.

A number of additional specification questions necessarily confront those involved in developing a linked system of country models. One of the most important concerns the question of uniformity of specification of component country models. At one extreme, each of the component country models might have the same structure, implying, *inter alia*, the exercise of a considerable measure of central guidance in their specification. At the other extreme, the country models could be built up in a decentralized way, with no attempt to exert central influence over their specification. The advantage of a harmonized specification is that understanding and control of the full system's results are improved. On the other hand, given the diversity of national economic structures, and differences in the availability of economic data among countries, to attempt to impose a rigid common specification across all country models would be inappropriate.

It has been found useful to distinguish two different aspects of standardization of the specification of equations, involving economic relations on the one hand and technical aspects on the other. Economic standardization is often desirable in that it facilitates the understanding and operation of an inevitably-large multi-country system. Indeed, homogeneity of specification of each country model's external sector – in terms of level of disaggregation of trade flows and international financial relations – is an essential feature of a coherent international linkage model. It is unavoidable, however, that differences in institutional arrangements – particularly those involving fiscal and monetary systems – and differences in data availability, lead to some diversity of economic specification among models for different countries in the system.

The other facet of standardization involves technical aspects, such as functional form of equations, and common 'input' and 'output' channels. Lack of technical standardization can be troublesome for overall system management, in that it renders the setting up and subsequent interpretation of multi-country simulation results difficult. It is in general useful that, wherever possible, equations for a given variable should have a common functional form, common 'input channels', through which policy and other exogenous variables operate, and common 'output channels', to ensure that forecasting or simulation results can be linked to existing or envisaged operating procedures.

The need for simplification in order better to understand and forecast economic developments gives rise to an inherent conflict between the reality of the model and its manageability. To be useful, a model must be 'realistic' in the sense that it must incorporate the main elements of the processes of interest. It must be sufficiently rich in structural detail to allow it to absorb quickly and efficiently any new information upon which forecasts depend importantly. The structural specification must also provide for sufficiently detailed policy instruments to permit analysis of various policy alternatives. These are forces tending to push models to increasing levels of complexity. At the same time a model must also, to be useful, be capable of being drawn on regularly, be relatively easy to maintain, and, importantly, be easy to understand. These are forces militating in favour of simplicity of specification.

Hence, at one extreme there are models that are highly realistic in the detail and disaggregation of coverage, and comprehensiveness of structure, but which have become so unwieldy as to render them all but useless in practical forecasting and policy-analytic applications. At the other extreme, a very small – and hence highly manageable – model may be so devoid of important structural detail as to be of little use to analysts engaged in forecasting and policy analysis. In the end, the specification necessarily represents something of a compromise – a structure sufficiently rich to be able to yield useful insights, yet simple enough to permit its regular use. In practice, a certain simplification of structure can be compensated by adopting a core model structure that can be complemented, as circumstances require, by imposing judgement on existing equations via 'add factors', and/or by adding, temporarily, an equation, equations, or equation block related to phenomena of current policy concern.

The size of the model naturally depends in part upon the resources available, and the size and experience of the team running the model. In practice, most models start small, as devices designed to capture key relationships which are the current focus of policy attention. In this phase they are generally well understood by all of the members of the team, which is usually small: most participants become so familiar with the model that they are generally well able to intuit the answer it will give to most questions.

If the model is successful, it is typically expanded, to take in more relationships and be able to examine more issues. The team manning the model also may well get bigger. Specialization occurs, so that not all members are familiar with all parts of the model, and certainly may not be familiar with all its system properties. This may not matter if the team continues with a core of members who retain overall understanding and control. But there is a risk, if the model and the team get still bigger, and if the originators of the model leave or become preoccupied elsewhere, that the model can become something of a monster, with system properties that are ill-understood and perhaps even odd. And by being larger the model becomes harder to maintain and to change; it may not move with the times. These problems are familiar to most model users, and they can be guarded against.

The specification of a model will also be influenced by data considerations. From the point of view of forecasting, it is desirable that the exogenous variables (other than policy variables) included in the model should themselves be no more difficult to project than the endogenous variables for which forecasts are to be made. To the extent that projections of a model's exogenous variables are subject to more uncertainty than are the model's endogenous variables, little would be gained, from a forecasting point of view, by their inclusion. On the other hand, in applications where the emphasis is directed at, for example, the sensitivity of economic performance to alternative assumptions rather than forecasting per se, this consideration would not apply.

Once the variables that are to be treated as endogenous, and those that are to be treated as exogenous, are identified, the model is cast into formal algebraic statements, in the form of equations. The choice of appropriate functional form for each equation is an integral part of the specification process. Decisions must be made about whether an equation should be linear or logarithmic, and whether data are to be expressed in levels or first differences, nominal or real magnitudes, as stocks or flows, in total or per capita quantities, and so on. Further, the nature and form of lagged relationships must be made explicit.

The choice of periodicity is an important consideration. Macroeconomic models are typically quarterly, half-yearly, or annual.

The main advantage of a shorter interval is that it is possible to portray the sorts of short-run cyclical fluctuations that so often are the main concern of forecasters, policy-makers, and businessmen. On the other hand, the shorter the time frame, the more difficult it is to find reliable, usable data. The choice of time horizon over which the model is to be used can also influence specification. It is often the case for example that, in models used for short-term forecasting, less attention is given to ensuring long-run stability properties and long-run equilibrium conditions than is suggested by economic theory. It is increasingly accepted, however, that even where a model is intended only for use in relatively short time frames, adequate consideration of long-run properties is important, particularly to ensure that short-run properties are fully compatible with them. This issue is returned to in chapter 11.

Assembly of data

In order to permit estimation of the parameters of equations relating economic variables in a way suggested by theory, and subsequently to support the model in forecasting and policy-analytic applications, a set of data is required, corresponding to each of the variables in the model. This may sound rather obvious; but many a modelling effort has foundered for want of sufficient attention to the assembly, scrutiny and organization of the necessary data.

Most data used in macroeconomic modelling for forecasting and policy analysis are time series, based on periodic observation of variables in successive time periods. The primary sources for most of these economic data are government agencies; important secondary sources are international organizations, such as the IMF, the IBRD (World Bank) and OECD. For the most part, the raw data series these agencies supply require subsequent processing to put them in the form suitable for forecasting, policy analysis, and other model-related activities. For example, data used in connection with economic modelling at OECD are typically seasonally adjusted. Removal of the seasonal component from series can permit a clearer picture to emerge of underlying developments. Seasonal adjustment methods cannot, however, be applied purely mechanically, as this might in some cases obscure underlying trends, and lead to erroneous profiles. Adjustment must be made for holidays and other such factors. Special factors, such as strikes and bad harvests, can be erroneously 'picked up' by seasonal adjustment methods, and embodied in the seasonal components, unless care is taken to exclude them. Further, the use of seasonally adjusted series when estimating the equations of the model can, in some cases, result in distortions of lagged relations, because seasonally-adjusted data are themselves constructed from moving averages of lagged and leading values of the series.

Other transformations necessary to render raw statistical data supplied by official agencies suitable for modelling and forecasting include: re-basing of a given country's data obtained from different sources to a common base year, adjusting fiscal year definitions to a calandar year basis, merging of data obtained from different sources, splicing a current data series to a discontinued series, temporal aggregation and/or interpolation of time series, aggregation from components to totals (or inferring detail from broader aggregates), and temporal aggregation of high frequency data to periodicity used by the model. In a multi-country modelling context, additional adjustments are required, such as rebasing data across countries to a common base year for purposes of trade volume, trade price, and financial linkage, reconciling data reported at 'actual' rates and annual rates, rebasing indices to a common form, and standardizing units of measurement.

There are many other considerations involving data that are important not only to model construction but also to its subsequent operation and use in forecasting and policy analysis. Perhaps the most troublesome data problem encountered in model construction is the lack of requisite data in a form that matches economic theory, and the purposes to be served by the model. Examples include capital stock data (needed in the development of production function and potential output measures), asset holdings (which may play an important role in consumer behaviour), price deflators for internationally-traded services, and international capital flow data (required for analysis of the international transmission of monetary influences). Where suitable data are not available in the requisite form, proxies have to be used. This applies particularly to inherently ill-defined or unmeasurable concepts such as permanent income, potential output, 'real' interest rates, and expectations.

Other data problems may manifest themselves in a number of

ways, depending on the country, in terms of: coverage (not sufficiently disaggregated), frequency (available annually, but not quarterly), reliability (subject to substantial measurement error, or to frequent revision), form needed (flow data, but no stock data), and timeliness (updates with delays of a year or more).

The question of reliability of a given data series is of great importance to macroeconomic modelling for forecasting and policy evaluation: do the data really provide a measure of what they purport to measure, or are the errors and/or approximations involved in compiling them so large as to make pointless any attempt to use them for analytic purposes? The reliability problems associated with data for stockbuilding (inventories), for example, are notorious. These result from the fact that, in many OECD countries, much of the discrepancy among different measures of GNP is put into the stockbuilding data. Yet because this variable is one of the biggest sources of fluctuations in GNP, it is important to have as good a basis as possible for understanding its past behaviour, in order thereby to be able to forecast it.

Examples abound of series that do not in fact provide a good measure of what they purport to measure or, indeed, of what they are assumed to measure. Classic examples of series that may be deficient in the former respect are employment statistics, particularly the statistics for self-employment. This is largely because self-employment figures are themselves based on estimates obtained, by difference, from employment figures (established by surveys of business firms), and labour force statistics (which are based on surveys of households). When the component series are moving in opposite directions, this gives rise to sharp fluctuations in the number of measured self-employed, which in fact is generally considered to be one of the most stable of all employment series. This problem is avoided in some countries, but not truly overcome, where the statistical office makes the technical assumption that the number of self-employed is fixed. An example of a failure of a series to measure what it might unwittingly be assumed to measure is provided by construction permits issued which, in at least one OECD country, are issued only *after* the completion of construction, whereas in most countries such permits would be issued prior to construction, and regarded as a leading indicator of construction. When using data in model construction, the builder should always read the statistician's fine print.

Economic time series are often plagued by a lack of continuity, with breaks in series due to changes in definition, rebenchmarking, and so on. Unless factors are available for linking the 'new' series to the 'old', it is not possible to have a long, consistent continuous run of data, which hampers model development, and thereby forecasting and policy analysis. In such cases, it is necessary to resort to mechanical 'splicing' of series, linking them, for example, through rates of change. Further problems arising from data revisions were discussed in chapter 5.

Data reliability problems become particularly acute in multi-country modelling. Data collection, estimation and reconciliation practices under the national accounting framework upon which most national models are built have been developed and refined over several decades. However, there have as yet been no comparable concerted efforts at the international level to ensure the completeness and consistency of international payments and financial data. The growing global disparity in current account figures, with reported world imports (of goods, services and factor income) exceeding reported exports by some \$100 billion per year, is a current striking example.

Estimation and initial evaluation

Estimation of the behavioural equations of the model involves the application of statistical methods to data in order to determine the most satisfactory explanation of the variable of interest, according to some statistical criterion. Methods derived from classical 'least squares' constitute the most widely-used statistical approach to estimating values of the parameters of the behavioural equations of a macroeconomic model. (See, for example, Goldberger (1964), Johnston (1972) and Malinvaud (1970).)

Classical least squares regression is appropriate, however, only if a number of assumptions involving error distribution hold. If these assumptions are violated, the regression method should be altered. Indeed, it is an emphasis on the development and application of estimation methods applicable under a much wider range of conditions than classical ordinary least squares that is a hallmark of modern econometric methods. Various well-known statistical tests are available as a standard element in most regression packages to help determine whether, in any particular estimation context, the ordinary least squares method is valid or whether it must be supplemented by some other more appropriate estimation method.

Further, the interdependence of economic variables means that, on this count alone, the classical least squares regression model is not strictly applicable, because of the problems of 'simultaneous equations bias' associated with estimating simultaneous equation relationships. The classic example of this problem involved attempts to estimate the consumption function, in which consumption expenditure is expressed as a function of current income. Economic theory suggests that income is an important determinant of consumption expenditure, and the results of early econometric investigation lent support to this. At the same time, however, consumption expenditure is itself a major component of national income. The 'two-way' causality involved would, unless properly allowed for, generate spuriously high estimates of the propensity to consume out of income, and hence poor forecasts, and possibly inappropriate policy.

A number of methods have been developed to deal with the problem of simultaneous equations bias in the estimation of simultaneous equations systems. While theoretically appealing in terms of eliminating this bias, however, these methods are not widely used in practice; the ordinary least squares method (OLS) still predominates. One reason for this is the simplicity with which this estimation method can be applied. Another, frequently-invoked reason has to do with the minimum variance property of OLS estimation. In forecasting applications rooted in applied econometric methods, some small amount of bias in estimates of an equation's parameters can often be accepted, in return for reduction of dispersion of those estimates about their true value. Error properties for the equation as a whole may thereby be improved. Finally, the OLS technique has been shown by experience to be rather robust, even when the data might not strictly speaking warrant its application.

The testing, at the time of estimation, of the economic theory embodied in each equation against actual data is an important aspect of the initial evaluation of a model's equations. This evaluation involves examination of each equation, in turn, on the basis of a number of criteria, including:

- does the equation fit historical data well, tracking major turning points correctly?
- are the signs of the estimated coefficients consistent with those predicted by economic theory?
- are the values of the estimated coefficients consistent with prior beliefs, and with other evidence?
- do the estimated coefficients satisfy tests for statistical significance?
- have all specification problems been appropriately dealt with?

If any equation does not satisfy the preliminary evaluation criteria, then, depending on the circumstances, that equation is respecified or re-estimated using an alternative estimation technique.

Frequently, two or more alternative specifications of an equation may appear plausible on *a priori* grounds, with the results of the estimation process being used to choose between them. In other instances, however, the available estimation techniques often do not make it possible to distinguish, on statistical grounds, between alternative specifications of an equation. Indeed, where differences of functional form are involved, comparison of regression results is not a statistically valid procedure. The final choice may, therefore, depend on out-of-sample tracking properties, and on how each equation interacts with the full system.

Further, because economic theory provides little guidance about the nature and timing of the lag adjustments involved, there are no formal statistical tests that can be applied to reject or not hypotheses concerning lag lengths. Rather, lag lengths are largely imposed on the basis of information from other sources, or knowledge of technical relations underlying the adjustment process (such as planning delays, delivery delays, and search delays). In all, there is not only scope, but a need, for the exercise of judgement when deciding on the specification of an equation to be retained for use in the model.

It would, of course, be unreasonable to expect any equation to provide a perfect 'fit' to the variable whose behaviour it is intended to explain. One important reason for this is the simplification of relationships involved in specification of a model of manageable proportions. One or more explanatory variables may have been omitted on this account alone. Variables otherwise thought to have been important determinants may have been omitted because their influence in the past has been too small to permit detection by the statistical techniques used. Or a variable may not have been included simply because no data were available for it, or because the variable does not lend itself to quantification. Examples include factors such as business and consumer confidence, and factors related to non-price competitiveness in international trade. Certain institutional relationships, simplified in the form of tax equations, for example, also change over time. Finally, of course, the behaviour of economic agents is not governed by immutable laws, such as those governing physical processes. Tastes and technology change over time. And there is an inherent random element in behaviour, which accounts for a significant part of observed regression residuals.

Only when each equation has satisfactorily met the preliminary evaluation criteria can it be considered ready for tentative inclusion in the model. And only when the full set of behavioural equations has satisfactorily passed the preliminary evaluation phase, can the model as a whole be considered ready for full-system validation.

Validation of the model

It is wise to put considerable effort into delineating the range within which it is appropriate to use the model, as well as to establishing confidence in the model's properties when used within these limits. These exercises are known as model validation. Their purpose is to determine the robustness of the model under different operating circumstances, to determine the sensitivity of properties and/or projections to variations in values of key parameters, to determine the sensitivity of properties to alternative specifications of key equations, and to determine the plausibility of the model's responses to alternative disturbances applied to selected policy and other exogenous variables.

The term 'validation' is used in particular to denote a set of procedures for ascertaining that the model's tracking and multiplier performance is satisfactory. The preliminary evaluation criteria for individual equations, applied at the estimation stage, provide a first yardstick in determining whether the model can be expected to perform satisfactorily for its purpose. The results of statistical tests at the estimation phase do not, however, provide an adequate validation of a model consisting of one or more dynamic relations, nor of a model consisting of several, interacting, simultaneous equations. There is no guarantee that a model, each of whose equations may 'fit' historical data well, will, when taken as a whole, track well, or have reasonable simulation properties, when solution values are passed among equations, or even when, in a single equation context, a dynamic evaluation of an equation is involved.

Solution of the model. The 'solution' of a macroeconomic model is the process of computing values for each of the endogenous variables in one or more periods, given the structure of the model, and given the values of policy and other exogenous variables, and lagged values in the system. In any given period, the lagged endogenous variables operate on the system in the same way as policy and other exogenous variables. That is, they influence the solution, but are not themselves influenced by the solution in that time period. When solving the model over several time periods, however, the values of these variables are determined as endogenous variables.

The behavioural characteristics of a macroeconomic model can, in general, be established in two ways – analytically, or by numerical methods. Analytic methods are generally applicable only to small, linear models, although they may be applied to larger models, and to linearized versions of non-linear models. In general, however, the structural characteristics of large, non-linear dynamic models must be established via simulation experiments, involving the use of numerical solution methods. Such methods typically start with some initial approximate solution for the endogenous variables; this is then successively refined through iteration. Simulation tests, which involve solutions of the full model under various assumptions, permit the identification of equations, or blocks of equations, that are not performing satisfactorily in the sense of either poor tracking performance, implausible dynamic multiplier properties, or both. Once an offending equation, or block of equations, has been identified, remedial measures can be taken – which may involve action ranging from simple correction of a transcription or data input error, to reformulation and reestimation of one or more equations.

It is customary to distinguish time horizons involved in model

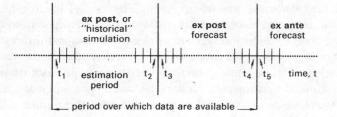

simulations into *ex post* (or 'historical') simulation, *ex post* forecasting, and *ex ante* forecasting (see diagram above).

In *ex post*, or 'historical', simulation, historical values of lagged endogenous variables are used up to period t_1, and actual historical values are used for policy and other exogenous variables over the period t_1 to t_2. From period t_1 on, however, lagged values of endogenous variables are progressively replaced by solution values of subsequent periods. The solution results generated in this way, when compared against actual historical data for the period, provide a test of the model's ability to reproduce observed movements in various economic variables, such as cyclical behaviour and turning points.

The term *forecasting*, used here in a strictly technical sense, involves solution of the model beyond the sample period used in estimating its equations. Two types of forecast simulation are distinguished: *ex post* and *ex ante*.

Ex post forecasts involve starting model solution at the end of the estimation period, and solving the model from then to the present. Lagged values of endogenous variables are initialized at period t_3, and actual values for exogenous variables over the period t_3 to t_4 are used. Again, solved values of endogenous variables are carried forward, to be used as values of lagged endogenous variables in successive time periods. The procedures are essentially the same as with *ex post* simulation, except that the simulation is run on the basis of data not available when the equation coefficients were estimated. The results of *ex post* forecast simulations, when compared with recent data, provide useful insights as to the model's ability to track historical experience beyond the period over which its equations were estimated.

An *ex ante* or 'future' forecasting simulation involves solution of the model beyond the most recent period for which data are available, using assumed values of policy and other exogenous variables (from t_5 onwards). Again, the model itself generates values that are subsequently used as lagged values, in each succeeding time period. *Ex ante* forecasts are a useful device for examining the dynamic properties and stability of a macroeconomic model over a long time horizon. For it frequently occurs that a model, while performing well in historical simulations, exhibits explosive behaviour, or other signs of dynamic instability, as the time period is extended.

Static and dynamic simulation. For equations containing lagged values of an 'own' dependent variable among the explanatory variables, it is useful to distinguish between a 'static' and 'dynamic' simulation of an equation. By static simulation is meant evaluation of an equation, during the solution process, on the basis of actual values of 'all' explanatory variables, exogenous as well as both current and lagged endogenous variables. In this way both the cross-equation and intertemporal processes are isolated. In a static simulation, in which each equation is evaluated singly, the solution mode is referred to as the 'null' or 'residual check' solution because, over the sample period used in estimating a given equation (t_1 to t_2), the solution residuals should correspond to the estimation residuals. Alternatively stated, the solution path of variables in null mode should be identical to the fitted values of the corresponding regression equation. This is so because, in both cases, actual values of explanatory variables are used to evaluate the equations. Thus, the null solution results provide an important check that a model's equations have been correctly coded. By dynamic simulation is meant evaluation of an equation, during the solution process, in which actual values of explanatory variables are used, except for 'own' lagged values for which, over successive solution periods, solved values from previous periods are used.

For the period beyond the estimation period, but for which actual data are available (t_3 to t_4), the null solution residuals provide important information about how a given equation can be expected to perform in forecast applications. Indeed, the information contained in the residuals can be, and customarily is, integrated into the forecast process. Evaluation of post-estimation-period residuals generated by an equation solved in null solution mode can provide a useful way of choosing between alternative equations for inclusion in a model, when it is impossible to choose on the basis of conventional statistical techniques associated with regression methods alone. Purged from cross-equation error propagation, analysis of residuals generated by the null solution constitutes a basis for 'add factor' adjustments (taken up below) when using the model for forecasting. The null solution helps to identify equations that may be the victim of structural shift in the post-sample period, and hence for which respecification may be required.

In a dynamic simulation the solution values of 'own' lagged endogenous variables are used in evaluating the equation. Even when solved in a single equation context, the dynamic simulation of an equation will not reproduce the fitted value resulting from the regression equation, because the values taken on by one or more ('own' lagged endogenous) explanatory variables are based on preceding period solution, rather than on actual data. Single equation dynamic simulation provides a more rigorous test of an equation's tracking properties than do measures of fit obtained from a regression equation (which corresponds to single equation static simulation) because the solution values obtained for endogenous variables in one period become the values of lagged endogenous variables in subsequent periods.

Properties of the complete system. The error characteristics (or 'tracking performance') of a simultaneous equations macroeconomic model cannot be established simply by examination of the error characteristics or simulation properties of the equations taken individually. This is because, in a simultaneous equations model, actual values of explanatory endogenous variables are replaced by calculated values passed from other equations. Errors from any one equation will be passed to others, and so on, so that they may accumulate and mutually reinforce one another. Further, in equations with dynamic elements – reflecting lags in adjustment processes – model solution involves replacing actual values of lagged endogenous variables with solution values obtained in previous periods. This in turn may result in intertemporal error accumulation. For these reasons, it is important to establish the error properties of the complete system.

In general, errors from the equations when solved in the context of the complete model will be greater than those obtained from single equations. In a full system solution, endogenous explanatory variables in any given equation will take on solved values passed from other equations. These values will tend to be subject to error, whereas when estimated on a single-equation basis, exact values of the explanatory endogenous variables will be used. Hence error tends to build up. This is not necessarily the case, however, because cross-equation cancelling of errors also can – and does – result on occasion.

There are both qualitative and quantitative aspects to the validation of a macroeconomic model. When first examining the results of a dynamic historical simulation, a number of qualitative issues are first reviewed, before proceeding to more elaborate quantitative measures of performance.

The model needs to exhibit both cyclical and trend properties that are characteristic of the economy. Short-term cyclical properties will depend on having adequately captured the various stock-flow, financial-real, and volume-price relations on which cyclical fluctuations seem to depend, as well as their attendant lags and non-linearities. In addition to exhibiting reasonable multiplier properties, the model should exhibit damped oscillatory behaviour. As the projection horizon is extended, the steady-state properties exhibited by the model must be consistent with the implications of long-term behaviour derived from economic theory. In practice, these long-term conditions may be imposed on the structural equations, as part of the estimation process.

Other qualitative issues in the validation of the model include:

– do the solution paths for variables follow the actual historical series acceptably closely?
– are model responses to changes in exogenous variables plausible in magnitude and sign, and are they in conformity with what is expected on the basis of economic theory?
– does the model exhibit the same cyclical properties as the actual historical series – are turning points correctly captured, and do the solution paths avoid 'false' turning points?
– is the model inherently stable in dynamic simulations, or are there signs of explosive or undamped oscillatory behaviour?
– do the projection paths in the *ex ante* simulations seem reasonable?

Any assessment of the qualitative properties of model behaviour depends, of course, on the judgements and *a priori* beliefs of the analyst making the assessment. But such exercises are important in instilling confidence in the model, through ensuring that the results make good economic sense, and that the model succeeds in reproducing the behaviour typically observed in key economic variables.

Any serious shortcomings of the model revealed by a qualitative assessment of model properties would, of course, give rise to remedial action – typically involving respecification of one or more of the model's components. Sources of domestic instability might arise from an explosive wage-price spiral, for example. Sources of instability at the international level in a multi-country linkage model could arise from, for example, failure of the trade equations to satisfy the 'Marshall-Lerner' conditions, or the interaction of capital flow equations and the exchange rate determination process. Once the model's component blocks, and the system as a whole, exhibit acceptable qualitative properties, a number of quantitative measures of performance can meaningfully be applied.

It is natural to expect that values generated by historical simulation of a model will reflect observed behaviour over the period. That is, it would be hoped that a close correspondence would be observed between simulated values for each endogenous variable and the actual historical series. Indeed, it is useful to have a quantitative measure of how close the association is.

Quantitative measures of model performance are of interest both in their own right, and in providing a benchmark of model behaviour, against which the effects of subsequent changes or alternative specification can be assessed. In many cases, quantitative measures of full model performance are analogous to measures applied to individual regression equations. A number of other quantitative techniques, however, are specifically designed to assess performance of the model, as a set of interacting simultaneous equations (Dhrymes, et al. 1972). In contrast to statistical measures customarily applied to regression equations, however, there are no formal tests that can be appplied to the performance of a full macroeconomic model. This is because there is no statistical theory applicable to a situation in which forecasts are generated in part on the basis of their own lagged values.

It is also useful to establish the sensitivity of the model to changes in parameter values. This is an important, though typically too little-practised, part of the model validation process. Parameter sensitivity analysis is important in assessing the robustness of the model. Confidence in the model is usually increased where it can be shown that its essential properties are not critically dependent on particular parameter values, but hold over a range of parameter values. In this way, concerns with estimation error in regression methods and with the effects of structural change, and their implications for a model's usefulness, can be mitigated.

Remedial action. Identifying the causes of tracking error is as important as establishing that tracking errors are significant. Similarly, identifying the causes of unsatisfactory simulation properties is just as important as establishing that model properties are not satisfactory. Determination of which variables or parameters are most critical to a model's performance involves a systematic tracing through of the structure of the system, to isolate the offending equations. Once these have been isolated, alternative specifications may be substituted with a view to improving simulation and forecasting performance.

A systematic technique for decomposing the response properties of a macroeconomic model to a given shock, developed by Helliwell and Higgins (1976), is now quite widely used within the OECD Secretariat. Briefly, this involves:

   (i)   computing a control solution for the complete model;
   (ii) applying a shock to the complete model, and computing the alternative solution;
   (iii) computing a succession of alternative solutions, with selected blocks of the model suppressed in turn (i.e. with the corresponding endogenous variables made exogenous).

This procedure can be used to identify, for each type of shock applied, which blocks and/or equations are most associated with any implausible response in tracking properties that the model might exhibit. It is also helpful in identifying any features of the model to which results are particularly sensitive.

The next chapter describes how the various principles outlined in this chapter have been applied in developing an actual model system for international forecasting and policy analysis – OECD's INTERLINK system.

9 The INTERLINK system

Summary

The INTERLINK system is at the hub of the OECD Secretariat's regular economic forecasting and policy analytic activities. It helps ensure that forecasts and simulations are economically coherent, internationally consistent, and reflect an agreed view about the way the world economic system operates. The system consists of country models for each of the OECD countries, and eight regional models covering the non-OECD area.

The country models are basically demand-determined, based on circular income-expenditure flows. Supply effects are represented through the influence of labour market conditions on wage (and hence price) formation, and the influence of capacity utilization measures. Particular attention is paid to the specification of the numerous channels through which international trade volumes and prices, and financial variables, affect the domestic economy, and through which economies interact at the international level. Exchange rates and capital flows may be solved endogenously, or set exogenously.

Introduction

INTERLINK, the OECD Secretariat's model of the world economy, has been developed as an operational tool to assist in economic forecasting and policy analysis. It treats the world economy as an integrated whole, with countries' trade flows, capital flows and domestic economic developments determined simultaneously. The model thereby ensures that changes in the external trade and financial sectors feed back into the domestic economy, inducing further changes in countries' real, price, financial and other variables. These in turn influence partner country economies, and so on. INTERLINK is not a research vehicle. Rather, it is a framework for deploying the empirical work of the OECD Secretariat's Economics and Statistics Department, bringing to bear the power of system-wide consistencies, relationships, and identities on issues the Secretariat is regularly called upon to address. As such, it is a vehicle for formalizing thinking, and performing computations to show posssible responses, both domestically and abroad, to changes in policy and other exogenous variables.

The system helps ensure the coordination and smooth functioning of a multi-country forecasting exercise which necessarily involves thousands of data series, and in which all parts of the Department participate. It provides a focal point for the interchange of information, helping coordinate the contributions of staff involved. It ensures that domestic and international accounting identities are respected as forecast components are revised, and that the economic consequences of a revision to a given forecast component are appropriately reflected through the entire forecast set.

INTERLINK is regularly called upon to carry out a variety of functions, including:

- initiating each forecast 'round' with a 'climate run' in which the previous forecast set is updated for changed policy assumptions and other exogenous variables, with incorporation of initial judgemental information;
- testing the international consistency of a set of individual country forecasts and evaluating, country by country, the revisions to domestic demand, price and financial forecasts that would be needed to achieve international compatibility;
- facilitating the production of alternative projections, once the baseline forecast has been constructed;
- simulating the real, price, and financial effects of changes in (policy-induced) economic conditions in one country on the economies of other OECD countries and non-OECD regions, transmitted via international trade and financial linkages;
- evaluating the medium-term effects of alternative policies or behaviour on domestic activity and inflation, and hence, through trade, activity and inflation in other countries;

- helping assess internationally-coordinated policy changes in one or more countries that would be needed to achieve short- and medium-term policy targets (GNP growth rate, foreign balance, inflation etc.) in one or more countries.

The structure of the system

The structure of INTERLINK reflects the natural evolution in the use of international modelling techniques at OECD, which now have a rather long history. The world trade models elaborated over the period 1969-1976 (Adams *et al.*, 1969; Meyer-zu-Schlochtern and Yajima, 1970; and Samuelson, 1973, 1976) were a natural first step in this direction, given the OECD's traditional role in international economic forecasting. The primary contribution of these trade models was the provision of a rigorous framework for ensuring the international consistency of trade volume and price projections as the forecast round evolved. Further, the endogenization of countries' export volumes and import prices – making them explicitly dependent on trading partners' import volumes and export prices, as well as on relative prices and exchange rates – made it possible to take more fully into account the influences of policy and other factors on international trade flows. As the trade models were progressively refined, their geographic coverage was extended and trade flows further disaggregated by commodity group. An overriding principle underlying their development was that the structural specifications continue to ensure that, in simulation and forecasting applications, changes in a given country's import volumes and export prices have their full counterpart in trading partners' export volumes and import prices.

The development, implementation and progressive refinement of trade models marked the first significant introduction of computer-based techniques in the forecasting process. The trade models were initially used both to support the forecasting of countries' balance-of-payments positions and, in simulation applications, to purge countries' foreign balances of the effects of transitory fluctuations in activity levels – both at home and abroad – so as better to identify underlying (or 'fundamental') trade balances. Given incremental shifts in demand and/or relative price competitiveness, the trade models facilitated timely and coherent revision of import volume and export price projections, together with corresponding changes in countries' export volumes and import prices.

An important limitation of these trade models, however, was their inability to allow for feedbacks from the foreign trade sector into domestic demand and cost components. Hence, the trade models alone were unable to capture fully either the important international transmission and multiplier effects that characterize the interdependence of the OECD economies, or the interaction of OECD economies with non-OECD regions. These effects were captured as best the Secretariat could by a series of 'manual' iterations between the trade model and other parts of the system.

Events of the 1970s, and particularly those associated with the changed energy situation, highlighted the importance of international transmission effects. The mutually-reinforcing effects of synchronized fluctuations in OECD economies (considered in chapter 4) were clearly seen, and suggested that substantial improvements in forecasts might be made if these effects could be more systematically taken into account. Moreover, in a world characterized by rapidly changing economic events, and volatile exchange rates, it became increasingly difficult to cope with the analysis of the growing quantities of data required, and the increasing demand of OECD member governments for more frequently updated forecasts embodying, *inter alia*, a consistent assessment of the international forces at work. The data problem in particular is considerable: over 7000 series are regularly involved, in addition to which it is necessary to monitor a continuing flow of revised or updated economic data throughout each forecasting round. There was also the need to be able to incorporate into the forecast changes in countries' economic policies, and significant events external to the OECD area, when these occur in the closing stages of a forecasting round.

Accordingly, in 1976, work began on a simplified international linkage model, building on the, by then, relatively sophisticated trade model structure. The objective was to implement a system that would be comparatively easy to manage, understand, and maintain, yet whose structure would fit OECD's half-yearly forecasting procedure, and whose focus would be the effects of various international transmission processes.

The result was an international linkage model – INTERLINK –

which integrated the world trade model with small models for OECD and non-OECD regions – see Llewellyn and Samuelson (1979). These captured the principal domestic economic responses to foreign trade disturbances, and fed induced changes in import volumes and export prices back to the world trade model such that, on repeated iteration, a more economically coherent, as well as internationally consistent, set of projections would result.

Initially, the country models of the INTERLINK system consisted largely of reduced-form relations, derived from the simulation properties of large structural models used by, or known to, national administrations. These had the advantage of being relatively straightforward to implement. At the same time, attention was given to ensuring full specification of the various channels through which external developments would impinge on the domestic economy, and through which changes in domestic economic trends in any one country would influence the pattern of world trade, and hence ultimately affect its trading partners. This involved, *inter alia*, drawing on information contained in input-output tables, which was useful in two important ways. First, it permitted the weighting, for each trade commodity group, of various expenditure components according to their import content. This in turn enabled a more reliable assessment to be made of the likely influence of a given pattern of domestic demand on import volumes. Second, weights derived from input-output tables were used to help construct cost components – involving *inter alia* a weighted average of changes in import prices of various commodity groups – for use in various price equations. This helps ensure that changes in the price of internationally-traded goods and services – such as oil – are properly reflected in changes in various domestic and export prices.

Progressively, however, these reduced-form relations have been replaced by structural equations. Indeed, it is now standard policy within the Economics and Statistics Department that, wherever relevant, empirical macroeconomic analysis be designed from the outset to be compatible with the overall INTERLINK framework so that, if promising, results can be incorporated in the system with a minimum of effort. This in turn expands the capability of the system as a whole, making it a 'library' or repository of knowledge, agreed, and drawn on, by all concerned.

The principle that the country models, when used in single-country mode, should broadly reproduce the simulation properties of larger national models – modified, as required, by economic circumstances on the basis of discussion with forecasting experts from national administrations – has been, and remains, an important consideration in the development of INTERLINK. This serves to establish confidence in projections and simulations with the system run in fully linked mode, in which the results emanating from any one country or regional model influence projections obtained from the others.

An important feature of the development of structural features of the INTERLINK system is an attempt to ensure coherence of short and medium-term properties. This is in contrast to modelling efforts in some countries, where short-term forecasting and simulation is often undertaken on one model – which typically emphasizes demand-side processes – while medium-term studies, if undertaken, may be conducted within the framework of a different model, often with a different database and with more emphasis on supply-side phenomena.

Undertaking short and medium-term analyses on separate models frequently presents insuperable problems in linking the end of the short-term projection to the beginning of the medium-term projection. Certainly, this was the experience of the OECD Secretariat some years ago when attempts were made to link medium-term projections, derived from a separate medium-term identities model, to the short-term forecasts. Conducting short and medium-term projections on the same model is technically feasible, and offers considerable savings in resources, there being only one database, one set of software, and with many blocks of equations – such as those concerning taxation, government expenditure, imports and exports, and private expenditure – being common to both applications. Furthermore, ensuring that the model's behavioural equations have satisfactory theoretical and empirical medium-term properties also improves their usefulness in short-term applications, as well as increasing the confidence which can be placed in them.

In its present form, INTERLINK consists, basically, of:

(i)   twenty-three medium-size structural models (approximately 150 equations each) for the OECD Member countries,[1] which broadly reproduce the simulation properties of larger econometric models well-known to, and used by, national administrations;

(ii) reduced-form models for each of eight non-OECD regions, with properties established on the basis of empirical evidence available both within the Secretariat and in research centres and institutions specializing in the economies of non-OECD countries.

(iii) world trade and financial linkage models, which link the OECD economies and the non-OECD regions through merchandise and services trade volumes and trade prices, international capital flows, and other factors such as cross-country wage-rate emulation (Chart 9.1).

The OECD country models

The OECD country models are basically demand-determined, income/expenditure models, in which blocks of equations determine the main components of demand; wages and prices; foreign trade prices and volumes; the distribution of income; output and employment; and financial variables. Supply effects operate primarily through the effects of labour market conditions on wage rates and hence prices, as well as the effects of varying levels of capacity utilization on prices.

Each country model consists of about fifty behavioural equations, and around one hundred identities. Given that there are models for 23 OECD countries, it would be impractical to attempt to describe here the more than three thousand equations involved. The features that broadly characterize the country models of the INTERLINK system, however, are summarized below.[2]

Domestic expenditure. Three broad categories of domestic expenditure are distinguished: private consumption and investment, and government spending. Private consumption is related to real disposable income, and long-term real interest rates, with due allowance for adjustment lags. 'Real balance' effects and measures of 'consumer confidence' (for which proxy variables, such as the unemployment rate, and changes in the inflation rate, may be used) are theoretical determinants of consumption expenditure. Such variables are not included, however, as there seems little evidence in most countries that they play an important role.

Chart 9.1 The INTERLINK system
(basic structure)

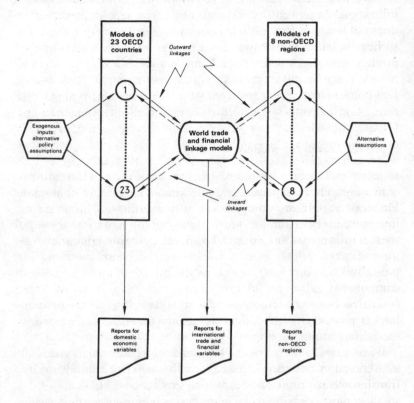

Note: *Outward linkages* correspond to a country's variables that directly affect partner countries. These include import volumes, export prices, net capital inflows, wage rates, interest rates, and exchange rates.

Inward linkages correspond to external variables that directly affect the domestic economy. These include export volumes, import prices and net capital outflows.

Private investment expenditure is, in most of the country models, divided into at least three components: business fixed investment, residential construction, and stockbuilding. There is further disaggregation for some countries. Business fixed investment is typically determined by current and past changes in private sector output and relative factor costs, with due allowance for profits and capacity utilization. In some OECD economies, residential construction does not lend itself to 'explanation' by econometric equations; it is so heavily influenced by government policy that it is most appropriately viewed as a policy instrument. For most OECD economies, however, the model treats residential construction as a function of real household disposable income and the long-term real interest rate, again subject to lagged adjustment. Inventory series, for many OECD countries, are so volatile and/or prone to measurement error that inventory investment (stockbuilding) is typically treated as exogenous. However, for some countries it has proved possible to relate this variable to a desired stock/sales ratio, which adjusts with a lag to both expected and unexpected changes in final sales. Financial variables, while theoretically exerting an influence on inventory investment, are not included in the equations because there is little consistent empirical evidence suggesting that they play a significant and stable role. Government expenditure, which is typically sub-divided into consumption and investment components, is treated as exogenous in nominal terms for most countries. For some countries, however, the nature of the national budget process is such that government expenditure is treated as exogenous in real terms.

Wages and domestic prices. Wage rates are determined primarily as a function of labour market conditions, trend productivity, transfer and payroll taxes, and price expectations. In some of the smaller, most open OECD economies, wages in larger neighbouring economies are also a determinant of domestic wage trends. Prices (deflators for private consumption and other expenditure components) are determined via a mark-up on costs – of which labour and imported materials are the most important – together with allowance for changes in indirect tax rates and trend productivity. The mark-up process is variable, reflecting variations in product market conditions as measured by capacity utilization or 'gap' between actual and potential output. The relative weights attached to various cost components are derived from information contained in input–output tables. Changes in labour costs and in import prices are typically assumed to be shifted into domestic prices within twelve to eighteen months.

Foreign trade – prices and volumes. Six trade categories are distinguished, of which five are endogenous: manufactures, energy, food, raw materials, and private non-factor services. A sixth category, consisting of government services and factor payments, are exogenous to the model, as are net foreign transfers.

Import volumes for each of the five commodity groups treated endogenously are determined by changes in the level, and composition of, aggregate demand, with expenditure components weighted according to their import content. Capacity utilization measures also play a role, with imports tending to be higher than would otherwise be the case when domestic capacity utilization rates are high. Expenditure elasticities for manufactured goods tend to lie in the range of 1½ to 2, and around unity for non-manufactured trade components. Relative prices of imported and domestically-produced goods are also an important determinant of countries' imports. Price elasticities typically lie in a range of −0.7 to −1.1 for manufactures and private non-factor services (lagged over two to three years), around -0.6 for energy (lagged over six to seven years), and close to zero for food and raw materials.

Export prices for manufactures are determined through a variable mark-up on costs – of which unit labour costs and an import-content-weighted average of import prices are the most important elements – with allowance for changes in competitors' export prices. Export prices for internationally-traded raw materials and food vary according to fluctuations in world activity and the world price level. In the case of food prices, allowance is made in the context of forecasting applications for the EEC's Common Agriculture Policy. While responses are dependent both on baseline conditions, and on the pattern of changes in activity, it is generally the case that a 1 per cent change in OECD area GNP in the model will induce, over a period of one to two years, a simulated increase of about 3 per cent in the prices of internationally-traded raw materials, and of about 2 per cent in the prices of internationally traded food. In forecasting applications, export prices of oil move in line, by technical assumption, with the average OECD export price of manufactures, though in some simulation applications the price of internationally-traded oil is determined as that equilibrating world demand and supply.

For the commodity groups treated endogenously in the system, export volumes are determined primarily on the basis of changes in 'market growth' (a weighted average of changes in partner countries' imports) and in relative price competitiveness. Market growth is the key notion underpinning world trade models: it is the channel through which countries' projected exports are made to depend upon partner countries' imports. Its elasticity is usually assumed to be unity for commodity groups other than manufactures trade where, for some countries, this elasticity seems to be slightly above or below unity – although, of course, it has to average out at exactly unity for all countries taken together. Price elasticities for manufactures and non-factor services (export prices relative to those of competitors) typically lie in the range of -1.0 to -2.0 (lagged over three years). For other commodity groups (oil, food, raw materials) relative export price elasticity effects play little role over the short to medium-term simulation horizon for which the system is typically used. For a given country, import prices for each of the five commodity groups treated endogenously are determined primarily as a weighted average of partner countries' export prices to that country. The trade linkage block, described below, ensures the international consistency of countries' trade volumes and prices.

Distribution of income. Appropriation accounts for households, business and government are constructed by identifying first the different sources of income on the revenue side, while the disposition of each sector's income is determined in the expenditure account.

Income of households consists primarily of wages and salaries, income of the self-employed, and transfers received. These income elements, together with property and other income, are adjusted for direct taxes and transfers paid to derive households' disposable income. Consumption – and hence household saving – is a function of this variable. Households' net lending is then determined by further subtracting exogenously-given capital transactions.

Current receipts of government are the sum of direct taxes on households and business, indirect taxes, various transfers received, and property income of government. Current disbursements of government are the sum of government consumption and investment expenditure, and various transfers, subsidies, and property income paid, including interest payments on government debt. Net lending of government is given by government saving (current receipts less current disbursements) net of investment and other capital transactions.

Business taxes are a lagged function of business income. The remaining components of the business appropriation account are derived as residuals: business income is GDP minus the net income of the three other sectors (households, government and foreign); business net lending is determined residually as the difference between the foreign balance and net lending of the other two domestic sectors.

The supply side. Supply effects manifest themselves in the country models primarily through the influence of labour market conditions on wage rate determination, and the influence on prices of capacity utilization terms. As already noted, capacity utilization measures also play a role in investment and import equations. Private sector dependent employment is determined as a function of current and lagged activity and real wage rates. Self-employment is typically assumed to move in line with private sector dependent employment, while government employment is exogenous. Unemployment is defined as the difference between the labour force and total employment. Industrial production, unit labor costs, productivity, and capacity utilization measures are also determined in the supply block. At the international level, supply-side effects manifest themselves primarily through the effect of variations in demand conditions on trade commodity prices, which in turn feed into OECD countries' domestic cost and price structures. This is an important area, often overlooked from the vantage point of a forecast or policy-analytic exercise of any single country, for the cumulative effects of changes in demand conditions in a number of countries can powerfully affect the inflation rate via commodity price responses.

Financial influences. The transmission of monetary influences – whether within a given economy or internationally – is a particularly complex area. Further, the empirical literature does not reveal a consensus as to the relative importance, or indeed existence, of the channels through which monetary influences operate, and the lags involved. In view of the vigour of the monetarist/Keynesian debate in recent years, such a lack of consensus is perhaps not surprising. Further, the widely differing institutional arrangements in OECD Member countries preclude a common approach to modelling financial mechanisms.

For most country models within INTERLINK, the approach adopted has short-term interest rates determined via an inverted demand-for-money function, with the money supply either given exogenously, or, for example, determined via unsterilized changes in net foreign asset holdings of the central bank. For some of the smaller OECD economies, allowance is made for the influence of partner countries' short-term interest rates in the determination of domestic monetary conditions. For countries where interest rates are administered directly by the central bank, this variable is treated as exogenous. The short-term interest rate is the immediate response variable, and influences, *inter alia*, international capital flows. The long-term rate, which typically feeds into the expenditure equations, is determined through a distributed lag of short-term interest rates, with allowance for the expected inflation rate. The influences on the money supply of a country's balance of payments, and of alternative means of financing public sector deficits, are represented explicitly in most of the country models.

A recent development in the model, and which has already proved particularly informative in policy discussions, has been the modelling of international capital flows, determined on the basis of changes in interest rate differentials, expected exchange rates, world wealth, and other factors, such as trade-related credit, and the recycling of OPEC surpluses. The financial linkage block, described separately below, ensures the global consistency of international capital flows, in either fixed or floating exchange rate modes.

Non-OECD regional models

The eight non-OECD regional models included in the INTER-LINK system cover the countries which are not members of the OECD. These countries are grouped broadly according to similarity of economic characteristics, as follows: less absorptive OPEC countries; more absorptive OPEC countries; other oil-producing countries; newly-industrializing countries; low- and middle-income developing countries; USSR and Eastern European countries; China and selected Asian countries; and other non-OECD countries. Details of the countries in these groups are given regularly in the *OECD Economic Outlook*.

The non-OECD regional models are much less detailed than the models for OECD countries. They do not, for example, include structural equations for determination of domestic expenditure, domestic wages and prices, and income distribution. Rather, they are cast in the form of reduced-form equations characterizing import volume and export pricing behaviour.[3]

Import volumes in each non-OECD regional model are expressed as a function of changes in each region's foreign exchange resources (export earnings, transfers, borrowing), adjusted for changes in the terms of trade. The rationale underlying this approach has been discussed extensively (see, for example, Polak and Boissonneault, 1960). The foreign exchange resources of most non-OECD countries tend to be limited. For this reason, changes in imports tend to be closely related to changes in export earnings, whether the result of price changes or volume changes. In cases where export earnings fall, for example, imports tend to be reduced, in order to protect the foreign exchange position. Conversely, an increase in export earnings tends to give rise to a loosening of import restraint.

In simulation applications with the system, capital flows for non-OECD regions are assumed simply to be the counterpart of current balance positions, such that their international reserves are unchanged. In forecasting applications, however, this is not necessarily the case, changes in net capital flows being expected to have effects on non-OECD countries' imports analogous to those of a change in export earnings.

Debt interest payments account for a large proportion of the current account deficits of non-OECD regions (excluding OPEC). Because much of this debt is floating rate debt, with interest payments thereby related to world short-term interest rates, fluctuations in these rates can also play an important role in determining the foreign exchange resources of non-OECD regions. While their effects are not yet explicitly represented in the system, the effects of change in financial conditions affecting the non-OECD regions are taken into account via add-factor adjustments.

For most non-OECD regions, it is assumed that any changes in real foreign exchange resources will be fully spent in the course of a year or two, depending on the region. The lags involved are assumed to be the shortest for low-and middle-income developing countries (which have an assumed spending propensity of 1.0, distributed over one year), and the longest for OPEC low-absorbers (spending propensity of 0.7, distributed over two years).

The non-OECD regions are assumed to be 'price takers' for trade in manufactures: their export prices of manufacturers are assumed to follow the average of the OECD area. As with the OECD country models, export prices of food and industrial raw materials respond to changes in demand conditions in the OECD area and costs of production. Also, as with the OECD country models, the export price of internationally-traded oil is customarily assumed to move in line with OECD countries' average export price of manufactures though, in some simulation applications, the price of internationaly-traded oil is determined through a market-clearing mechanism which balances total OECD area oil requirements with indigenous production, non-OECD production (OPEC and non-OPEC), and changes in inventories.

International linkage

World trade and financial models link the OECD country models, together with those of the non-OECD regions, to provide internationally-consistent projections of trade volumes and prices, and international capital flows. The main structural features of the international linkage mechanisms and their interaction with the individual country models are described in OECD (1983). For some countries, other linkage channels can be important, as in the case of wage rate determination (where wage rate trends in small open economies are directly influenced by wage rate trends in a larger neighbouring country) and interest rate determination (where interest rate trends in some countries are related to those of the United States).

Trade volume and price linkage. The trade linkage procedures apply separately to each of the five trade categories treated endogenously: manufactures, energy, food, raw materials and private non-factor services. Within each country and non-OECD regional model, import volumes and export prices are endogenously determined for given values of, *inter alia*, exchange rates, import prices and export volumes. When the system is used in fully-linked mode, these individual country projections are passed to the central world trade block, where a consistent set of export volume and import price estimates is determined. These are in turn passed back to the country models as revised inputs into the determination of domestic demand and costs, so that on repeated iteration a convergent and internationally-consistent model solution is achieved. The linkage process therefore consists of allocating country-model-based estimates of global import demands between individual exporting countries, while also determining individual country import prices, given a global view of export prices, exchange rate movements, and the emerging patterns of international trade.

A number of approaches have been suggested for the consistent linkage of countries' trade volumes and prices in a multi-country modelling context (Hickman and Lau, 1973; Klein and van Peeterssen, 1973; Moriguchi, 1973; and Samuelson and Kurihara, 1980). While the theoretical underpinnings differ, they all provide for global consistency of results. A detailed review of these various methods may be found in Amano *et al*, 1980. Several of these approaches have been evaluated in terms of their tracking properties in both in-sample and post-sample simulation tests by staff of the Japanese Economic Planning Agency. The Samuelson-Kurihara approach to linkage has been adopted in the INTER-LINK system – see Samuelson and Kurihara (1980). There are three reasons for this. First, it exhibits robust simulation and tracking properties. Second, it is easy to interpret because of its resemblance to the specification of a traditional export equation found in many national models (in which some measure of relative price, of foreign activity, and possibly other variables typically appear). Third, it can be used directly in simulations carried out in single-country mode.

This approach involves export volumes adjusting as a function of changes in relative price competitiveness and change in 'market growth' – a weighted average of changes in partner countries' import volumes.[4] A disadvantage of this approach, in contrast to some other linkage methods, is that there is no *a priori* guarantee that this formulation will satisfy the condition that the sum of exporter shares of a given import market is unity. This follows from the fact that the equation used, while closely related to the global accounting identity set out initially, may depart from it in that the market growth elasticity need not be unity. Further, the coefficient associated with competitive performance corresponds to the relative price elasticity of export volumes averaged over markets. While a straightforward formulation of this sort has proven to be robust in application, as well as facilitating interpretation of the factors at work to influence trade volumes, it does not itself ensure global consistency of results. In practice, any inconsistencies, which are generally fairly small, are eliminated by the rescaling of exporters' shares on a proportionate basis. This revised 'share matrix' then constitutes the base-period market-share pattern used for export volume and import price projections in the next period.

From the vantage point of a given country model, export volumes and import prices can be viewed as being essentially exogenously determined. This is true to the extent that many of the factors on which they depend, such as market growth, partner countries' export prices, and competitors' prices in third markets, are indeed fixed when the system is run in single-country mode. These variables, being determined in the world trade model, become fully endogenous only when the system is run in linked mode. They can, of course, be manipulated by assumption in single country mode, with attendant effects on import prices and export volumes. Even so, some domestic variables can affect both import prices and export volumes, inducing endogenous responses even in single-country mode. Import prices, for example, adjust fully in single-country mode to assumed changes in the exchange rate; and export volumes adjust to changes in relative competitiveness, whether resulting from a changed exchange rate assumption or from changes in own export prices.

Thus, the effects of, for example, changes in competitive position on exports can be assessed in single-country mode, without necessarily solving the fully linked system. This does, however, entail loss of information about the effects of competitive price responses, and other adjustments, induced in other countries in fully linked simulations.

As is the case for trade volumes, international trade price linkage starts from an accounting relation; changes in a given country's import prices are related both to changes in partner countries' export prices, and to each partner country's share in the import market. Because it is not possible to infer movements in absolute price levels from changes in a weighted average of index numbers (except in a fixed-basket case), import price movements are related in percentage change terms to market-weighted percentage changes in export prices.

In forecasting and simulation applications, an element of discriminatory export pricing by market is introduced, reflecting the fact that, *ceteria paribus*, exporters tend to adjust prices across markets, in response to a changed competitive position with respect to domestic producers. For example, in a market where, relative to the average, competitive position with respect to domestic producers has deteriorated – whether because of better inflation performance, an exchange rate adjustment, or whatever, exporters tend to reduce prices in a given market below their average export price in order to maintain share in that market. Conversely, in a country where domestic prices have risen, exporters tend to take advantage of the opportunity to widen (or restore, as the case may be) profit margins, raising their export prices in that market. Thus, an important element of the international price linkage mechanism involves, for each exporter and subject to the constraint that average export prices determined in the country model be respected, shading export prices upwards or downwards to a given market, depending on whether domestic competitiveness in that market has improved or deteriorated relative to the average of export markets. These 'differentiated' prices enter the weighting scheme determining import prices.

Financial linkage. A world financial linkage model ensures the international consistency of forecast or simulated capital flows among OECD countries and non-OECD regions. This is a prerequisite in any quantitative consideration of the properties of the international economic system under the present exchange rate system. The main considerations underlying the design of the financial linkage block and the organization of related information flows are similar to those for international trade linkage, but there has been much less experience world-wide so far with this aspect of international linkage modelling. In both cases an essential operational requirement is that the system be able to be run both in single country and internationally-linked modes. For this reason it is again useful to decompose the main features of the financial linkage system into domestically and internationally-determined components. The relationships for the former category of variables have been described in the block structure of individual country models. Those for the latter group are computed in the financial linkage block, which may operate in either fixed or floating exchange rate mode – see Holtham (1984).

The principal behavioural equation involved is that for net international capital flows, which are a function of *ex ante* short-term interest rate differentials, the expected rate of currency depreciation/appreciation, world wealth and domestic and partner countries' current balances. Additional identity relationships are used to define reserve changes, both in domestic and dollar terms, and effective exchange rates, both actual and expected. As with the trade linkage block, the U.S. dollar is used as the numeraire currency, so that a country's effective exchange rate is defined as the ratio of the domestic-currency bilateral dollar rate to a weighted average of partner countries' dollar rates. The treatment of the expected effective exchange rate is fully analogous to that of the actual effective rate, with expected bilateral dollar rates replacing actual rates. Not surprisingly, the expected exchange rate exerts powerful effects – in the model and, it would appear, in the world. Considerable investigation is currently being undertaken, at OECD and elsewhere, into what determines expected exchange rates.

Consistency of international capital flows in the international financial linkage block is achieved by appropriately-defined weighting procedures for interest rates and exchange rates. A set of cross-country parameter restrictions embodied in the weights used in the net capital flow relationships ensures that, for given changes in interest rate differentials and expected exchange rates, the net capital flow resulting for any one country is exactly matched elsewhere in the system either by capital flows, of the reverse sign, or changes in foreign currency holdings.

In linked mode, each country's domestic interest rates and actual and expected exchange rates are passed to the financial linkage block. The linkage block in turn calculates for each country weighted-average actual and expected exchange rates, and weighted-average foreign short-term interest rates. The weighting procedures are geometric in form, consistent with usual IMF practices.[5] These weighted averages of actual exchange rates, expected exchange rates, and short term interest rates are then passed back to individual country models, where they influence *inter alia* net capital flows.

When run in single country mode, with actual exchange rates, expected exchange rates, and interest rates all exogenous by assumption, a change in the effective exchange rate induces a capital flow. In linked mode, changes in exchange and interest rates for any single country feed through via, *inter alia*, international capital flows, affecting exchange rates and interest rates throughout the system.

In a policy regime of fixed exchange rates, interest rates adjust in response to changes in the international reserve component of the money supply. In floating rate mode, exchange rates as well as interest rates are determined endogenously, in accordance with a specified international reserves target. The floating rate system is implemented through an option that in effect 'inverts' the identity relation defining changes in a country's international reserves. Essentially this involves the computation of a domestic exchange rate (in single country mode), or a full set of rates (in linked mode) which achieve prespecified reserve targets or intervention limits for all countries. In the case of 'exchange rate unions', such as the EMS, a joint float is achieved by directly linking a group of currencies to a chosen central rate, which in turn is permitted to float freely. A targeting facility within INTERLINK, whereby alternative assumptions concerning the response of monetary authorities may be taken into account, permits further policy options including reserve and exchange rate targeting through interest rate determination.

Adapting INTERLINK to recent policy concerns

The INTERLINK system was originally developed at a time when appropriate setting of demand management policy in increasingly interdependent OECD economies was of central concern to policymakers. It is therefore natural that the structure of the component country models of INTERLINK should clearly reflect the income and expenditure relations that were central to those concerns. And this is likely to remain the case, because the international transmission of demand impulses is likely to remain an important phenomenon which will need to be taken into account by policymakers, individually and collectively, when analysing and forecasting the behaviour of their economies.

But economic circumstances evolve, and policy requirements change. It is clear, for example, that the concerns of policymakers in many countries have shifted – in some cases quite fundamentally – over the past decade. Considerable effort has, therefore, been put into adapting or modifying the structure of INTERLINK so as to keep abreast of current policy concerns. At the present time, for example, there are four main areas in which further developmental work on INTERLINK is proceeding:

- a fuller representation of financial markets and, in particular, the floating exchange rate regime;
- a more complete modelling of expectations and, especially, effects that 'rational' expectations on the part of economic agents may have on overall economic behaviour;
- the modelling of the interactions of the OECD area with developing economies, particularly as regards their debt situation;
- the modelling of the way in which the supply side of economies operates, and the role of profitability in investment and output decisions.

The question of floating exchange rates is clearly one which by its very nature can be examined particularly conveniently in the context of a fully-specified international model. Given the well-known difficulty of establishing stable empirical relationships in this area, results will need to be regarded as markedly more tentative than those which flow from the international interaction of comparatively well-attested domestic relationships. That having been said, one particular facet of this work with potentially important policy implications concerns Mundell/Fleming 'export crowding out'. It is an as yet unresolved empirical question whether a fiscal expansion would result, under conditions of unchanged monetary growth, in a currrent balance effect on the exchange rate which would dominate the effect of increased capital flows resulting from induced higher domestic interest rates. Were it to do so, the currency would depreciate and, at least in the short run, impart an additional stimulus to demand by way of the induced change in the real trade balance. On the other hand, a relatively high responsiveness of capital movements to interest and exchange rate movements could cause the capital account effect to dominate, and the currency to appreciate, thereby imparting an offsetting effect on demand. This subject is returned to in chapter 11.

The way in which economic agents form their expectations, and the influence of changing expectations on behaviour, has become an important area of both theoretical and policy concern. There are many unresolved questions. For example, while it does seem clear that the way in which expectations are formed can have an important effect on the way that policy operates upon an economy, it is not so clear how expectations are in fact formed by market participants. The process may be essentially forward-looking, backward-looking, or something in between. Nor is it clear whether most market participants are implicitly using much the same model to trace through the consequences of their expectations, or whether individual market participants have widely differing views about how the economic system operates. Empirical work in this area in an INTERLINK context is at an early stage, and it would not yet be appropriate to attempt to draw any inferences – however tentative – from it. The key point for the work so far is not so much what expectations are formed, but rather to trace through the differences in the behaviour of economic agents that would result if expectations were formed in a consistent, forward-looking manner. Such behaviour differences in the particular – though potentially important – case of the financial markets are explored in Masson, Blundell-Wignall and Richardson (1984).

Economic forecasting and the formulation of economic policy for the OECD economies as a whole is increasingly dependent on taking careful account of conditions in the non-OECD area – particularly the developing economies – and the feedback effects from the non-OECD countries that actions in the OECD area can induce. The heightened importance of interaction of OECD countries with the developing economies is exemplified in recent policy concern over these countries' debt problems. For example, increased interest payments by developing countries over the three years 1981 to 1983 lowered their spending on imports, with a cumulative negative impact on GNP growth of the major OECD countries of perhaps 1½ per cent. Accordingly, the modelling of the effects of interest rate changes on ldc debt, and thereby on ldc imports, is one area where improvements in the INTERLINK system are envisaged. Another is the determinants and consequences of changes in primary commodity prices.

A fourth area of policy-analytic concern currently under development within INTERLINK concerns the modelling of the supply side. As noted earlier, supply-side effects are already present in the current version of the system, both at the national and the international level. Within each of the country models, supply-side effects manifest themselves primarily through effects of labour market conditions on domestic wages, costs and prices (including export prices). Factor demand equations for energy, capital and labour are derived consistently from a postulated three-factor 'putty-clay' aggregate production functions (see Artus, 1983). At the international level, supply-side effects manifest themselves in the model primarily through the effect of variations in demand conditions on trade commodity prices, which in turn feed into OECD countries' domestic cost and price structures. The attention now being given to improving the commodity price determination block of the system has been alluded to above. The primary thrust of recent developmental work, however, has been the enhancement of the supply side of the component country models of INTER-LINK. Conducting the exercise within an international linkage framework will enable the various supply-side relationships to interact with the relationships determining aggregate demand, both nationally and as transmitted internationally.

Data management

Considerable effort has been put into ensuring the provision of timely, accurate data, in the form required for forecasting and policy simulation. Hence the operation of the model is structured around a data base system, through which regular and timely data are provided for forecasting and policy analysis. It is through the data base that users can easily find and have access to national source data regularly used in these activities.

The degree of disaggregation undertaken in OECD forecasts is modest relative to that undertaken in many national administrations. But with 24 Member countries and the specification of their linkages through a six-way trade commodity split, capital flows, and other variables, the OECD Secretariat is thereby committed to handling approximately 7,000 time series. Further, the data base system has to be capable of handling add-factor series for the behavioural variables, so as to permit the imposition of judgement, as well as several thousand coefficients for the behavioural relationships.

Efficient, automatic, regular and – importantly – rapid updating of the data base is also required. At OECD forecasting rounds take place regularly twice a year, and in recent years there has been heightened interest in more frequent reassessment. Accordingly, it is not sufficient for the data base to be updated only two or three times a year. Continual updating, as well as accommodating the data revisions, rebasing, or redefinitions of one or more Member countries every month, is required.

An important feature of the INTERLINK data base is that all series are documented. This documentation, which is available to users 'on-line', includes information on the source of the primary data involved, whether they are seasonally adjusted, units of measurement, actual or annual rates in the case of flow variables, average or end-of-period values in the case of stock variables, base year in the case of indices and deflators, and transformations involved – if any. The availability of such documentation greatly facilitates the work of all staff involved, who thereby have a clear understanding of the particular series used in connection with given economic concepts, and the problems – if any – associated with it. This documentation is included automatically as an integral part of the magnetic tapes now distributed by the OECD, containing the most recent projections published in the *Economic Outlook*, together with their associated historical statistics.

Support facilities

The INTERLINK system must be accessible to a large number of economists – most of whom have only limited data processing experience – so that emphasis has been placed on ease of operation. This is reflected in a straightforward command structure. When used interactively – as is increasingly the case – operation of the system is conversational, with a succession of user-prompt messages guiding the flow of operations. This permits easy manipulation and display of data, parameter values, and add-factors. In addition, standard display and report routines permit automatic comparison of baseline and alternative simulation runs.

The production of tables of projection and simulation data is potentially a substantial task. Table-generation programs have therefore been developed as an integral part of the INTERLINK system. As a result, the entire set of forecast and related analytic tables for the 24 OECD countries and eight non-OECD regions can be run off on a high speed printer in a matter of minutes, in a variety of standard formats used for various OECD committee documents. As a result, it is now possible to undertake several major iterations during each forecasting round with all participants able to review and comment on a full set of multi-country forecasts. By removing a major production bottleneck, these table-generation programs have also made it feasible to move toward the regular construction and presentation of alternative projections, with coherence and international consistency ensured by INTERLINK.

Particularly important to any forecasting or policy analytic process is the alignment of equations of a model to those variables whose values are known for the recent past. This can be a tedious and cumbersome process and, given the several thousand equations in the INTERLINK system, would be prohibitively time-consuming if done manually. Therefore, an algorithm has been developed which automatically generates add-factors, whereby the model is obliged to 'lock-on' to historical data or a set of estimates. (For a description, see Llewellyn and Samuelson (1981).) Through this device, any single equation, set of equations, or the complete model can be obliged to track the path of history, or a given set of baseline projections. Any investigation of the consequences of different policies or alternative assumptions can then be calculated automatically and presented in the computer-generated tables as increments to the baseline forecasts.

A second algorithm permits the decomposition of the relative contributions of explanatory variables to movements in endogenous variables. By this means it is possible to evaluate automatically how much of, for example, a simulated change in import volumes is due to changes in simulated import prices, exchange rates, domestic prices, activity levels, and so on.

A control or 'targeting' algorithm permits the usual logic of the model to be inverted, so that instead of simulating the consequences of a specified set of policies, the model can instead solve for the set of policies that would be required to achieve given 'target' objectives, taking into account the national and international transmission of economic effects. This algorithm facilitates, in the context of the policy formulation framework developed by Tinbergen and Theil, examination of the feasibility of policy objectives, both at the national and international level.[6] It helps identify and quantify policy trade-offs, and permits calculation of policy instrument changes required to secure policy objectives in a number of countries simultaneously. Without such an algorithm, consistent solutions could only be approximated, by time-consuming trial and error. (See, for example, Samuelson (1977).)

Finally, a number of de-bugging aids facilitate the task of system maintenance, and the bringing 'on-line' of new or modified elements of the system. These include:

- a facility for running in 'residual check' (or 'null' solution) mode – in which all equations are evaluated on the basis of actual values of explanatory variables;
- a facility for display and comparison of values of variables at each successive step in the iterative solution process;
- an 'alert' facility, which produces a summary report of variables for which historical tracking errors, or add-factor values for the projection period, exceed a given threshold value.

The next chapter describes how the INTERLINK system is used to assist the production of internationally-coherent country forecasts.

10 Making international economic forecasts

Summary

A major contribution of a properly-conducted international fore-casting exercise is to provide a set of forecasts that is internationally consistent. Where to break in to the circular set of relationships which tie economies and their performance together is problematic. Forecasts made for individual countries by national forecasting institutes typically take the 'rest of the world' as given: export markets, commodity prices, capital flows and other variables can be considered as exogenous variables. For the international forecaster, however, there are virtually no exogenous variables apart from economic policy decisions and world supply conditions for certain key commodities.

The OECD forecasting round involves an iterative process among country specialists on the one hand – primarily responsible for individual country forecasts – and subject specialists on the other – primarily responsible for ensuring that various aspects of the multi-country forecasts are coherent and consistent across countries. Clear procedures have been established for updating values of policy and other exogenous variables, and for making explicit the judgement which is incorporated in the forecasts.

Introduction

This chapter describes how international economic forecasts are made at the OECD, and the role of INTERLINK in that process.

The OECD does not have a large team of full-time forecasters. Apart from a small central group responsible for maintaining the model and for organizing the regular forecasting 'round', OECD forecasts are made by a number of country and subject specialists who each devote only a part of their time to that activity. It was found at a quite early stage that it was much more satisfactory not to divorce forecasting responsibility from responsibility for analysis, reporting, and research in a particular area. Nevertheless, the conduct of an international forecasting exercise that successfully incorporates the diverse expertise of country and subject specialists involved, while at the same time retaining overall coherence, requires that particular attention be paid to a number of aspects. These are basically similar to those involved in the production of national forecasts, although the number of active participants is larger than in many national administrations, and (as discussed in the previous chapter) the data management problem is considerable. Computerization and rationalization of activities, within the context of the INTERLINK system, minimize the seriousness of many of these problems, particularly those of ensuring that the various participants observe the 'rules of the game', maintaining effective and quick communication among the participants, and permitting an increased number of alternative projections to be produced, while keeping total costs within acceptable bounds.

The specialization of function inevitable even in a relatively small Department requires quick, efficient communication between its members if analytic and forecasting processes are to be effective. This is well-recognized in national administrations: those economists responsible for analysing or forecasting expenditure have to be in close contact with those responsible for forecasting income, who have to interact with those forecasting tax revenue, and so on. A formal modelling framework helps ensure economic coherence of a forecast, in that changes in exogenous variables, or add-factor changes based on judgement, are automatically carried through to all other variables in the system.

The equivalent requirement arises at the international level, but perhaps in a somewhat more acute form. Producing the internationally-consistent trade projections for 24 Member countries and eight non-OECD regions involves the projection of a 32×32 matrix, for each of several time periods, and for each of six categories of merchandise and services. This is a demanding exercise. A further task confronting the international forecaster, in today's world of increasingly-integrated financial markets, is to analyse incipient international financial pressures, and ways in which they might work themselves out.

In addition, the study of policy alternatives, which has become standard practice in many national administrations, is increasingly required at the international level, with emphasis on the trade and financial repercussions both among OECD countries and between the OECD area and non-OECD regions. Such analysis involves large numbers of calculations, the handling of a considerable body of data, and the specification of a large number of international trade and financial linkages (as described in the previous chapter).

Ensuring international consistency

One of the most important features of the OECD forecasting exercise is that of ensuring the international consistency of a set of forecasts produced simultaneously for all OECD countries and non-OECD regions. There is considerable power to be realized from ensuring that consistency requirements embodied in various accounting identities are respected in a forecasting exercise. This is a familiar matter to all national forecasters who nowadays, by working with formal computer-based procedures, routinely ensure that their historical data are reconciled and that forecast data obey the national accounts rules. But at the level of international forecasting there is less experience of enforcing this consistency; given the substantial discrepancies in important areas of external payments data, the task can be troublesome. Even the past, as recorded, is not consistent – although this is something that can be handled in the forecasting process (see below).

If a set of country forecasts is inconsistent, in any of a number of possible ways, one or more of the forecasts in the set must be wrong. Unfortunately the converse does not hold: achieving an internationally-consistent set of projections is no guarantee that any of them is right: international consistency is a necessary but not a sufficient condition for an accurate set of country projections.

There are several facets to international consistency. These include:

- trade volume consistency. Changes in countries' export
  volumes must have their counterpart in changes in partner
  countries' import volumes;
- trade price consistency. Each country's import price has to
  have its counterpart in the export prices of the countries from
  which it imports its goods or services;
- financial consistency. The projections for current accounts,
  capital accounts, interest rates and exchange rates have to be
  compatible.

The first two facets – trade volume and trade price consistency –
involve international accounting identities, and hence complete
consistency should be aimed at and achieved. The third facet –
consistency between the balance of payments, interest rate and
exchange rate projections – is somewhat more problematic. Current and capital account projections should each sum to zero for the
world as a whole, but in practice past data do not. The so-called
world current account discrepancy seems broadly to depend upon
the movements of variables which are forecast, however, so that the
discrepancy itself is forecastable, and hence there is no reason to
depart from overall rigour when making the balance-of-payments
projections.

But the consistency between the balance of payments projections
and those for interest rates and exchange rates is a matter of
behavioural rather than accounting consistency. Hence while this
facet of consistency is of central importance to a set of international
forecasts, it is not possible to define and hence achieve accounting
consistency: it is possible only to draw attention to those cases
where behavioural evidence points to potential inconsistency.
Inconsistency in this sense is liable to be present in OECD forecasts,
because (see below) they are made on the basis of present policies
and unchanged exchange rates. The forecast 'on present policies'
may well make the assumption of unchanged exchange rates
eighteen months hence look untenable. This apparent logical
inconsistency may not in practice be a disadvantage, however,
because identification of potential pressures in the system is one of
the features of the OECD forecasting process which Member
governments most value.

Where to start the forecast process

The generation of a set of national forecasts could start – and indeed used to start at OECD – with each country desk officer making a largely independent single country forecast, based partly on an intelligent guess as to the likely growth of export markets and import prices. The resulting trade volumes and prices can then be inspected to see if they are internationally coherent and, if they are not, they can be adjusted, with consequential changes for countries' GNP and inflation, until they are. But this is not wholly satisfactory, because of the way the initial assumptions about import prices and export markets are made. Although it is unlikely that wholly inappropriate starting values would be taken, if only because the various participants keep in touch with the global economic environment, there is a risk that the process of reaching consistency could result in convergence to an inappropriate consistent forecast if the initial values are too wide of the mark.

Rather than start with an initial set of country projections that may be seriously inconsistent, the OECD Secretariat has moved to an alternative method of starting the forecasting round. This involves taking the latest-published (*Economic Outlook*) set of internationally-consistent forecasts, and using INTERLINK to modify them in the light of changes in policy, known data changes, and any clear forecasting errors which have become known by the start of the new round.

This procedure has a number of advantages. First, by starting with a set of forecasts that are internationally-coherent, that coherence is relatively easy to maintain throughout the round; instead of having to force consistency on a possibly inconsistent initial forecast, all that has to be done is to ensure that each *change* is internationally consistent. Secondly, the procedure ensures continuity in the forecasting process. While there is nothing sacrosanct about a previously-published forecast – indeed a prime purpose of monitoring and re-forecasting is to correct previous errors – the previous forecast does contain the product of considerable thought and judgement, and it would be wasteful to throw that away each time a new forecast was started. A possible disadvantage of the procedure is that an individual participant in the process might not adjust his previous forecast by as much as would be appropriate.

The preparatory stages of the forecast round, leading to the production of a first 'model run', typically involve relatively few people. The process starts with a review of recently available data, to identify any major divergences between the previously published forecast set and these data, and the reasons for them. For all equations, add-factors are automatically adjusted to align the model's equations to the most recently available data. An updated set of add-factor adjustments associated with key behavioural equations in the system is distributed to country desk officers and various subject specialists involved in the round. Where new historical data have given rise to very large changes in add-factors, for example because of a dock strike, a newly-imposed wage/price freeze, or an oil shock, some preliminary adjustment may be made to add-factors over succeeding half-years of the forecast period, to reflect possible persistence of special factors at work over succeeding half-years or, alternatively, to reflect possible reversal of the effects.

In the case of equations expressed in change form, or otherwise involving lagged values of the endogenous variable amongst the explanatory variables, some further adjustment or 'phasing out' of the effects of an add-factor in a given period is necessary.

The next step involves specifying the paths to be taken on by exogenous inputs. Three kinds of exogenous variables are distinguished in the forecast round: policy variables, technical assumptions, and other exogenous variables.

Policy variables, often the most important in terms of determining the overall profile of the projections, involve assumptions concerning the setting of the fiscal and monetary instruments. For example, values are specified for government expenditure components, various tax and transfer rates, government wage payments, and so on. Similarly, to reflect the conduct of monetary policy, values must be specified for reserve changes, required reserve ratios, the discount rate and other administered rates (depending on the country), credit rationing, interest rate ceilings, and so on.

At the OECD, the forecasting 'rules of the game' require that policy variables be set consistently with announced economic policies of Member governments as revealed, for example, in budget presentations, and in various announced financial targets. The implementation of such 'no policy change' assumptions, however, is not wholly unambiguous. For some countries, there may be no explicit policy statement covering the latter part of the forecast period. Further, the pursuit of current policies may have implications that are inconsistent with stated policy targets (unemployment, inflation, interest rates, balance of payments) suggesting that at least some adjustment to policy is likely over the forecasting horizon. A complicating factor is that sometimes the actual stance of policy will diverge from that stated in advance by the authorities, so that a forecast built on a literal interpretation of a government's stated aims can after the event prove to have been inappropriate. A particularly delicate situation arises when it looks as if policy may in fact change, as when new legislation is pending, but with the change subject to internal debate in the country involved.

A further set of inputs is established on the basis of 'technical assumptions'. This involves setting values for a few selected variables, without pretending that these be representative of most likely developments. Variables whose values are set on the basis of 'technical assumptions' are those which, while in principle endogenous, are nevertheless difficult to forecast, politically sensitive and partly determined by policy decisions in OECD countries, or in non-OECD regions. The two main examples are exchange rates (assumed to remain unchanged in nominal terms), and the price of internationally-traded oil (assumed to move in line with OPEC policy pronouncements, and to move in line with the average of OECD countries' export prices of manufactures where there is no such operative pronouncement).

Remaining variables to be specified include those for which there are no explicit equations in the model, either because they do not lend themselves to determination by econometric methods, or because information concerning their evolution may be drawn from other sources. Examples include growth of and shifts in population or labour force (based on demographic studies), and official aid flows from OECD countries to non-OECD regions (which may be imposed on the basis of known intentions or informed judgement).

A third preparatory step in setting up the model run involves a preliminary reconsideration of add-factor adjustments, apart from those related to accommodating recently available historical data, to reflect the influence of major new special factors expected to be at work. Supply-related factors, for example, may suggest a surge in commodity prices over the forecast period beyond what corresponding equations might project. Or adjustments to the wage-rate equations may be necessary to reflect recent developments in the wage bargaining process. Export pricing equations may have to be changed in a period of unusually sharp exchange rate movement. Import projections of non-OECD regions may need to be adjusted for the effects of unusually large fluctuations in foreign exchange resources available to them. And so on. For the new half-year being added to the forecast period, preliminary add-factors are typically set at their previous period values.

Finally, in some cases, parameter values associated with selected equations may, with the agreement of the various interested participants in the exercise, be modified. This could result, for example, from changes in tax legislation, which would require the adjustments in the marginal relations in tax equations.

Once these various inputs have been assembled, the preliminary model run, involving all OECD countries and non-OECD regions, is carried out in fully-linked mode. Compared with the previously-published forecasts, this model run provides the first systematic indication of the nature and extent of revisions to those forecasts resulting from:

- information conveyed by recently available data;
- analysis of previous forecast errors, and incorporation of implications for subsequent periods in add-factor adjustments;
- adjustments of the time paths for changed policy and technical assumptions;
- adjustment of add factors for additional special influences that might be at work over the forecast period;

This first 'climate run' is thus largely a mechanical update of the previous set of forecasts. Because the add-factors are largely unrevised at this stage, the judgemental element is, for the most part, that which had been incorporated in the previously-published set of forecasts.

The results of this run are carefully checked prior to distribution to participants in the forecasting exercise. Because of the large quantity of data involved this entails, in the first instance, ensuring that no major mechanical or transcription errors have contaminated the results. Should any be uncovered, these are corrected, and the model re-run. The preliminary projections are checked to make sure that results are plausible, and that there are no incoherencies amongst the forecast components. Major changes in the revised projections, compared with the previous forecast set, are identified, and the reasons for them identified. Given the number of variables involved, it is not feasible at this stage to examine each one in detail. Rather, attention is concentrated on key variables that are important in the sense that they either provide a summary expression of some major facet of the global forecast, or that they are an important determinant of other forecast components.

The results of the first climate run are circulated only to those actively participating in the construction of the projections, because they represent only a partial update, with only a limited exercise of judgement. The results broadly define the nature and extent of change in the overall economic 'climate', on the basis of which the more detailed forecasts will be prepared. On some occasions the alternative projections at this stage look little different from those previously published. On other occasions, however, for example when there have been important policy changes, major exchange rate changes, important new evidence on the importing behaviour of the non-OECD regions, or a substantial change in the price of internationally-traded oil, the alternative projections can differ quite considerably from their predecessors, particularly for individual countries or country groups.

Country desk officers and subject specialists active in the forecast round then proceed to prepare the inputs for the second climate run, which moves the projections further from their previously-published values. Revised historical data are entered, together with any new information on policy and other exogenous variables, and a further round of judgemental updates of other forecast variables. The exercise of judgement is still limited at this stage, though an attempt is made to incorporate new evidence which may materially affect a significant part of a forecast for a given country. Changes in consumer and business sentiment – variables not explicitly represented in the expenditure equations – may suggest some adjustment to the projections that the equations alone would not provide. Estimates must also be provided for lagged values of some variables, for which data are not yet available. In some cases, the model itself is used to 'project' these values, on the basis of other information available in the lagged periods. In other cases, estimates are provided judgmentally, either on the basis of partial information available (a few months' data, or a quarter's data, for example), or on the basis of movements in some other indicator believed to be related to the series in question.

Particularly important in the preparation for the second climate run is the entering of revised and rebased trade data by the trade specialists. Furthermore, rather detailed forecasts are entered for the United States and Germany, the two economies which, because of their large imports of manufactured goods, exert a particularly strong influence on other OECD countries.

The second climate run involves contributions from all country desk officers and subject specialists. Because data-entry errors are not uncommon at this stage, and could lead to misleading results in the model projections, the new inputs are passed through a filter which rejects any changes that are atypically large. Because it is essential that the whole forecast exercise proceeds according to timetable, the data base is scanned for missing data, and any gaps are filled initially on an *ad hoc* basis. In an extreme case a country can, if it is small, be excluded entirely from the climate run.

Once data entry is complete, the system is run again. The result of this second climate run simulation provides country specialists not only with estimates of the direction, magnitude and timing of domestic factors likely to affect each country forecast, but also a measure of the influences – via international trade volumes and prices, financial variables, and other factors -- originating in what, from the vantage point of a single country's forecast, is the external sector. The structure of the INTERLINK system ensures that the pattern of these external effects is consistent in an accounting sense, and coherent in an economic sense, in that the interaction of factors simultaneously conditioning international trade, financial, and other variables is taken into account.

Assessing the economic climate

An internal note is then prepared giving the key features of these new, essentially-mechanical, projections, and the reasons for the differences between them and the previously-published set. The amount of material that is presented depends mainly upon the importance of the changes and the reasons for them. These 'climate run' projections thus provide a numerical basis for a discussion of the economic climate, a discussion which, involving virtually all members of the Department, is deliberately kept broad. The aim of the projections is not so much to produce a fully-fledged forecast, even though a complete set of numbers is produced. Rather the purpose is to inform each country desk officer what sort of international climate his or her country seems likely to be facing.

The ground rules for the procedures to this point are rather like those which underlie voting in a democracy. Each individual – in this case each country desk officer or subject specialist – knows that, taken by themselves, the revisions that he or she is making may not make a great deal of difference to the projections of others. But taken in sum, the changes can and often do add up to something quantitatively significant. Hence each country desk officer or subject specialist makes any judgemental alterations as carefully as possible. At the same time, no forecaster is constrained at the next stage of the round from making changes on the basis of new evidence, including of course the discussion that has taken place at the 'climate meeting', which is typically held two weeks after the beginning of the round.

By this point the link with the previously-published set of forecasts is becoming more tenuous. The subject specialists enter into the system revised projections for government wage and non-wage expenditure, tax rates, money supply growth or interest rate targets, oil and non-oil commodity prices, wage rates and import volumes of the non-OECD countries. More importantly, country desk officers then enter revised projections for the seven major countries, which together account for about 85 per cent of OECD GDP. The way in which these projections are made differs from one country desk to another. But in every case the close scrutiny of each projected variable, period by period, becomes important at this stage, so as to take into account the full range of information that is available to the country specialists.

When the country desk officers for the seven biggest countries have completed this task, INTERLINK is then locked on to the domestic components of these projections and, taking them as datum, produces a further revised set of mechanical projections for the 17 smaller OECD countries. The country desk officers for the smaller countries then review these projections and enter revisions to produce their first detailed forecasts, in much the same way as their colleagues responsible for the larger economies. Typically, however, the model input into the forecasts for the smaller countries is rather less, in part reflecting the paucity of reliable data for a number of them.

Making the detailed forecasts

At this point the forecasts are reviewed closely, variable by variable, for internal consistency and plausibility. Matters where the evidence is insufficient to be conclusive are discussed, often at considerable length, and involving on occasion most of the people involved in the forecasting round. Finally a judgement is made. This exercise of judgement, which appears as an add-factor in the formal forecasting apparatus, is discussed below. An iterative process, involving successive revisions to the forecasts, made at discrete intervals, occupies the remaining part of the round. Desk officers revise their forecasts, especially of domestic demand components and inflation, in the light of internal discussions. Revisions are also made to non-OECD demand, commodity prices and exchange rates at pre-defined stages in the round. This process is repeated iteratively, until a convergent, globally coherent set of forecasts for all OECD countries and non-OECD regions is obtained.

About four weeks into the round, the overall set of domestic and international forecasts is discussed at the 'intradepartmental meeting'. This meeting gathers all the economists most directly involved in the forecasting exercise as well as a number of 'generalists' and aims, for each country and for the OECD area as a whole, at thoroughly reviewing various features of the forecasts. Some may feel, for example, that assumptions concerning the underlying policy stance, various technical assumptions, the consideration of expectational effects, and so on may be inappropriate. Others may feel that too much weight, or perhaps insufficient weight, is being given to current indicators. And so on. In each case, agreement must be reached during the meeting about the eventual modification of certain forecast components. Where necessary, forecast elements are revised, entered into the system, and a complete set of revised forecasts circulated in the Department three to four working days later.

One of the most useful roles the model plays in the forecasting process at this stage is in the decomposition of contributions of individual factors accounting for differences between the new central forecasts, and those previously published. This involves two aspects: first, use of the model to help identify and quantify the extent to which forecast revisions depend on changed assumptions concerning policy and other exogenous variables; and second, use of the model to help identify the extent to which forecast revisions are attributable to changed judgemental elements for key variables, as embodied in add-factor changes. This decomposition of changed forces acting in the forecasts may ultimately lead to the preparation of 'alternative forecasts'. These embody different assumptions from those contained in the 'central forecast', where particular events are thought not only likely to occur, but also to have important implications for the main economic aggregates being projected, and consequent policy decisions.

About two weeks after the intradepartmental meeting, the forecasts are finalized and submitted to experts from OECD Member governments. Shortly afterwards, these experts meet at OECD to comment on the Secretariat's forecasts and present their own. This review process helps not only refine and bring up to date policy assumptions embodied in the forecast, but also affords representatives from each country a first opportunity to see the implications of an internationally consistent set of forecasts for their respective country's exports, trade prices, market growth, relative competitiveness, and so on. Indeed, one service the Secretariat often performs at this meeting is examination of the mutual consistency of national authorities' forecasts taken together.

In a formal sense, the main purpose of this meeting of national experts is to prepare the regular meeting of the Economic Policy Committee, which gathers together top-level officials from economics and finance ministries and central banks. The Secretariat prepares policy-analytic documents for this group, addressing current and future issues in the light of the forecasts and related simulations. Much of this material is subsequently published in the *OECD Economic Outlook*.

Further modification of the forecasts may be made in the light of comments made either by the experts or in the course of the Economic Policy Committee, as well, of course, as to embody new information that has become available. After each revision,

INTERLINK is run to explore the implications for export market growth and trade prices, and the revised forecasts are 'corrected' accordingly. A final set of internationally consistent forecasts for all OECD Member countries is ultimately published in the *OECD Economic Outlook*. Including the two climate runs a normal round can involve the production of six or seven internationally consistent sets of forecasts.

Keeping the model current

Continued maintenance of a macroeconomic model to ensure that it continues to perform well, and is ready for use at all times, is a demanding task – certainly as demanding as the original formulation and estimation of the model itself. This is particularly so of a multi-country model. The structures of the economies represented in the system change over time, new issues (or shocks) become important, the concern of policy shifts, and so on. The model must be kept current in these respects, as well as with respect to a continuing flow of new data.

Some decentralization of responsibility is involved in any modelling effort, in order to achieve an optimal division of analytical labour. In a national modelling effort, this typically takes the form of charging different individuals with primary responsibility for development and maintenance of blocks of the model, subject to some measure of central control. Protocols are established, to ensure that the blocks fit together. Further, timetables are required, to ensure that updating and use for forecasting purposes is properly synchronized. Such arrangements are all the more necessary in an international modelling effort.

Without such arrangements, model development, rather than being systematic and coordinated amongst all those involved in its use, would tend to be unduly subservient to current applications, with the inevitable consequence that development would be haphazard. 'Quick-and-dirty' solutions needed for current applications, for example, would tend to become permanent features of the master version of the system, without adequate prior checking of the implications for simulation and tracking properties, and without adequate documentation. This is not to deny the occasional need for ad-hoc changes to the model, or the important role that those using the model in current applications should play in model development; rather it is to argue the need for a well-defined model development responsibility, to complement the model applications.

It is a generally held view in the OECD Secretariat that the model must be stable for significant periods. To have the model's properties shifting during the preparation of a forecast or during the course of a policy analytic exercise would result in unacceptable confusion. Hence once an agreed master version of the model has been produced, it is typically 'frozen' for the duration of the current forecasting Round. During that period, suggested modifications are collected and discussed and the appropriate checks (including re-estimation of equations, and testing simulation and tracking properties) are carried out. Agreed changes, however, are incorporated only at previously-agreed times, generally speaking at six-monthly intervals.

In principle, the model is altered only exceptionally during the forecast round, as in the case where an error is found, where minor changes are made to parameters or where poorly-performing equations are simply overwritten. Inevitably, however, in the heat of a forecast round, and in response to changing issues, rapid solutions to current operating problems are required, and are perhaps unavoidable in a rapidly-changing world. These, however, are normally implemented in an experimental version of the system. To avoid a proliferation of 'experimental' versions, systematic follow-up action is taken and the results incorporated in the master version at the time of its next update.

Each person involved in the forecast round has clearly-defined responsibility for maintaining blocks of the model directly relevant to his or her work. The 'model manager' fosters discussion among these block managers as well as those involved in research that might be relevant to model development, and establishes the implications of new equations for system tracking, simulation properties, and so on. Only those changes on which widespread agreement is possible are incorporated in the model.

The exercise of judgement

OECD forecasters, in common with most professional forecasters today, use macroeconomic models, and thereby take account of evidence from the past. But however painstakingly the individual relationships are rooted in past evidence, there is invariably a call for the exercise of judgement.

Questions requiring the exercise of judgement can arise in many ways, as discussed in chapter 7. The net result is that in many forecasting rounds new problems emerge for which the model may be relatively ill-equipped, either because it was not expected that the sort of problem in question would arise, or because even if it had been expected, there was no evidence upon which to estimate the requisite relationships.

A further practical problem is what to do with the residuals, often disturbingly large, that are 'inherited' from each forecasting equation at the information cut-off date. While it is possible to specify mechanical rules for dealing with these, there is no substitute for finding out *why* each residual exists, and then on that basis reaching a judgement about how it is likely to behave in the future. Indeed, it is in the setting of the residuals that much of the art, as distinct from the science, of forecasting resides.

Given that the imposition of judgement is unavoidable, the practical task facing the forecaster, as discussed in chapter 7, is to make the judgement explicit rather than implicit. In the OECD forecasting exercise this is achieved by the specification of add-factors. In the case of individual country forecasts based importantly on INTERLINK country models, these add factors may be entered explicitly by the country desk officer to produce the intended result. In the case of country forecasts which are made initially by a more judgemental process, the add factors are implicit, generated by INTERLINK. It is possible to extract the add factors resulting from either approach and filter them, leaving for inspection only those which exceed specified threshold values. These form a basis for critical discussion during the forecast round; and after the forecast is complete, the performance of equations which were heavily add-factored is monitored, to establish the extent to which the imposition of those add-factors proved warranted by subsequent events. Where it was, there is a clear case for modifying or supplementing the equations which were successfully add-factored. In the other cases, where the imposition of add factors proved not to be warranted by events, the attention of the country desk officer or subject specialist involved is drawn to the fact, and harder questions are asked in the future if similar add-factoring is again suggested.

The process of setting add-factors may be thought of as the 'fine tuning' of a model-based forecast. At the limit the forecaster, through the add-factor facilities, can take complete control of the model, to the extent of imposing a completely judgemental set of forecasts on the equation set. The setting or changing of add-factors is a process that is not taken lightly. Rather, there must always be solid reasons for imposing the judgemental view that fundamental factors, causing departures from observed past behaviour, are likely to be at work, or that indeed special influences not otherwise explicitly captured in the equation system are expected to play an important role.

Add-factors are one way of introducing new information into the model. It may also be important on occasion to alter *marginal* relations among variables judgementally, thereby overriding regression parameters estimated on the basis of historical experience that may be considered to be no longer fully relevant. In this way, the forecaster and policy analyst can allow for the possibility that the current and future economic environment may be significantly different from the past.

Monitoring and post-mortems

The continual monitoring of events in relation to the forecasts, and the conduct of periodic post-mortems, are in the process of development at OECD. The task is considerable, in part because of the large quantities of data involved and because of the effort needed to document the forecasts adequately. But it is being persevered with because it is beginning to look as if the pay-off in terms of greater forecast accuracy could be considerable.

The desirability of confronting the current forecast with the continual stream of incoming data, in order to establish particularly those cases where the economy was not working in the way assumed when the forecast was constructed, was discussed in chapter 5. There are two basic purposes in doing this. The first is an essentially practical one, of using high-frequency data, such as monthly trade, price and industrial production figures to form a view about how well the forecasts, which are semi-annual for most countries, and annual and quarterly for the rest, are faring. When four or five months' data are in, it is possible to infer with reasonable accuracy what the six-month figure for the series in question will be, and compare that with the most closely corresponding aggregate in the forecast. But making use of the first two or three months of data is much more subjective.

The second purpose in monitoring, again as discussed in chapter 5, is to develop warning signals that one or more assumptions or behavioural relationships used in the construction of the forecasts is proving inappropriate. This is a much more difficult task than is required if the aim is merely to establish the extent to which the forecast may be off track. What is involved in addition is the formulation, preferably *ex ante*, of hypothetical configurations of the incoming data which, if they were to occur, would either tend to support the basis upon which the projection was made, or refute it. But this is not always easy to do, and experience in this area so far is rather limited.

With economic forecasts resulting from the interactions of the forecasters and the model, forecasting error can be decomposed to trace its causes. There are conceptually three distinguishable sources of forecasting error: assumptions concerning policy and other exogenous variables that were not realized, judgemental information inappropriately imposed on the model solution through add-factors, and the model itself. When it is considered important to examine the matter, the following procedure is used to identify sources of forecast error.

First, total *ex ante* forecasting error is established by comparing actual outcomes with forecasts, these latter having been generated by running the model with assumed paths for policy and other exogenous variables, and both explicit and 'mechanical' add-factor adjustments. Next, the contribution of unrealized assumptions concerning various policy and other exogenous variables is isolated. This is done by feeding into the model the actual values taken by these exogenous variables over the period for which the forecast was made, running the model, and again comparing the actual outcomes with the projected paths of endogenous variables. The change in forecasting error observed in this run, compared with the *ex ante* forecasting error, is attributed to the effects of error concerning the policy and exogenous inputs.

Next, the contribution of the judgemental inputs, embodied in the add-factors, is established. This is done by running the model in 'null' mode, using actual values of both exogenous and endogenous explanatory variables in each equation. The resulting equation residuals are then compared with the add-factors used in producing the forecast. This provides, on an equation-by-equation basis, an indication of the extent to which add-factors were over- or under-adjusted. In some cases, the actual contribution of any significant errors in setting add-factors for the system as a whole is assessed by simulating the incremental effects of the corresponding over- or under-adjustments in fully simultaneous dynamic mode.

Finally, the error contribution of the model itself is established by running the model with all add-factors set to zero, and using actual values of policy and other exogenous variables as inputs. It is typically observed that the model, while perhaps accurately capturing turning points, or directions of change in a variable, will tend to underestimate the magnitude of change. This is because models, by their very construction, involve specifications that tend to average, or 'smooth', time series. It would be unreasonable to expect a model to be able to reproduce the sudden, sharp fluctuations in variables that are often observed in the historical period. Similarly, a model typically will not project sudden sharp movements in series in the future.

A broad summary of the accuracy of economic forecasts by the OECD and other forecasters was presented in chapter 6. The major problem in producing more detailed post-mortems is that this proves very time-consuming, particularly for a set of internationally-linked forecasts. A number of procedures are being developed to do the job more economically. In this way it would be possible to conduct post-mortems regularly, and in somewhat greater detail.

Use in forecasting is perhaps the most spectacular application to which a macroeconomic model, particularly a world model, may be put. But perhaps more important than the generation of a point forecast is the role of the model in identifying the importance of critical assumptions on which a given forecast depends, the sensitivity of the forecast to alternative assumptions, and the shedding of light on the forces shaping the international economy.

Indeed, some writers have argued that economists have placed undue weight on the forecasting application of their models or other analytic apparatus, while putting insufficient effort into using these tools to study the responses of the economic system to a variety of shocks (see, for example, Mason (1983).) This may well be so. More generally, it is probably fair to say that the potential analytical scope of medium and large macroeconomic models, particularly linked ones for the world economy, has widened rather faster than the imagination of the people who built them. Certainly the experience to date at OECD has been that the major limitation to a more effective and informative use of INTERLINK has been an inability, perhaps combined with a little timidity, to identify major policy issues early enough to undertake the work necessary before it is possible to produce fully worked-through simulations.

A second factor limiting the application of linked-model simulation and alternative-forecast results to policy discussion has probably been that, just at the time that this technical possibility was becoming available, policy thinking in a number of major countries moved away from its earlier more activist stance, with policy-makers instead tending to espouse both a less active, and a more medium-term, approach to policy-making. For this sort of policy-making, which is discussed in the first chapter of Part III – chapter 11 – economic forecasts, and the analysis of policy alternatives, may seem less necessary. But, in fact, this policy approach has not solved all or even the major economic problems of the day, in part perhaps because insufficient attention has been paid of late to the importance of economic impulses which are transmitted internationally. Accordingly, chapter 12 considers how policy, in part aided by linkage analysis and the products of linkage models, might do better in the future through enhanced international cooperation in economic policy-making.

Part III
The international dimension in improving economic performance

11 Recent approaches to policy

Summary

Since the second oil shock in 1979, countries generally have concentrated on lowering inflation while seeking to improve the supply-side responsiveness of their economies. On the macroeconomic policy side they have attempted to maintain a steadier stance, often with a medium-term horizon: initially tight in the face of strong inflation but intended to be progressively less so as inflation came down. For a number of the larger countries, this approach has been based importantly on the pursuit of targets for the growth of monetary aggregates; many of the other countries have put greater weight on the exchange rate as an intermediate target of monetary policy. Nearly all countries have been engaged in trying to lower budget deficits, or at least their 'structural' component, thereby severely limiting the extent to which fiscal policy could be used for counter-cyclical purposes. There has also appeared less scope than had earlier been thought to manipulate the mix of monetary and fiscal policy.

By 1983, the approach followed had brought about the most thorough disinflation since the Korean war, and had also had some success in shifting income shares towards profits. But the cost in terms of unemployment and lost output was high; and recovery was at too early a stage to judge how far the behaviour of OECD economies had been changed in fundamental ways.

Introduction

Some major currents in macroeconomic policy thinking from the 1950s to the 1970s were traced in chapters 2 and 3. This chapter attempts to bring the account of views underlying policy-making up to date as of the time the book was finalized: 1983. The coverage is mainly of the period since the second oil shock in 1979, though most of the ideas have their origins considerably earlier.

The immediately striking feature of this recent period is that in terms of conventional measures of macroeconomic policy the stance in most countries has been tight for a longer period than in any earlier cyclical episode. Partly this reflects the importance attached to bringing inflation down as well as the expected difficulty of doing so in the face of stubborn inflation expectations. Partly, however, it reflects also a fairly widespread change of view on the best way of bringing about a recovery of activity that will prove sustainable. There has been greater emphasis on steadier macro-policy settings, often with a medium term horizon, while at the same time seeking to strengthen the well-springs of economic growth on the supply side of the economy. Related to this, there has been a fairly general shift of short-term emphasis from the final objectives of economic policy such as growth and employment to intermediate targets, notably for monetary aggregates.

Away from fiscal activism

These various changes of emphasis came about for a variety of reasons. In the course of the 1970s, many governments became increasingly sceptical of the efficacy, and even the desirability, of discretionary fiscal policy to affect the level of activity. In part this stemmed, in some countries, from a dislike of the growth in the relative size of the public sector that had accompanied – without necessarily being the result of – several decades of fiscal activism. It was argued for example that the growth of the public sector was adversely affecting economic performance by increasing the range of activities where market forces were inoperative, and that the tax rates needed to finance the growing government share were sapping initiatives and even the willingness to work. To some extent what was at issue involved questions of political philosophy, not of direct concern here. But the question of the efficacy of fiscal policy is a more technical one, on which a body of empirical work can be brought to bear.

One objection to the use of discretionary fiscal policy is that it cannot be applied with sufficient precision. While the evidence of the 1960s is that, in a number of countries, stabilization policy *did* succeed in reducing the amplitude of fluctuations over the cycle taken as a whole, even if deviations were increased in some individual years, the difficulties of forecasting GNP accurately in the early 1970s suggested that, for a period at least, governments should give up the attempt at discretionary stabilization policy, and rely instead upon the so-called automatic stabilizers.

Automatic stabilizers, such as personal and corporate income taxes on the revenue side, and payments to the unemployed on the expenditure side, operate to damp variations in disposable income associated with changes in economic activity. But unlike discretionary policy, these stabilizing mechanisms are automatic in the sense that once they have been legislated they require no further policy action before they take effect. Because they come into play only in response to cyclical variations in the level of activity, they can never entirely eliminate economic fluctuations, but they can constrain the magnitude of such fluctuations as do occur. Hence, in principle they solve the two key timing problems at once: they overcome the need for a forecast, because they come into play automatically in response to a change in cyclical position, and they do not require the passage of enabling legislation, the correct timing of which may be hard to achieve.

For many years the effectiveness of automatic stabilizer mechanisms in promoting economic stability was taken largely for granted. Early studies suggested they were doing their job well.[1] There were indeed suggestions for reinforcing or augmenting existing automatic stabilizer mechanisms by converting them from passive damping mechanisms to more active instruments of stabilization policy – termed at the time 'formula flexibility'. For example, government expenditure programmes, tax rates, and so on could be made to vary automatically with changing economic conditions. Early theoretical experiments using what would now be regarded as relatively simple models of the United States economy suggested that appropriately-formulated mechanisms could significantly moderate cyclical movements in the economy.[2]

An important operational question in implementing formula flexibility concerned the choice of index, or indexes, to trigger the mechanisms at the appropriate time. But at the same time as this discussion was taking place, more fundamental questions were being asked about the effectiveness of any type of automatic stabilization mechanism.

The possibility that automatic stabilizers might not work as well in practice as their protagonists were suggesting had been raised early on by Friedman (1953), who argued that the uncertainty of impacts might lead to destabilization with a policy which under certainty would be stabilizing. Moreover, because stabilization policy is concerned with fluctuations, the effectiveness of automatic stabilizers could be appraised appropriately only in a dynamic context. Early inferential attempts to examine the validity of this criticism employed either relatively simple static relationships, or models with limited structural detail and simple lag structures. Furthermore, attention was generally limited to the impact effects of those mechanisms. The general conclusion was that there was little force in the Friedman criticism. But as economic models became larger, with a fuller articulation of the main identified behavioural mechanisms in the economy, and with considerable attention being paid to lag structures, more doubt started to be cast on the efficacy of automatic stabilizers.

For example, Smyth (1966) constructed a simple model with plausible dynamics, in which he demonstrated that automatic stabilizers, while cushioning the impact effect of shocks, subsequently reinforced the fluctuations induced by those shocks. Helliwell and Gorbet (1971), using the RDX2 model of the Canadian economy, found that a number of so-called automatic stabilizers, although cushioning impact effects on real final demand, could have destabilizing effects when the economy was subjected to continuing random shocks, essentially because of complex interactions of lags involved in the stabilizing mechanisms. Progressively the conclusion was reached that automatic stabilizers might actually destabilize the economic system. The problem of timing, it seemed, was not necessarily solved by the use of an automatic stabilizer.

Structural and cyclical budget deficits

Even if there was some loss of faith in the ability of automatic stabilizers to smooth the course of activity, their effect on the government budget balance remained of central analytical interest. Seeking to reduce budget deficits, yet thwarted in their efforts to do so by the effects on the deficits of the recession, a number of countries began to pay attention to the evolution of the *structural* budget deficit. Conceptually this was no different from the high-employment budget balance popularized in the United States in the 1960s, when confidence in the demand-management properties of fiscal policy was at its height. What was different in the recent period was, first, the increased difficulty of calculating the measure because of the greater doubt surrounding the level and rate of growth of economies' productive potential; and, second, the purpose for which it was used, which was less a question of seeking to calibrate the stance of fiscal policy than of assessing the progress made in the medium-term objective of reducing budget deficits and thereby restoring financial stability.

That there was a need in most countries to reduce deficits over time was doubted by few policy-makers. By 1983, the public sectors in virtually all OECD countries were in deficit, by amounts ranging up to 12 per cent of GDP, and on average by over 4 per cent of GDP. The latter was double the figure for 1979, and could be compared with an average deficit of less than ½ per cent of GDP in the first half of the 1970s. Where views differed was about the speed at which it was appropriate to effect the reduction. Some policy-makers and observers who attached importance to the effect of deficit reduction on interest rates, and of lower interest rates on private spending (in other words, who saw relatively quick and complete 'crowding out') favoured the most rapid feasible reduction of deficits; indeed, in some countries it was held that the act of bringing down deficits would create a reinforcing positive impact on business confidence. Others, however, were more impressed by the short-term weakening of demand that would result from vigorous deficit-cutting if their economies were not yet firmly on the road to recovery.

In practice, there was widespread reduction of structural deficits. The major exception – and an important one – was the United States, where the Reagan administration's tax cuts and stepped-up defence spending pushed the structural balance from a surplus of about 1 per cent of GNP in 1979-80 into small deficit by 1983, with much higher structural deficits expected later in the decade.[3] In Europe and Japan the average movement was in the opposite direction, seemingly taking some countries into structural surplus, a remarkable political achievement at a time of recession. For the

OECD area as a whole, the structural deficit remained broadly unchanged. Because it was a time of recession, however, the cyclical component of deficits increased on average by between 2½ and 3 per cent of GDP between 1979 and 1983. As suggested in chapter 4, the fact that a large number of countries were simultaneously seeking to reduce structural deficits was a factor making for weakness of demand and hence tending rather generally to increase the cyclical component of countries' budget deficits.

But with depressed conditions continuing for some years, doubts were beginning to be expressed about the usefulness of the structural/cyclical distinction. A 'cyclical' component cannot be convincingly described as such for years on end. And even though this component should be reduced, and finally eliminated, when recovery takes place, it will itself have added to future structural deficits by increasing the outstanding stock of government debt and hence future interest payments. Only if the bonds issued to cover cyclical deficits were redeemed by future budget surpluses would this not be the case. Over the period 1979 to 1983, when, as noted, the collective structural budget balance of OECD countries remained broadly unchanged in relation to GDP – and improved by over 1 per cent of GDP if interest payments are excluded – the combined debt/GDP ratio increased by some 10 percentage points of GDP to 50 per cent, and was still increasing at the end of the period.

Because country circumstances and priorities differ, there is no generally optimal ratio of debt to GDP. As well as the 'normal' demand for government debt on the part of financial investors, the role of government as an investor in nationalized industries and public infrastructure must be recognized. Some forms of government expenditure – for example, in infrastructure, research or education – may yield a rate of return sufficient to cover the interest payments and to repay the loans. Some governments may appropriately choose to run a long-run budget deficit, and perhaps even allow for an increasing public debt/GDP ratio over protracted periods. But persistently-increasing government debt/GDP ratios may be a sign of fiscal instability if they go along with increasing amounts of public debt in private portfolios, relative to other assets, and rising interest payments. Over the last few years, it seems that debt/GDP ratios have risen faster in a number of countries than is consistent with longer-term stability of public finances. Fulfilment of governments' medium-term plans for deficit reduction would lead to eventual declines in debt/GDP ratios. Their achievement seemed, however, to require a return to high levels of resource utilization, yet without resort to fiscal easing.

Monetary targets

The desire to base policy on a 'rule' rather than on 'discretion' has been even more marked on the monetary side. Friedman in fact had been arguing since 1948 that economic forecasts are so inaccurate, the problem of timing policy measures so severe, and the short-run impact of policy measures so unpredictable, that policy could be directed only towards longer-term stabilization. And the use of the policy instruments for short-term stabilization should be firmly constrained by well-defined rules.[4]

The most commonly-suggested rule has been a relatively invariant, or steadily declining, growth of the nominal money supply, which fits also with Friedman's views about the importance of monetary growth in its effect on the economy, and hence its importance as an intermediate policy target. But the case for a policy rule can be made independently of monetarism. It became widely accepted that there had been undue emphasis on nominal interest rates under earlier approaches to monetary policy, entailing excessive monetary growth in conditions of accelerating inflation. And economists of quite different persuasions have come to emphasize the need to set policy instruments in response not to immediate economic conditions but instead in the light of the desired medium-term configuration of the economy.

Targets for the growth of monetary aggregates began to be set in the United States and Germany in the mid-1970s, and by the latter part of the decade most of the larger countries had targets for some measure of money or total credit. This approach to policy was pursued with increased vigour in the face of the oil-induced spurt of inflation in 1979-80. Thus the United States moved to a new procedure whereby money was targeted by operating on banks' reserves rather than on very short-term interest rates in the Federal funds market. The new Conservative government in the United Kingdom affirmed its whole-hearted attachment to money targeting, and announced a series of declining target ranges for several years ahead. Germany and Switzerland, which (as described in chapter 4) had earlier been driven off their money targets by currency inflows related to the weak dollar, now gave priority to them anew.

Considerable emphasis was placed on pursuit of money targets, at least until 1982. In reviewing this experience, the relevant questions are perhaps:

–   how closely were monetary authorities able to achieve their targets?
–   to the extent targets were achieved, was the course of nominal income broadly as expected?
–   did the particular approach being followed improve the 'credibility' of the authorities and/or the expectations of the private sector, such that the output/price split of nominal income was more favourable; in other words, was inflation brought down at a lower cost than it might have been otherwise in terms of lost output?

The first two questions, controllability and predictability, have to some extent to be considered together, as there is a degree of trade-off between them, related to the choice of aggregate. On theoretical grounds, the 'money' of textbooks is more closely approximated by relatively narrow measures, essentially non-interest-bearing. Demand for such aggregates should be relatively interest-sensitive and they should accordingly be relatively easily controllable. On the other hand, narrow money constitutes such a small part of total financial assets that it would be surprising if its control were sufficient to bring about the desired evolution of the economy. The relationship to the overall course of the economy (nominal GNP) tends to be closer for broader aggregates, which include a substantial interest-bearing component. Control of these via interest rates can be problematic; at the limit, control of the aggregate may have to proceed via control of the economy itself. M1 in Canada may exemplify the first kind of problem, £M3 in the United Kingdom the second.

From 1979 to 1982, most countries were reasonably successful in achieving their money targets, especially if very short-run changes are disregarded. If anything, money growth tended to be in the upper part of target ranges or slightly above, and, at least on a year-to-year basis, relatively smooth.

But if policy turned out broadly as intended in terms of the monetary aggregates that countries were targeting, the same was not true, by the end of the period, in terms of end results for the economy as a whole. For a time, developments unfolded very much as most policy-makers and forecasters had expected. Policy succeeded first in checking, then in reversing, the boost to inflation from the second oil shock. Real growth declined, but remained positive on average in both 1980 and 1981. With interest rates, both nominal and real, remaining high, however, OECD output fell slightly in 1982 and inflation was sharply lower. Particularly weak components of demand were stockbuilding and exports to the developing countries, which were obliged to reduce their imports in response to steep increases in their debt payments as a result of protracted high interest rates.

Thus the relationship between the targeted money aggregates and the final objectives of policy did not turn out as expected. Both output and prices were weaker than expected or, presumably, intended. At the root of this phenomenon is what is often referred to as the 'velocity puzzle'. To be sure, there had for a long time been a well-attested tendency for velocity to move cyclically, but in 1982 it appeared in a number of countries to be particularly low. After the event, there has been considerable debate about whether what happened was a 'puzzle' or not; but, at the time, the surprise was real enough.

A complicating factor in some countries was the impact on the targeted aggregates of financial innovation, often in response to deregulation. This factor had the effect of increasing the growth of some aggregates while reducing the growth of others. In either case there is the problem that when the money stock as defined changes in meaning, the relationship between the targeted aggregate and the variables of ultimate concern to the authorities becomes less certain than previously.

Did the fact that inflation came down more quickly than expected constitute evidence that the new approach to policy had in itself had the favourable expectational effects that many had claimed for it beforehand? It would appear not, because output too was lower than expected; there was no clear sign that the split of nominal income growth, and hence the output cost of reducing inflation, was different from what would have been expected under the earlier policy regime.

In summary, getting inflation down was the over-riding priority in the period following the second oil shock; and policy was successful in this aim. The growth of money as defined and thereby measured was broadly as envisaged, and nominal income growth slowed down if anything more than expected. But the way this was split between output growth and inflation was probably not radically different from experience in earlier episodes.

There has been a widespread supposition that the monetary authorities of the major countries became converted to monetarism in the late 1970s, and that the period since 1979 represents something of a test-case for monetarist ideas. A few policy-makers indeed seem to have been influenced by monetarist ideas, though in the main rather by those of Friedman than by those of Lucas and the rational expectations school. This is suggested by the fact that most authorities aimed to reduce money growth only gradually, not 'at a stroke'. Friedman, it should be noted, in contrast to the rational expectations school, had always stressed that there would be some costs of disinflation, even though he tended to suggest that they would be 'modest'.[5]

Mainstream central bank thinking seems, on the contrary, to have continued to be pragmatic. Money targeting was adopted because it seemed the most suitable response in the circumstances of the time. In the early 1970s, too much attention had been paid in many countries to (nominal) interest rates at a time of increasing inflation. Central banks were determined that the sort of money growth rates that occurred then would not be repeated, and therefore would have needed to place greater emphasis on money growth whatever variables were notionally being targeted. An attractive feature of targeting money aggregates was seemingly that interest rate increases could be de-politicized; central banks might have found it difficult to push interest rates up to the sort of levels reached at the beginning of the 1980s had they been the avowedly-targeted policy variable.

By 1983, the pragmatism of monetary authorities could be discerned with increasing clarity. The length of the recession, the partly-related intensification of international debt problems, the unpredictability of velocity and doubts in some cases about the meaning of the aggregates being targeted had led a number of major countries to adopt a more flexible approach to monetary policy. This took the form partly of permitting temporary overshooting of targeted aggregates, and partly of paying greater attention to a wider range of indicators, both financial and real.

Even so, there was little sign of active ease. Interest rates remained high by the standards of previous recovery periods. Central banks were alive to the fear, especially prevalent in financial markets, that it can be but a short step from 'flexibility' to the abandonment of financial discipline. It seemed probable that they would continue to announce money targets and aim broadly, on a year-to-year basis, to achieve them. But with most central banks seeking to be more responsive to events as they unfolded, it appeared unlikely that they would attempt to meet their targets rigidly over short periods.

The mix of monetary and fiscal policy

Recent years have also seen a change of view regarding the potential for influencing the combination of output and price outcomes (the 'split' of nominal GNP) by varying the 'mix' of monetary and fiscal policy.

In the years following the first oil shock, as countries learned to live with floating exchange rates, there was a tendency to 'assign' monetary policy to inflation control and fiscal policy to the level of activity. 'Non-accommodation' of inflation was nearly always discussed in terms of monetary control, operating both domestically and via the exchange rate. 'Reflation' was discussed almost exclusively in terms of fiscal expansion. Although the point was generally not made explicit, there appears to have been an underlying assumption that a particular level of nominal income could be achieved by different mixes of monetary and fiscal policy, and that a mix involving tighter money and easier fiscal policy would tend to improve the output/price split of that given nominal income.

Few policy-makers would now believe that there was much scope to tilt the mix of policy in this way. First, both monetary and fiscal policy are seen as operating simultaneously on both output and inflation; the two instruments are seen as more collinear than supposed earlier. Second, in many countries it is considered that monetary and fiscal instruments cannot be operated as two independent levers, or at least that a point is reached beyond which they cannot be. This is because of perceived or actual links between budget deficits and current or future money creation. Various channels may be at work. In countries where the money stock formation process is viewed in terms of the 'credit counterparts', it is customary to see a direct short-term link between the budget deficit, less an allowance for a reasonable sale of government bonds, and money creation. Alternatively, in the longer term (and less closely dependent on particular institutional arrangements), there may be 'wealth' effects on the demand for money (and hence bonds), which effectively limit the proportion of government bonds that will be willingly held in private portfolios and, thereby, the size of deficit that can be financed in a non-monetary way.

Despite the increasing acceptance of this sort of view, which emphasizes not so much the flow aspects of fiscal/monetary policy as the stock consequences over a run of years, the policy-mix issue was live in the recent period because the United States, not entirely by express design, has since 1982 been pursuing – and over the period seemingly benefiting from – a markedly unbalanced mix. The beneficial effect on the output/price split has come from 'export crowding out' – that is, the mechanism, associated with Mundell, whereby for given growth of the money stock, a more expansionary fiscal policy will lead to upward pressure on interest rates, an appreciation of the (real) exchange rate and, over time, a widening current-account deficit to accommodate the incipient capital inflow resulting from higher domestic interest rates. According to this reasoning, tight money and easy fiscal policy have brought about the strong dollar, and thereby made it possible to achieve a fortunate balance between domestic demand growth and the terms of trade. The high dollar has helped bring down inflation; meanwhile the associated reduction of net exports has not seemed unduly worrying because total output has nevertheless been rising strongly in the recovery phase. Where export crowding out is well-established, a mix of tight money and expansionary fiscal policy may thus appear to have substantial short-run advantages, whatever the longer-term implications for economic structure.

But there may be important limitations to the apparent efficacy of such an unbalanced policy mix in the longer term, even for the United States. First, it has implications for resource allocation, some of which may be thought undesirable. On the real side of the economy, the attendant loss of international competitiveness increases the penetration of domestic markets by imports, and weakens the U.S. penetration of markets abroad, so that there is a continued adjustment away from the 'tradeable' to the 'non-tradeable' sectors. On the financial side, the large U.S. budget deficit is accompanied by an inflow of savings from abroad, and lending and borrowing patterns in the rest of the world shift to reflect this. At least until end-1983 the various adjustments had been relatively orderly, and judged not to have been particularly serious. But there was no experience of adjustments on this scale for a long period: with the U.S. current account deficit projected to widen to unprecedented levels, it was by no means certain that such orderliness would persist.

The second limitation to an 'unbalanced mix' policy as a deliberate strategy would be that it does not generalize. If export crowding out were equally characteristic of all economies, each might be tempted by a tight money/easy fiscal policy mix, and associated currency appreciation. But it is evident that the benefits of a stronger exchange rate cannot be enjoyed by all at the same time: not all can experience currency appreciation. Furthermore, even considering countries individually, it may be that for many of them export crowding out may well not be as pronounced as it is in the United States. For example, it may be that, because of the relative independence of the Federal Reserve, markets are more convinced for the United States than for other countries that deficits will not be monetized. In the absence of such confidence they may regard a budget deficit as a harbinger of future inflation and currency depreciation, and so not respond to higher interest rates. More generally, the export crowding out hypothesis requires that the current account deficit resulting from fiscal expansion will raise risk premia by less than the induced rise in interest rates; the United States may well be a special case in this regard.

If export crowding out is less operative in the majority of other countries, there may be little incentive, outside the United States, to use policy asymmetrically. The trade-off between longer-term costs of an unbalanced mix and short-term benefits from the terms of trade would be unfavourable. And it is noticeable that in practice few countries have sought to emulate the United States policy mix. Further it would seem that, even in the United States, export crowding out cannot go on for ever. The logic is that eventually the dollar would have to depreciate, not just to restore the balance of trade (including non-factor services), but to make possible interest payments that cumulative foreign indebtedness, through the current account, would require.

Exchange rate objectives; the European Monetary System

The prolonged period of dollar strength at the beginning of the 1980s heightened differences of view among countries about the role of the exchange rate in policy formulation. With the advent of floating rates, many of the smaller countries had continued to make stabilization of the exchange rate the principal intermediate objective of monetary policy. Moreover, during the second half of the 1970s, each of the major countries had at some point been influenced in setting monetary policy by the course of its exchange rate; and each had on occasion intervened in the exchange market. But the episode of dollar strength at the beginning of the 1980s was marked in the United States by the authorities' reluctance to accept that the stance or mix of fiscal and monetary policies should be influenced by exchange rate developments. In these circumstances, other countries decided, no doubt correctly, that exchange market intervention on their part to stem the dollar's rise would be ineffectual, and saw themselves as having little alternative to accepting the implications of pressure on the dollar for their own effective exchange rates. Many countries claimed that they were forced by exchange rate pressure to maintain higher interest rates than were desired for domestic reasons; but with money growth generally towards the upper end of target ranges (where they existed), the validity of this claim is difficult to establish.

There are broadly two kinds of reasoning which lead countries to have objectives for their exchange rate, or at least to have a view on its appropriate level or range. One is based on the desirability of maintaining a rate that is appropriate from the point of view of the pattern of external payments a country wishes to have (at high employment); this approach will tend to emphasize maintenance of an exchange rate that is sufficiently low from the point of view of international competitiveness. The second kind of motivation derives from anti-inflation objectives, and the view that a small country can best counter inflation by pegging its currency to that of a larger partner with a good inflation record; this 'hard currency option' will involve seeking to maintain a relatively high rate.

The apparent trade-off between competitiveness and anti-inflation desiderata only exists in the short run, however. Over a longer period, a seemingly 'high' nominal rate will either be validated by relatively low inflation in the country in question – the outcome hoped for by those pursuing the hard currency option – or be driven down to levels consistent with less-good inflation performance.

In the recent period, the main interest in exchange rate objectives has been for their counter-inflation potential – as 'anchors' for economies' price levels. A literature has appeared analysing the respective merits, for 'small' countries, of money targets and exchange rate targets in the face of different kinds of shock.[6] Not surprisingly, the conclusion is typically that no single target performs better in the face of all the various shocks liable to impinge upon an economy. It is therefore perhaps not surprising, for example, that Switzerland should have opted to give high priority to a money target while other small central and North European countries have tended, formally or informally, to peg their currencies to the Deutschemark. Equally, it is not surprising that no country has pursued either objective in a totally rigid way.

Among the OECD countries, the most structured exchange rate arrangement is that of the European Monetary System, which was brought into operation in 1979 and includes all Community members apart from the United Kingdom and Greece. In effect, the eight participating currencies are held together by a grid of parities, around which only limited divergencies are permissible, and float jointly *vis-à-vis* other currencies such as the dollar. In the period of its operation, the System has been successful in its aim of reducing exchange rate variability: average month-to-month changes in the *effective* (weighted) exchange rates of participating currencies have been considerably smaller than those of the dollar, yen or sterling. The existence of the arrangement seems to have had some favourable effect on expectations, and has brought participants – individually all very open economies – an element of greater stability in their operating environment. Partly this has been made possible by the fact that the arrangements include one dominant currency which is held more widely than the others – the Deutschemark. Realignments have taken place sufficiently frequently – at least once per year – for currencies not to seem to get obviously 'out of line', and have generally been accomplished with relative calm.

On the other hand, there has been less progress towards the more ambitious aim of Community members to bring about greater 'convergence' in their economic performance. In particular, since 1979 there has been less convergence in inflation rates between other EMS participants and Germany than there has been that country and the other main international currency centres: the United States, Japan, the United Kingdom and Switzerland. There may, of course, have been greater convergence within EMS than there would have been in its absence; but this is virtually impossible to test.

More generally, individual Community initiatives cannot be assessed on economic grounds alone. Whatever contribution it may have made to economic performance, establishment of the EMS has helped maintain momentum in the Community. Certainly, the participants appear to feel that it has provided a focus for discussion of policy coordination among themselves. But in the wider world outside the Community, there has not been much sign that other countries have judged that there was much in the EMS experience that could usefully be generalized.

What happened to incomes policies?

It is perhaps surprising in the light of earlier experience that the period since the second oil shock has seen little tendency for countries to experiment with prices and incomes policies, whether conceived as an arm of counter-inflationary policy or – against a background of non-accommodating monetary and fiscal policy – as 'employment' policy.

To be sure, in countries which can be thought of as operating a long-term incomes policy, existing well-tried arrangements remained in place. This went not only for countries like Austria and Norway where a formal incomes policy occupies a central place in the regular discussions between the authorities and the 'social partners' on a wide range of economic and social policies, but also for countries like Japan and Germany where an implicit understanding could be said to exist about what constitutes a reasonable basis for the distribution of income without this being enshrined in any official texts. But, elsewhere, there was no sign of the short-term incomes policies, aimed at achieving rapid inroads against inflation, that had been a feature of earlier episodes.

As already mentioned, the perception was general that tight policies, particularly on the monetary side, were essential if inflation was to be contained and then brought down. And most countries could point to a considerable degree of success in this endeavour. Indeed, the fact that deflation was general meant that there was considerable downward pressure not only on domestic costs and prices in each country, but also on prices determined in international markets, notably for primary commodities; each individual OECD country may therefore have experienced a greater improvement in inflation than might plausibly have been expected by its own policy-makers relying on traditional domestic relationships. Be that as it may, there can be no doubt that the authorities in most countries could justifiably feel that deflationary policies were serving to bring down inflation, and this probably reinforced the already quite widely-held view – in keeping with the greater attachment in principle to market-oriented approaches to policy – that there was no role for prices and incomes policy.

The other traditional concern of prices and incomes policy, like that of governments' strategy in this period, has been with the distribution of income between wages and profits. By 1982 or 1983, with aggregate demand weak, it was becoming possible in a good number of countries to observe what is variously described as 'wage moderation' or downward flexibility of real wages. The average share of labour in national income declined to close to the levels of just before the first oil shock.

The collective bargaining scene was characterized by a number of developments that were making for increased flexibility in wage-setting. They were due in large part to labour's weaker bargaining position, while actively encouraged in a number of respects by government. For example, public sector wages were increasingly decoupled from those in the private sector, in a number of cases being frozen for a time. (This was one of the ways in which governments sought to redress budget positions.) In the private sector, there was a tendency towards greater decentralization in wage bargaining, thereby giving greater weight to local conditions and ability to pay. At the same time, there was a widespread trend towards deindexing wages from past inflation, and correspondingly closer linking of wages to productivity and profits. In North America, there was even a round of wage 'give backs' (reductions within the contract period of wage rates already agreed upon). In a number of other countries, at least where inflation was reasonably low, it was no longer unthinkable for some groups of workers to receive zero wage increases in the annual round. And negative 'wage-drift' became widespread. The overall effect was to weaken both wage-price links (*de facto* or *de jure* indexation) and wage-wage links (rigidity in relative wage structures).

The economic forces at work here were closely inter-twined with more socio-political ones. Many analysts, of different economic schools of thought, had reached the conclusion by the late 1970s that a significant part of unemployment, in Europe at least, was attributable to labour costs having grown more rapidly in real terms than productivity. In these circumstances, calling for (real) wage moderation is not necessarily 'anti-labour'; in a longer-term sense it could be thought of as 'pro-employment'. But at a time when anti-union sentiment was evident in some countries, misinter-pretation was widespread. The call for greater flexibility in wage *structures* – thought by many to be an important element in smooth structural adjustment – was equally subject to misinterpretation. This was partly because it was often supposed that greater flexibility of wage relativities was a code for increased inequality – which is by no means a necessary concomitant. More specifically, however, resistance to the notion came from union leaders in some of the heavy industrial sectors in relative decline which are traditionally highly unionized and whose workforce stood to lose its position in the wage hierarchy.

What was unclear was how lasting the wage 'moderation' was likely to prove. Where governments had succeeded in repealing formal indexation arrangements, they certainly had no intention of restoring them. Most governments, it seemed, had relied on bringing about 'greater realism', in the sense of a closer conformity of wage-setting to market forces, rather than on seeking to establish longer-term consensus. Such realism would presumably operate symmetrically in a situation where demand for labour was strong – though in most countries such a situation did not appear imminent.

The supply side

Part and parcel of the more medium-term approach to policy has been the increased attention paid in policy pronouncements to the 'supply side'. This is particularly evident in the Anglo-Saxon countries, where there is a long-standing tendency for economic commentary to concentrate on one thing at a time. The approach in Japan and the continental European countries has generally been more pragmatic; indeed, in many of those countries, it had been less exclusively demand-directed in the earlier period.

The expression 'supply side' itself has different connotations in different countries. In Germany and a number of other European countries it refers above all to the perceived need to raise profitability (ensure that real wages rise less rapidly than productivity) and to reduce budget deficits (with a view to lowering interest rates and boosting private sector confidence). Both of these strands have been considered earlier in this chapter. In countries with a more interventionist tradition, such as France and Japan, the supply-side orientation is to an important extent embodied in their industrial policy.

In the United States, where the term was reincarnated, 'supply-side' economics is concerned above all with increasing incentives, notably via cutting taxes and removing 'unnecessary' regulation. For example, Craig Roberts (1978), considering what had gone wrong in economic policy-making, and thereby caused 'the crisis in Keynesian economics', argued that this 'is almost embarrassingly simple. Today in the United States, public economic policy is formulated in bland disregard of the human incentives upon which the economy relies. Instead it is based upon the Keynesian assumption that the gross national product (GNP) and employment are determined only by the level of aggregate demand or total spending in the economy.' In its extreme form, as expressed for example in the 'Laffer curve',[7] supply-side economics asserts that tax cuts will be self-financing in the fairly short run, as a result of increased economic activity and the consequent wider tax base. This conclusion bears a significant resemblance to that of closed-economy Keynesian economics, but with sharpened incentives rather than additional demand calling forth increased activity, and with the time-lags collapsed.

Influenced in part by these ideas, the Reagan administration in the United States enacted a substantial programme of tax cuts in 1981. Exactly what the results were expected to be is not clear. Official quantitative estimates, and indeed official projections, were scarce at that time, and there has been little empirical investigation of the Laffer curve. In general the large macroeconomic models, being of 'eclectic-Keynesian' origin and not concerned with the phenomenon at issue, could be of little use, because they did not contain the postulated mechanisms. Even some years later, however, Keleher (1982) noted that 'There is little evidence bearing on the so-called Laffer curve.' On the basis of such evidence as had been collected, mainly relating to the effects of taxes of specific sectors, he concluded that tax cuts probably did result in some increase in supply, although not by enough to prevent a fall in revenue; and savings might rise in some cases, making the deficit easier to finance.

After the event, it is hard to know the effect of the tax cuts on the budget, in part because they were accompanied by greatly increased defence spending. Overall the Federal budget deficit rose to its highest level since the Second World War in relation to GNP. Recovery, when it came in 1983, was strong, but so also was the increase in the 'structural' budget deficit, so that the cyclical improvement made little impression on the deficit overall. With the Federal Reserve keeping money growth broadly on track, the mix of monetary and fiscal policy became problematical, posing some of the questions evoked above as to its sustainability.

In general, many governments, in their approach to the supply side of their economies, have sought increasingly to rely on market mechanisms, in Japan and the United Kingdom for example 'privatising' successful public sector enterprises. In practice, however, the approach has not been easy to follow across the board, as the attempts to restructure traditional industries such as steel and shipbuilding exemplify. The motor car industry (which accounts for 8 per cent of world trade) has also been extensively managed by the state in many countries.

One sector where the question of the appropriate degree of intervention in the market is both difficult and yet of macroeconomic significance is energy. The energy market is characterized by very low price elasticities of demand and supply in the short run, but much higher ones in the longer run; and stocks are typically high in relation to current consumption. Energy is quantitatively important, the value of energy consumption in OECD countries amounting to about 9 per cent of OECD GNP, with oil accounting for about half of that. Given these characteristics, there has been increasingly general agreement that, over the medium term, prices are key; and it was noticeable that the second major round of oil price rises was passed through to final users of energy more swiftly and fully than the first. Energy consumption per unit of GNP fell much more sharply in the wake of the second oil shock than after the first. At the same time, there is room for significant differences of view as to how far it is appropriate for the authorities to intervene at times of short-term disruption of energy supplies to share out available quantities or draw down stocks, with a view to containing the abrupt price rise – and its macroeconomic effects – that might otherwise result.

Assessment

Increased attention to the medium-term seems appropriate. Although some views heard today are based on a caricature of post-war economic history, it is no doubt plausible to attribute *some* of the recent economic difficulties to undue concern with the short term in earlier periods. For example, while, as argued in chapter 2, the rapid increase in the relative size of the public sector was not itself due substantially to the pursuit of demand management policy, a more rational structure of public expenditure and taxation might well have been achieved in a number of countries had their evolution been governed by a longer-term strategy. What does seem to emerge from the history sketched in chapters 2 and 3 is that a key determinant of the efficacy of short-term policy activism is whether or not policy has a medium-term anti-inflation orientation. Under the Bretton Woods regime this was provided, so long at least as the United States pursued non-inflationary policies, by pegging the exchange rate to the dollar. In a country with a floating exchange rate, the authorities have to be more directly responsible for maintaining price stability in their own economy. This is now generally accepted; and it seems probable, despite the recent greater pragmatism, that countries will continue to monitor carefully the development of the various definitions of the money stock, in the hope of retaining a medium-term 'anchor' for nominal variables.

The shift of focus in the setting of policies has been paralleled, at the analytical level, by increased interest in the longer-run 'equilibrium' properties of economies. This in itself also seems a healthy development. Some of the builders of models designed for short-term forecasting and policy analysis may in the past have been careless in neglecting to ensure that beyond the short run their models displayed tendencies towards equilibrium consistent with economic theory. To the extent the models were used only in short-term applications this may not have appeared to matter much, but could have contributed to myopia in assessing the total effects of policy.

As it happens, there may be a substantial measure of agreement among economists of differing persuasions about some of the key long-run properties. Many would agree, for example, on long-run tendencies towards neutrality of money; towards full 'crowding-out' when fiscal policy is not accommodated by monetary policy; or, internationally, towards purchasing power parity. Controversy arose, however, when some commentators and policy advisors, perhaps as a result of carrying over the assumptions of the 'rational expectations' literature into the real world, began to suggest, or at least imply, that these were tendencies at work in the short run. Some policy-makers may have believed them, or at least have found that the policy implications that followed fitted comfortably with the orientation they wished policy to have.

In these circumstances there was inevitably a gap between what some policy-makers believed and what the empirical evidence – at least that relating to a policy-relevant time horizon – could substantiate. Indeed, an international survey[8] was able to conclude that in various key respects models being used for short-term forecasting and policy simulation in a number of national administrations did not capture some of the economic properties on which policies, at least at the level of public announcement, were being predicated. It seems reasonable to suppose that this was due in part to the inability of modellers to capture empirically certain effects that nevertheless are widely supposed to be significant in particular circumstances – certain kinds of wealth effect, for example, appear to come into this category. But in part it was attributable to policy announcements being vague about the time horizon over which policy effects were expected to come about, or to their ignoring the time-lags likely to be involved.

Time-lags are the very essence of macroeconomics. If all markets cleared instantaneously, much of the interest in the subject would disappear. Macroeconomists, and policy advisers, have traditionally interested themselves in the extent to which the adjustment of an economy to a new equilibrium, in response, for example, to policy changes or external shocks, is partitioned between price and quantity responses, the *timepath* by which the economy moves towards that equilibrium, and the *costs* that may be incurred along the way. It is one of the theses of this book that policy-makers should be provided with the best possible assessment of such timepaths and costs.

Whether policy-makers should act on such assessments is another matter. They may judge that the risks and uncertainties involved (discussed in chapter 5) make policy intervention unwise. A medium-term approach does not, however, necessarily rule out shorter-run adjustments to policy. In the period since 1979, which is the particular focus of this chapter, most governments have in principle sought to avoid short-term discretionary adjustments to demand that might risk blunting the overall anti-inflationary thrust of policy or conveying misleading signals to financial markets. As suggested by the discussion above of automatic fiscal stabilizers, and of monetary policy flexibility within a target-oriented approach, there is room for interpretation of what constitutes an unchanged stance; and a number of governments have taken some advantage of this. Some countries, for example, have found it useful to distinguish between *target stability*, which it may well be possible to maintain over the medium term, and *instrument flexibility*, which may be possible within – or even be necessary to – broad achievement of the targets.

By and large, however, governments have eschewed short-term demand support to moderate the costs of recession – which would indeed have tended to run counter to the fundamental strategy being pursued. At the same time, they have found themselves drifting into a variety of defensive measures of a microeconomic kind, whether at the frontier or domestically, to protect particular sectoral interests – sometimes in response to similar action abroad. The sectors concerned are typically ones whose relative importance in the OECD countries was declining as patterns of comparative advantage shifted world-wide. But the prolonged recession itself has made the required structural shifts inside OECD countries markedly more difficult. The measures taken have themselves often had implications for the public finances; and generally have the characteristic of delaying the structural change that would be indicated by market forces or by shifting comparative advantage, thereby tending to lower productivity, make the economy more inflation-prone, and reduce its potential growth-rate. Needless to say, such an approach at the microeconomic level is quite inconsistent with – even if, in the short run, partially to be attributed to – the thrust of macroeconomic policy.

In summary, the OECD economy had, by 1983, undergone its most thoroughgoing disinflation since the Korean war, and recovery was beginning. But how far the lower inflation rates would be sustainable as activity recovered; how far it would prove possible to effect the needed supply-side adjustments while unemployment and spare capacity remained large; and how far the costs of recession and structural change could be mitigated without nullifying the basic thrust of policy; all these remained unanswered questions.

12 International cooperation in economic policy-making

Summary

Today's close interdependence of national economies has not always been matched by a comparable degree of cooperation in the formulation of economic policies. Two key notions on which the case for international cooperation rests are that the properties of the international economic system are not the straightforward addition or averaging of the properties of individual national economies; and that the perceived loss of sovereignty involved in international cooperation is more apparent than real, and can on occasion even be helpful to policymakers. The relevant economic theory is not clear-cut, but it suggests that it is possible in general to achieve a better collective outcome with cooperative than with non-cooperative setting of policy. There are, however, considerable practical and political difficulties in making this finding operational.

Two examples of macroeconomic cooperation, based on systematic economic analysis and leading to quantified commitments, have been the Smithsonian realignment of major currencies in 1971 and the programme of concerted action agreed upon at the Bonn Summit of 1978. In each case, the effects of the agreement reached appeared to influence the course of the OECD economy in desired ways, but in each case, too, unforeseen events intervened that overwhelmed those effects.

Introduction

Much of the earlier part of this book has been concerned to address, at the analytical level, the implications of industrial economies' greater openness to international influences, or interdependence.

This chapter looks at some attempts that have been made to come to terms with interdependence at the policy level.

It was suggested in chapter 4 that for a typical OECD country, between a quarter and a half of the effects of domestic policy action on economic activity might be felt not at home, but in other economies. By the same token, it could be expected that over time a significant part of changes in activity in any given economy would be attributable to developments, including policy action, abroad. Moreover, financial linkages and related exchange rate variations are all-pervading in their effects. In such conditions, tolerably good control of domestic economic activity by the national authorities requires, at a minimum, knowledge of economic developments and policies in other countries as well as a view on how economic forces are transmitted internationally. Many would go further, and argue that policy formulation itself needs to be coordinated internationally. This issue, which is controversial, is returned to later in the chapter.

Impressive international agreements on the coordination of policy have been achieved on a few occasions. International economic meetings are held frequently, at all levels from technical experts to Ministers, and even – for the seven largest economies – Heads of State and Government. And monetary authorities have shown themselves able to move rapidly and cooperatively to defuse incipient financial crisis – from the support packages for sterling in the 1960s to those for Latin American debtors in 1982-83. Nevertheless, efforts at cooperation at the policy-formulation stage, at least as regards macroeconomic policies, must be regarded in general as limited in their scope and intensity in relation to today's close degree of international linkage. As Wallich (1983) has observed in this connection, 'growing world interdependence is not yet matched by growing ability or willingness to cooperate in dealing with the results of interdependence'. Later in the chapter, there is some discussion of why this is so, whether it is inevitable, and the form that international economic cooperation has come to take in recent years.

Some general considerations

It is convenient, following Hamada (1974), to think of international cooperation as a two-stage process. At a first stage, countries set up the framework for international economic relations – some basic rules and understandings and the multilateral institutions charged with enforcing or applying them. These are the 'rules of the game'; Bryant (1980) calls them 'supranational traffic regulations'.[1] At a second stage the countries play the game itself – setting their policy instruments as best they can to achieve their aims within the opportunities or constraints provided by the policies and performance of the other players.

At the first level, cooperation in the post-war world can be thought of generally as having been strong. The Articles of Agreement of the International Monetary Fund and the General Agreement on Tariffs and Trade defined the post-war international financial and trading systems, to which industrialized countries at least were keen to belong. To be sure, the Bretton Woods system broke down at the beginning of the 1970s, and the present arrangements as defined in the amended Articles of the Fund are a good deal looser. And it is also true that freedom of international trade has been increasingly fettered in the last few years by a wide variety of measures, both domestic and at the border. On the other hand, international financial transactions have become freer than ever before, a number of countries having moved towards greater, or even complete, freedom of capital movements. Overall, while it is certainly the case that there has been some weakening of the international traffic regulations, and some loss of traffic discipline, the volume of traffic remains considerable. Countries have not attempted autarkic solutions to their problems. The tissue of economic cooperation is still in place – somewhat frayed at the edges, perhaps, but still quite serviceable.

The remainder of the discussion of fiscal and monetary policies takes as given this institutional framework, within which individual countries can set their policies either cooperatively or not. Accordingly, even if a country's policies are set *non-cooperatively* – that is to say, on the basis of the best information available about developments in other countries, but set nonetheless unilaterally – this is not taken to mean that the country is renouncing the advantages and obligations of belonging to a broadly liberal international order. Countries can be said to set their policies *cooperatively* if as a result of negotiation they commit themselves to policy settings which are different from what they would have been without the negotiation (and consequent commitments by others).

Turning then to the second stage, policy cooperation itself, the starting point is the evident interdependence of national economies and hence the interdependence of their policies. This has been discussed at some length in chapter 4. At a common sense level, the closeness of international linkage – the fact that developments in one country strongly affect, and are strongly affected by, developments in other countries – might make it seem obvious that international cooperation in policy-making is desirable. The issue is, however, not quite so simple.

It is for example argued by some that all that is required by way of cooperation is an exchange of information among countries. According to this view, provided a country knows what is in place, or envisaged, by way of economic developments and policies in other countries, it can set its own policies in consequence, offsetting as desired any unwelcome effects on itself of developments elsewhere.[2] The difficulty with this line of thought is that in practice the degree of offset that is possible is typically quite limited, as many of the cases described in chapter 4 make clear. If, for example, policies abroad are exerting an influence perceived in a particular country as unduly deflationary, there is ample evidence that attempts to compensate for this by domestic demand expansion can quickly encounter constraints which subsequently force the country concerned to change tack.

The fact that the individual country cannot on its own reach a desired position does not however clinch the argument in favour of joint policy-making. Indeed, some of the frequently-heard calls for international cooperation are little more than cries of despair; in a difficult environment it is all too tempting to suppose that if only other countries would follow more 'reasonable' policies the nature of the policy choices available would be transformed out of all recognition. It may be that the country concerned simply has an unrealistic appreciation of the trade-offs, notably between growth and inflation control, that it and others are facing – or different preferences from the average of other countries. The combination of the outcome in the country concerned, even though viewed as unsatisfactory in itself, and those in all other relevant countries *might* still be 'Pareto-optimal' – a situation where no country is able to improve its position, in terms of its own preferences, without at least one other's being worsened.

Will then the outcome of non-cooperative national policy-making normally tend to be Pareto-optimal, or 'efficient'? Or is the global economic situation typically such that it would be possible by means of joint action to bring about an alternative situation in which all countries are better off – or at least where none is worse off? It is instructive first to turn to the theoretical literature on this point. Bryant has summarized the (not very abundant) work done in this area using the techniques of game theory.[3] The analysis has been done both on so-called Cournot–Nash assumptions (whereby each country takes as given the stance of others, ignoring any effect its own actions may have on others' policies) and according to a Stackelberg solution (in which a dominant country makes allowance for the fact that the behaviour of others will depend on its own actions). At least for the kinds of model and policy regime that have been examined, the general conclusion is that non-cooperative national policy-making is 'inefficient' – the outcome can lie far from a Pareto optimum. In particular, the world economy can be subject to an overall policy thrust that is over-expansionary or over-restrictive.

The discussion in chapter 4 suggests that this is not merely a theoretical possibility. Uncoordinated policy contributed to over-strong booms in 1968-69 and again in 1972-73, and to serious recession in 1980-82. Is the theoretical finding that it will generally be possible to bring about a better global outcome with cooperative setting of policy any less relevant to real world conditions? The evidence is difficult to interpret, partly because there have been few examples of cooperative setting of macroeconomic policies, and partly because of the usual problem in applied economics of determining what would have happened had circumstances, including policies, been different. Emerging empirical work in this area may eventually help provide further insights on the extent to which a better global outcome can be achieved through internationally co-operative policy setting, though it is still too early to be able to draw firm inferences from it. (See, for example, Brandsma and Hughes Hallett (1983), Oudiz and Sachs (1984), and Pauly (1983).)

The Bretton Woods period

The Bretton Woods regime provided a convenient framework for international cooperation in macroeconomic policy-making – at least in the setting of the 1950s and 1960s. The era was characterized by one dominant economy (the United States), limited capital mobility, generally low inflation and a relatively low incidence of large macroeconomic shocks. And over time something close to a consensus evolved as to how economies worked and the effect of policies upon economic activity, a consensus which for shorthand purposes can be described as 'Keynesian'. In these conditions, international demand management with fixed exchange rates was a logical extension of national demand management.

This is not to suggest that countries met regularly to agree on an internationally-coherent set of demand management policies. That would be a caricature. But over time certain presumptions of action came to be accepted.[4] In the first place, there was a presumption that an *individual* country in a weak balance-of-payments position should deflate its domestic demand, and that one in a strong position should expand domestic demand. Put into an *international* demand-management context, if demand pressure in the OECD area as a whole was excessive, or judged likely to become so, there was a presumption that countries in a weak balance-of-payments position should take the lead in curbing demand; if demand overall was deficient, countries in a relatively strong balance-of-payments position would, by the same token, take the lead in stimulating demand.

The applicability of this sort of conceptual framework depended on the major participating countries not being in 'fundamental disequilibrium' – a situation where the appropriate response to balance-of-payments weakness or strength would have been a change in the exchange rate. For most of the period this condition would seem to have been met, or at least was thought at the time to have been met. Admittedly, there was considerable latitude in arriving at an assessment of a country's 'fundamental' position: even when appropriate allowance for the effects of divergent cyclical positions had been made, a country's current account – and, even more, its capital account – would typically be subject to other temporary influences on the importance of which there was significant room for differences of view. There was a tendency to give countries the 'benefit of the doubt'. Changes of parity were rare events, charged with political significance; and partner countries were generally loth to force them, lest they find themselves in turn in the 'firing line'.

The Smithsonian realignment

In the end, this was one reason why the Bretton Woods system broke down. Parity changes were delayed too long, with attendant erosion of the credibility of the system itself. The biggest test the system had to face was its ability to accommodate a devaluation of the dollar itself. From the mid-1960s onwards, the dollar was showing increasing signs of overvaluation. To be sure, the United States did not move into current account deficit until 1971. (Though the initial estimates and data at the time were less favourable than the revised data now available for the period.) But the current account surpluses that were being recorded were increasingly inadequate to cover the regular outflows of official and private capital. The rest of the world needed the United States to run *some* overall deficit in order to provide increases in the global stock of international liquidity; yet if the deficit exceeded some critical amount, confidence in the dollar was threatened. When U.S. monetary policy was tight, as in 1969, inflows of short-term capital served to mask the weakness of the fundamental position, but when it was relaxed, as in 1970-71, the overall deficit was liable to become massive.

For a time, many regarded dollar depreciation as an impossibility – not only unthinkable for economic reasons, but legally impossible because of the link between the dollar and gold at the heart of the system and the fact that other currencies were defined in relation to that apparent fixed point. The legal issues are of no relevance to the present discussion, but the economics of the Smithsonian realignment are of considerable interest. It was based on what is almost certainly the most elaborately-quantified macro-economic analysis and discussion ever to underpin an international agreement, a process described by one journalist at the time as 'econometric diplomacy'.

Preparatory discussions took place in the second half of 1971, largely among the Deputies of the Group of Ten and the OECD's Working Party No. 3 (essentially the same participants). Working Party No. 3 was charged with establishing the extent of the payments disequilibria that needed correction, a task in which it received analytical support from the OECD Secretariat. The exchange rate changes corresponding to the 'needed' balance-of-payments swings were estimated by the IMF staff, and formed the starting point for the discussions among the Ministers of the Group of Ten at the Smithsonian Institution in December 1971. Throughout the period, technical cooperation between the IMF and OECD on the various aspects of the analytical work was particularly close.

The Working Party No. 3 exercise was the culmination of attempts that had been made for some years to judge current and prospective trends in payments balances in relation to the standard of a generally acceptable international pattern. Both arms of the exercise were fraught with difficulty. In today's environment it may be difficult to imagine countries putting so much effort into analytical discussion of this kind; it is important to remember that what was in train was the first major repegging of exchange rates for over twenty years, and countries were negotiating a new set of rates that they expected to abide by for a considerable period.

Turning first to the *actual* pattern of payments, the outstanding feature was the weakness of the United States, which had recorded a negligible current surplus in 1970, completely inadequate to cover the regular capital outflow. Moreover, this was at a time when activity in the United States was cyclically low while in some other major OECD countries it was cyclically high: developments both at home and abroad were serving to improve the look of the U.S. current account. Adjusting the figures for this, the U.S. position would have looked still weaker, and those of some other countries still stronger; such adjustment was desirable in the attempt to assess countries' underlying positions. The OECD Secretariat therefore developed the concept, and empirical estimates, of cyclically adjusted current accounts. The notion itself was not new; but the systematic calculation of internationally-consistent estimates was. This required an internationally- compatible set of cyclical indicators,[5] as well as a set of import and export functions for the various OECD countries and for the non-OECD as a group. The essential feature of the calculation of each country's cyclical component was that it allowed for the cyclical situation of all other countries as well as its own; by construction, the cyclical components of current accounts summed to zero across countries.

The calculation of cyclically-adjusted balances, though allowing for differences in cyclical position among countries, was not sufficient to give countries' 'underlying' positions a year or two ahead, which in principle were what the political discussion would focus on. Arriving at these involved extrapolating the trend of the cyclically-adjusted balances (to the extent one was discernible) and allowing in addition for any special factors judged to be significantly affecting the outcome in the recent past.

The *desirable* set of payments balances with which these prospective underlying positions were to be compared derived from several years' discussion in the Working Party of balance-of-payments 'aims'. Some of these aims were drawn from national statements or planning documents; some were formulated for the purpose of this exercise; a few had to be attributed to countries by the OECD Secretariat as a basis for discussion. The general principle was that aims, though announced in terms of the current account, were actually arrived at from the capital account side, and corresponded to each country's 'desirable and sustainable' net capital movements. For most developed countries there was generally a presumption that it was appropriate to aim for some current surplus, to match net capital outflows; for the OECD countries as a group, the sum of their aims had to correspond, apart from statistical discrepancies, to the group's (desired) net flow of resources to the rest of the world (mainly developing countries: the complications created by large OPEC surpluses were still in the future).

As might be expected, there was significant lack of international consistency in countries' aims as announced at the outset of the process, as well as in national assessments of prospective underlying positions. It was estimated by the OECD Secretariat that the combined OECD current surplus[6] in 1972 would amount to $11 billion – about ½ per cent of OECD GNP. Countries' aims added up to some ¾ per cent of OECD GNP; and their assessments of their own underlying positions added up to only ¼ per cent of OECD GNP. There was an evident 'mercantilist' bias here; wishing to limit their appreciation against the dollar, countries were playing safe in both the assessment of their underlying positions and their announced objectives. The OECD Secretariat produced a set of scaled-down aims which totalled $11 billion, as, perforce, did the consistent set of underlying positions. The implied swings in current account positions for individual countries – the differences between scaled-down aims and underlying positions – amounted to about 1 per cent of GNP for the United States with the counterpart widely spread, though Germany and Japan accounted for sizeable amounts.[7] The IMF's Multilateral Exchange Rate Model[8] was then used to determine the set of exchange rate changes that could be expected to bring about the hypothetical swings in current balances.

Discussions at the technical level went a good way towards establishing the basis for a consistent set of exchange rate changes. Considerable further discussion had to take place at the political level, however, before agreement could be reached. In the realignment finally agreed upon, the dollar was devalued by 8 per cent against gold and by varying amounts in relation to the other major currencies, amounting to 9 per cent on an effective, trade-weighted basis. There were effective revaluations of some 11 and 6 per cent for Japan and Germany, respectively, and mostly rather small effective changes for the other major currencies.

Those who had followed the analytical work closely tended to feel that these changes were if anything on the small side, but the trade elasticities and other elements in the calculations were anyway subject to considerable uncertainty. All agreed that the new rates would help bring about a considerably more balanced pattern of international payments. Cooperation among the major countries had been impressive, and the repegging of exchange rates, though ultimately the outcome of political negotiation, had been based to a significant degree on economic analysis. Many hoped that this series of discussions would be a model for the future.

This was not to be. Inflation was accelerating, and inter-country inflation differences were widening. The volume of potentially mobile capital was increasing rapidly. The major imbalances on current account were slow to adjust, partly because of the inevitable time-lags, and partly because domestic demand grew particularly rapidly in the United States relative to other countries in 1972. Exchange market participants, having seen one dollar devaluation, no longer expected that rates would stay fixed virtually indefinitely. The view that the Smithsonian realignment had been 'not enough' gained ground. In February 1973 the dollar underwent a second devaluation, arranged on this occasion in the course of a 'whistle-stop' tour of foreign capitals by Paul Volcker, then Under-Secretary for Monetary Affairs at the U.S. Treasury. The new rates for major currencies lasted only a few weeks, giving place in March to floating rates.

The situation after the first oil shock

With the abandonment of fixed exchange rates, the industrial countries lost one of the cornerstones of the intellectual edifice within which they had been accustomed to consider balance-of-payments questions. At the end of the same year, 1973, they lost another: the combined current surplus of the OECD countries as a group. The first oil price shock pushed it far into deficit, one effect that was perceived immediately and generally. In view of the disconcerting new circumstances in which countries found themselves, it was remarkable that they were prepared to agree immediately, partly on the basis of analysis provided by the OECD Secretariat and other international organizations, that the oil-induced negative swing in the current accounts of oil-importing countries was something that had for a time to be accepted, and that they should not – and hence would not attempt to – shift their current account deficits to others.[9] The understanding was that it would be appropriate, rather, to redress their external positions by reducing oil consumption, by stepping up exports to the OPEC countries, and by recycling financial flows (and hence purchasing power) to the non-oil developing countries.

This seems to have been an occasion when the industrial countries approached a new situation in a genuinely cooperative spirit. (Other aspects of this were the setting up of the International Energy Agency, the establishment of the IMF 'Oil Facility', the adoption of the OECD Trade Pledge, and the negotiation in the Organization of a 'Financial Support Fund'.) On the other hand, they were not prepared to undertake any quantitative commitment that would permit their agreement to be monitored. Some would have liked to see established a set of balance-of-payments 'aims' appropriate to the new situation, but little progress was made towards that end. Partly this was because any scheme for attributing aims consistent with the large current deficit for the OECD countries as a group would necessarily have assigned to most countries deficits of a size they could not publicly agree to, even as interim objectives. Equally important, the intellectual climate of the time was strongly influenced by the view that with flexible exchange rates any such quantified agreement would be redundant, and perhaps even harmful.

In practice, the key feature determining the evolution of countries' external positions in this period was the differing intensity of their anti-inflation policies, an aspect described in chapter 3. It seems, indeed, that countries' policies were not primarily motivated by the objective of redressing current account positions, even though there was fierce competition for bilateral export deals with the OPEC countries. The OPEC surplus was shorter-lived than most people had feared would be the case, but the distribution of the counterpart deficits was uneven. By 1976, the 'external constraint' on a number of OECD countries, in the form either of downward exchange rate pressure that threatened inflation objectives or of an unsustainable pace of foreign debt accumulation, forced them to give priority to reduction of current deficits.

'Locomotive' and other theories: the Bonn Summit

As they emerged from the 1974-75 recession, OECD countries aimed for 'moderate but sustained' growth. At the time, this was taken to mean an average growth rate of 5 per cent a year or somewhat more between 1975 and 1980.[10] Judged against that yardstick, the recovery, after an initial spurt in 1975–76, was thought by many to be disappointingly slow. The United States was recovering relatively rapidly, with unemployment falling. As a counterpart to this, its external position was deteriorating. Germany and Japan had relatively low inflation rates and strong current account positions, but their domestic demand was expanding relatively slowly. The United States felt that these two countries were not taking their share in maintaining a reasonable pace of world demand growth, and was particularly critical of Japan's large current surplus. Most OECD countries other than these three largest had weak payments positions and perceived these as constraints, more or less binding, on any policy action by themselves.

Against this background, various ideas or plans for joint – or 'concerted' – action began to be formulated in 1977. These tended to be categorized under the heading of the 'locomotive theory', a term which was often at the time, and more frequently since, employed pejoratively. It is true that the term 'locomotive' itself conveyed a misleading, over-simplified impression of what was in the minds of those who were seeking to design a programme of concerted action. To begin with, the programme had a number of elements, of which demand management policy was only one. Other key features were the freeing of energy prices in countries, most notably the United States, where they were significantly below world levels, and a range of policies to promote freer trade and a more rapid adjustment of output and employment to changing patterns of demand. Furthermore, where demand management was concerned, the idea was *not* simply that two or three countries in strong external positions could expand demand and 'pull' the rest of the OECD countries out of low demand by boosting the latter's exports and thereby creating an adequate rate of growth internationally. The point of the approach was rather that the boost to the exports of the 'non-locomotive' group would ease the external constraint on their freedom of action, thereby providing them with 'elbow room' and enabling them to sustain a higher level of domestic demand than would otherwise have been the case.[11]

This point was illustrated by the OECD Secretariat with the help of a pair of simulations, performed with an earlier version of the system described in chapter 9. In the first simulation, five countries in strong balance-of-payments positions (Japan, Germany, the Netherlands, Belgium and Switzerland) were presumed to take stimulatory action. As a result of their higher simulated imports, other countries received higher simulated exports and hence higher GNP. Their simulated current account positions also improved. In the second simulation, in addition to the action by the five strong countries, other OECD countries also were presumed to raise demand, by just enough to move their current accounts back to where they were at the starting point. Obviously, this example was unrealistically fine-tuned. But it was one way of showing that the properly-specified version of the approach, more aptly called the 'convoy theory', which allowed for appropriately-differentiated policies, was considerably more powerful than the simple version. Indeed the second simulation suggested more than twice as much 'locomotion' (incremental demand) for the OECD area as a whole, markedly more than this for the non-locomotive countries, and with somewhat higher demand even for the locomotive countries themselves.

The action assumed in the simulations took the form of fiscal expansion, reflecting the policy-level discussions taking place at the time. Monetary policy, which figured rather little in those discussions, was assumed in the simulations to be accommodating. As the premise underlying the convoy approach was that the critical constraint facing most countries was the weakness of their external position, the simulations paid particular attention to countries' current account responses to different impulses. But the effects on inflation were also examined with some care. The concerted action analysis made available to policy-makers was unambiguous that the boost to demand under discussion could be expected to be accompanied by some increase in inflation. Because, however, the simulations had to be performed under the assumption that exchange rates would remain unchanged, the estimates of the inflation effect for individual countries were less solidly-based than the estimate for the OECD area as a whole.

The OECD was used more intensively in the preparation of the 1978 seven-nation summit than for other summits either before or since. The Organization was well placed for this, not least because the overall summit package also involved elements other than macroeconomic policy (most notably energy policy), but also because the apparatus available to perform the preparatory analytical work was better developed there than elsewhere.

By the time of the summit itself, the macroeconomic priority for the United States had become the countering of inflation, and various measures to this end too were announced as part of the overall programme. But most importantly from the point of view of the other participants, the United States committed itself to various energy policy measures, notably the decontrol of domestic oil prices by end-1980. Germany agreed to undertake within six weeks fiscal expansion equivalent on an impact basis to about 1 per cent of GNP. Japan pledged itself to achieve a real growth target in fiscal 1978 1.5 per cent higher than in fiscal 1977, and took action shortly afterwards equivalent to 1 per cent of GNP. It also agreed to keep the volume of Japanese exports for fiscal 1978 at or below the level of fiscal 1977. Canada, France and Italy agreed to modest additional stimulus; the United Kingdom, which had already enacted fiscal stimulus of over 1 per cent of GNP shortly beforehand, pledged itself to continue the fight against inflation.

Anthony Solomon, who as Under-Secretary for Monetary Affairs at the U.S. Treasury helped prepare the Bonn Summit, has written:[12]

'It was the only summit [of the eight up to 1982] where the final agreement clearly represented a coordinated package, in which actions were pledged by each country in return for specific undertakings by others – all of which were capable of being implemented. In that sense, it was unique because it meant that countries were willing to make commitments that they had not necessarily planned to make on purely domestic grounds, but they were willing to undertake as part of an overall deal. The circumstances of 1978 were especially suited to this kind of package. Therefore, the potential benefits from the package as a whole appeared to far outweigh any of the potential costs.'

Viewed in this light, the Bonn Summit appears as a paradigm of international cooperation – at least at the policy-formulation stage. How far were such hopes borne out? Unfortunately the effects of the agreement reached are extremely difficult to disentangle. A few months after the summit the Iranian revolution began, triggering the second oil price shock. The inflationary effects of this struck oil-importing countries in the course of 1979. Policies began to move to restriction; in particular, the United States adopted new operating procedures for monetary policy, which in the circumstances of the time led to high and volatile interest rates and a strong dollar. These two factors – the second oil shock and countries' fairly uniform policy response thereto – became the overwhelming proximate influences on the course of OECD economic activity and inflation (see chapters 3, 4 and 11).

Although a rigorous disentangling is hardly possible, a few elements relevant to assessing the effects of the Bonn Summit agreements can be put forward. To begin with, however, it is difficult to judge how much of the demand boost agreed to by Germany and Japan was truly attributable to the summit discussion. In Germany, the progressiveness of the tax scales is such that fiscal drag is strong, and a number of expansionary fiscal packages of up to 1 per cent of GNP had been enacted in the course of the 1970s in order to broadly offset this. In Japan, too, there had been a number of expansionary packages. It might well have been, therefore, that Germany and Japan would have taken fiscal action of some size in 1978 even had there not been a Bonn Summit agreement.

Be that as it may, expansion got under way, and was more widely spread, in 1978 and 1979. From mid-1978 to mid-1979 unemployment in Europe was reduced for the only time, and productive investment showed its only significant upturn, in the post-1973 period. Indeed, activity can now be seen to have been picking up before the summit action was taken. This has led some observers to suggest that a 'fine tuning' mistake was made: reflation where none was required. Others have argued that demand picked up in anticipation of the concerted action measures, which were foreshadowed some time in advance.

Another aspect of the situation which developed in hoped-for ways was the pattern of external current accounts. The effects of exchange rate movements in 1977-78, notably the depreciation of the dollar and appreciation of the Deutschemark and yen, combined with the changing relative cyclical positions to push the United States back towards surplus and Japan and Germany towards deficit. When the second oil price rise put the OECD area into large combined deficit in 1980, Japan and Germany sustained 40 per cent of it. This was a very different configuration from that at the previous peak OECD deficit in 1974, when Germany, virtually alone among OECD countries, had been in very substantial surplus. Germany's relatively large deficit in the later period also helped the new European Monetary System get off to a remarkably smooth start, Deutschemark strength taking longer to assert itself than had been expected.

Almost certainly, however, the most successful aspect of the programme has proved to be the decontrol of U.S. energy prices. The ensuing large rise in energy prices in the United States, particularly in the case of natural gas, has done much to reduce energy demand in relation to GNP at the international level. In turn this has contributed to a marked weakening of real energy prices, and reduced the likelihood of further large oil price shocks.

On the other hand, inflation in most countries accelerated far more than expected in 1979-80, mostly because of the OPEC oil price hike and induced secondary effects on prices generally. Some have gone so far as to blame the Bonn Summit for the second oil shock. This seems far-fetched. To be sure, in a medium-term perspective the oil price increases must be seen as endogenous to the world economy, rather than as unfortunate exogenous accidents. Any increment to global demand would ultimately have been liable to contribute its part to *ex ante* excess demand for oil at a time when supply was disturbed. But it hardly seems reasonable to attribute the oil price rises of 1979 to the concerted action of mid-1978, given that Iranian deliveries were cut by 2 mbd and consuming countries added nearly another 2 mbd to demand for a time through a scramble to build up inventories. More generally, however, the world economy may have been rather closer to capacity than realized. Non-oil commodity prices grew more rapidly than expected from mid-1978 to early 1980, and measures of capacity utilization in the industrial countries probably failed, as they still may do, to make full allowance for the part of the capital stock that had been rendered prematurely obsolete by the change in the relative price of oil, and hence the change in the structure both of demand and production that resulted. It has also been argued that countries where relatively little progress had been made against inflation by 1978 should have used the occasion of the Bonn summit to tighten their policies further.

The rise in inflation rates led some policy-makers to be sharply critical of the Bonn package. In particular, as German inflation moved above 5 per cent in 1979 and the current account swung into deficit for the first time since 1965, the authorities in that country took a strongly negative view of the concerted action episode, even though the adverse effect on both inflation and the current account seems clearly to have owed much to oil, and subsequently Deutschemark depreciation.

It is perhaps more appropriate to return a verdict of 'not proven' on the concerted action programme as a whole, but to recognize that the decontrol of U.S. energy prices was clearly beneficial.

The period since the second oil shock

Subsequent summit meetings have stopped well short of the quantified interlocking agreements of Bonn. The summit theme coming closest to traditional international policy cooperation has been the concern for 'greater stability' of the international monetary system, which, it is suggested, would be brought about by 'convergence' of the various countries' policies. Both the implicit diagnosis and the cure appear somewhat imprecise. In context, the concern appears to have been mainly with the short-term variability of exchange rates, though most economists would argue that a bigger problem in recent years has been an increasing tendency towards medium-term misalignment – or 'overshooting' – of a number of major currencies. And convergence is not the same thing as cooperation, at least in the sense in which it had been understood until recently; it seems to imply, rather, the parallel pursuit of similar policies in a number of countries.

Indeed, there has been an increasing tendency for international cooperation to mean – at the level of governments and the international organizations – agreement to pursue together policies to deal with afflictions which are recognized as essentially domestic in origin, though they may well have international implications. When the policy action considered necessary to deal with a problem is politically difficult, it can strengthen governments' hands significantly if they can point to the widespread nature of the agreement that exists internationally about the appropriate solution.

This aspect of international cooperation is of course not new; for most of the post-war period policy pronouncements have systematically stressed the importance of supply, demand, and the achievement and maintenance of a liberal international system of exchange. But the emphasis has varied. Since the end of the 1970s, the focus of attention has tended to move away from demand to the other two elements. For example, in 1980 (shortly after the second great oil price rise) OECD Ministers considered that they faced three main macroeconomic tasks: bringing inflation under control, ensuring a 'sufficient' level of activity, and positive supply-oriented policies. The communique that they issued at the time[13] seems to have accorded approximately equal importance to the demand side aspect and the supply side aspect, while reaffirming the need to maintain an open international trading system. By 1983 concern with the policies to improve supply-side performance of economies had heightened. Thus while the importance of international linkages was recognized[14] much of the concern of Ministers was with policies to secure a better supply-side performance. These covered measures to control inflation, increase profitability, improve collective bargaining, promote positive adjustment, improve the functioning of labour markets and achieve stronger social consensus.

Outside the official sphere, ideas for effective coordination of monetary and fiscal policies under the prevailing regime of floating exchange rates have been scarce. One interesting idea for a new approach has been that associated with McKinnon.[15] His proposal does address misalignment. And it yields policy recommendations that contrast sharply with those of 'convergence'. The proposal is concerned with international cooperation in monetary policy, and has two main aspects. First, the major countries (at the level of practical exposition McKinnon talks in terms of the three largest – the United States, Japan and Germany) would agree on a growth rate for their combined money stock that is suitably non-accommodating of inflation for the group as a whole. This would go far towards determining inflation in individual countries. Second, the way in which the overall money growth would be apportioned among the individual countries would pay attention to international demand for the various currencies. If, for example, international holders substituted into assets of country X out of assets of country Y, this would put upward pressure on currency X and downward pressure on currency Y; the policy response would be for monetary authority X to step up its money growth and for authority Y to slow down money growth.

McKinnon gives a plausible account of the last dozen years. He shows that there have been two big bulges in the growth of the combined money stock of the industrialized countries as a group, in 1971–72 and in 1977–78, followed, in 1973–74 and 1979–80, by accelerations in their combined inflation rates, reflected in the rates of most individual countries. The two bulges in money growth occurred in periods when there was substantial substitution by international holders out of dollars into other currencies. Money growth was thereby boosted outside the United States; but U.S. money growth continued at much the same rate as before, the effects of dollar intervention by other countries being automatically sterilized by the Federal Reserve. McKinnon argues that the United States should have reduced its money growth in these periods, responding to the reduced international demand for dollars; correspondingly, he argues that U.S. money growth was too low in 1981–82, when there was substantial shifting *into* dollars internationally, and that it ought to have been expanded. The (world) recession would on this argument then have been less severe.

There are clear limitations to this prescription, which by its nature does not address those aspects of the international problem caused by, for example, inappropriate fiscal policies or terms-of-trade shocks. Further, there are clear practical difficulties with the approach. Even abstracting from political considerations, the task of controlling the combined money stock of the United States, Germany and Japan would clearly be formidable. McKinnon argues that it would actually be easier to control the combined money stock of the three countries than that of a single country, because instability of demand for money resulting from international portfolio shifts would tend to cancel out within the group. But demand for money can be unstable for many reasons other than currency substitution. Equally, experience has shown that typically it is difficult to know at the time what factors are creating exchange rate pressure; and the monetary adjustment required to offset a particular degree of pressure is unknowable with any precision.

Nevertheless, the McKinnon proposal is one serious attempt to face the problems of macroeconomic policy cooperation in the modern environment. The problems which would be involved in attempting to make it operational are the kind of issues that need anyway to be faced if monetary cooperation is ever to be more than a catch-phrase.

Assessment: is greater cooperation possible?

Summing up at this point, cooperation in the setting of macroeconomic policy may on the one hand be directed at generating an appropriate overall thrust of policy for the group of countries considered, or may seek to achieve a better balance in some sense among the various participating countries. In practice, there may well be elements of both. The Bonn Summit proposals, for example, aimed at the general level to generate faster expansion world-wide (and hence provide the opportunity for better performance in each individual country), but were based in detail on the perception that achieving this faster expansion required a different balance of policy among the OECD countries. Analogously, the McKinnon proposal would seek to achieve both an appropriate growth of the 'world' money stock (in practice, that of a group of major countries) and a distribution of this money growth among the issuing countries that would be determined by the evolution of the international demand for the respective currencies. On the other hand, the Smithsonian realignment was, more or less by definition, concerned virtually exclusively with bringing about a better-balanced set of exchange rates, and hence balance-of-payments positions, among the major countries. Recent notions of policy 'convergence' seem also to be concerned with improving balance among countries, notably by reducing exchange rate instability, but have generally been in terms which were too vague to have operational significance – as well as devoting relatively little attention to what the converging policies would add up to at the global level.

Overall, it is difficult to avoid the conclusion that although international cooperation at what was called above the first stage has generally been strong, the case-book of cooperation at the second stage, involving joint commitments to specified policy actions, is disappointingly slim.

In view of the theoretical findings cited earlier – which seem intuitively plausible – that cooperative outcomes will generally be superior to non-cooperative ones, why is it that cooperation in macroeconomic policy-making has not been more active? One important reason is that such ideas do indeed seem theoretical; policy-makers are not accustomed to thinking in terms of 'Pareto optimal' outcomes, or at least not explicitly. And it is of course difficult to give the notion operational content. The distribution of the gains from cooperation will be unclear. Even if there is strong political will to cooperate, institutional and timing differences in different countries' policy arrangements, and imperfect information and communication, undoubtedly make cooperation difficult in practice.

But such arguments can be overplayed. There are circumstances in which policy-makers will perceive that better performance need not be merely a theoretical possibility. Evidently 1978 was an occasion when policy-makers internationally considered that a better outcome could be achieved by cooperation. It seems probable that, had there been a general realization at, say, end-1971, of the intensity of the inflationary pressures that were in store one-and-a-half to two years later, there would have been preparedness to agree that a better outcome was possible; and each individual country would have found it politically easier to soft-pedal its expansionary policies if others had been doing likewise. It is also possible that countries might have been prepared to apply reasoning symmetrical to this in 1980-81 had there been a general appreciation of the prospective seriousness the recession would take on in 1982.

What seems typically to have been lacking at the macroeconomic level, therefore, is a common understanding not only of how the world economy was developing, but also of the range of 'efficient' outcomes that was available. Making good this lack would of course pre-suppose a consensus about how the world economy works, a point that is returned to later.

There are also more 'political' reasons why international macroeconomic cooperation is not pursued to the point consistent with generation of efficient outcomes. International cooperation is a 'public good'.[16] A country participating in it will tend to be more conscious of the costs to itself – particularly the perceived loss of national sovereignty – than of the prospective benefits, even supposing that it trusts its partners to fulfil their part of the bargain. Still less, in general, will the country make adequate allowance for the beneficial effects of its own actions on others. Typically, then, there will be inadequate realization of the benefits that can accrue world-wide from cooperative action. Less cooperation will be forthcoming than would be optimal.

Then there is the 'free rider' problem. In the international macroeconomic field this typically arises as between large and small countries. Developments in large economies tend to have bigger effects on the fortunes of small countries than vice versa. Small countries therefore tend to seek action by the large countries while having little to offer in return. Since, however, action in the large countries will affect small countries whether or not the latter are involved in the discussions, the large countries should normally still have an interest in involving small countries and extracting whatever agreement from them they can – so long as the extension of the number of participants does not make the negotiations too unwieldy. It has to be remembered, too, that international economic policy is a part not only of overall economic policy but also of foreign policy.

Clearly the obstacles to international economic cooperation of the form espoused in the 1960s and 1970s are considerable. Yet international cooperation is a question not of altruism but of enlightened self-interest. Because it is a public good, the 'supply' of it will tend to be inadequate unless the largest countries display a degree of international statesmanship and give the process impetus.

There would seem to be two broad ways in which international economic cooperation can most usefully proceed at present. The first is to achieve international agreement on the appropriate policies to follow to improve supply side performance, through measures to accelerate structural adjustment, raise profitability, encourage labour mobility, and promote freer trade – in short movement generally towards more market-conforming behaviour. There can be little doubt about the importance of agreement on actions to these ends at a time when protectionist attitudes are gaining ground, reflected both in measures at the border and in market-distorting domestic measures that may have similar international repercussions. Indeed, it has been economic cooperation in this sense that has been the main concern of policy-makers internationally over the last few years.

The second way forward for international cooperation might involve intensified exchange of information among countries. It would certainly seem possible to go considerably further in this direction than is habitual at present. It would be possible, for example, for countries to be franker about their current policy motivations, their plans for the period ahead, and the ways in which they would be likely to respond to various contingencies – though the latter is admittedly made difficult in practice by the fact that national negotiators cannot know in advance how the necessary domestic bargains among various interest groups would be struck. At a more technical level, there could be more sharing of research results, particularly those relating to international transmission of economic impulses, so as to move closer to an internationally-shared view, or 'model', of the properties of the world economy as a whole and of the interaction of its constituent parts.

At the limit, if all nationally-available information – giving this term its broadest meaning – were pooled internationally, each country would be able to set its policies, if not in a situation of complete certainty, at least as well-equipped with knowledge of policies, and of 'policy reaction functions', in other countries as those countries themselves. If in addition all the participating countries had a common view of how the international economy worked, 'enlightened rational' policy-making by each country would make due allowance for probable induced responses in other countries, and the global outcome could in principle approach that which would result from actual negotiation of a joint set of policies to achieve a chosen 'efficient' outcome.

This is obviously a grossly stylized vision. The real world is just not like that, even with modern techniques of information handling. Nonetheless, there can be little doubt about the potential value of larger and franker interchange among countries, especially given that at present the lack of a common view of how the international economy works may be an even greater barrier than lack of political will to more intense international cooperation.

Greater exposure of policy-makers to such a process would seem certain to impress upon them the validity of the two key premises on which the case for international cooperation rests. The first of these premises is that the properties of the system as a whole are not the straightforward addition or averaging of the properties of individual national economies. As demonstrated in chapter 4, there are some national actions which can be efficacious if pursued by a single country but which will be nullified if also pursued by a large number of its partners; and there are other lines of action which can have unexpectedly strong mutually-reinforcing effects if followed by many countries simultaneously.

The second premise is that the loss of sovereignty involved in international cooperation is more apparent than real, and can on occasion even be helpful. An individual nation is in fact nearly always heavily constrained in its feedom of action; pre-paredness to cooperate, involving in a formal sense some infringe-ment of sovereignty, will in many cases not further reduce its freedom, and may indeed tend to open up a greater effective freedom of action.[17] As Bryant (1980) has observed: 'a tendency exists, inside a nation's government as well as in the private sector, to underestimate the disparity between formal sovereignty to manipulate instruments and effective ability to control national target variables'. The persistence of this anachronistic tendency is attributed to '… the continuing dominance in domestic politics of ideas, symbols and institutions that are exclusively national in orientation'.[18]

It is this dominance that needs continually to be challenged by confrontation with the facts of interdependence.

13 Some concluding thoughts

What then are the lessons of the past decade? Does the experience of the quarter century from the late 1940s have any relevance to today's conditions and problems? Or are still earlier epochs likely to offer better guidance to what the future may bring? What has been learned about the way economies function individually, about the ways that they interact, about the way that policy affects them individually and collectively, and about the way that policy should be made and implemented?

The view of this book is that, in the present state of economic theory, and given the impossibility of knowing what shocks may lie ahead, a degree of humility is in order in answering these questions. It seems that, over the last decade, a modest amount has been learned about the way that economies function and interact, and that rather more has been learned about the principles that could usefully guide the formulation and implementation of policy. What is proposed is a rather general way of approaching the analysis and making of policy. The book emphasizes the importance of policy, together with the need for careful monitoring and forecasting of the evolving economic situation. It cautions against uni-causal explanations of events, or single-variable prescriptions for policy. And it suggests that considerable attention needs to be paid to the international dimension.

Economic mechanisms

A few new lessons, and many old ones, have been learned over the last decade. For example, those who may have doubted it before must now concede that money does matter. Monetary growth well in excess of the potential rate of growth of an economy is bound to result in inflation; furthermore, monetary growth can be so slow as to provoke tight monetary conditions and lead to a slowdown in the rate of growth of activity. The mechanisms are not all fully understood and quantified, particularly as concerns the transmission of monetary impulses between countries, but the importance of money cannot now be questioned. Fiscal policy matters too. The evidence of the last decade is quite consistent with the previously-prevailing orthodoxy that fiscal policy tightening will reduce the level of activity, and that fiscal easing will tend to support activity, at least for a time, albeit with some effect on the price level also.

But recent years have ' also shown that there is much less independence of the two macro-policy instruments than had previously been thought, or at least assumed. If, in the individual economy, fiscal stimulus is the main support to demand over a run of years, the accumulated stock of government debt may become so large in relation to the total wealth of the private sector that a point is reached beyond which it is possible to sell yet more debt only if interest rates are increased, perhaps markedly. This can considerably limit the scope for fiscal action, at the limit rendering fiscal policy impotent. And the scope for independent monetary policy too may be significantly circumscribed. Monetary policy that is too loose risks capital flight and currency depreciation; while too tight a policy can dramatically raise the interest burden on the stock of government debt and thereby the size of the public sector deficit itself. Fiscal and monetary policy may represent more than a single instrument, but – it is now generally agreed – significantly less than two independent ones.

The recent period has provided evidence of a number of effects that had previously been difficult to capture empirically – or not much thought about. For example, wealth effects have been found to be important, disinflation in a number of countries in 1982 and 1983 leading to a sharper fall in personal savings ratios, and thereby stronger consumption, than predicted by conventional consumption equations. Exchange rate determination is not well understood, but rates have been seen to be influenced importantly at times not only by countries' current account developments, but also by the relative stance or mix of monetary and fiscal policy between countries. Expectations appear to have been important on occasion in influencing interest rates and exchange rates in a number of countries. Labour productivity growth, and perhaps total factor productivity growth also, has been found to be affected not only by its traditional supply-side determinants, but also, within limits, by squeezes on profitability imposed by high interest rates or currency appreciation. And there has been at least suggestive evidence of a tendency for employment growth to be relatively strong where real wages have kept relatively well in line with productivity.

Policy-making

Of greater importance than the knowledge gained about individual economic mechanisms, however, may be what has been learned about the appropriate way to analyse and make economic policy, particularly given the importance of the interaction of policies and performance between countries.

Perhaps the most constructive general development has been the recognition of the need to formulate macroeconomic policy in terms of objectives and likely outcomes over the medium term. A frequent criticism of policy-making in the 1950s and 1960s is that policy was destabilizing, in the sense of tending to cause output fluctuations over the cycle as a whole to be larger than they would have been otherwise. While the evidence does not support this as a general conclusion, it is nonetheless probably the case that, to the extent that policy was framed by looking only a year or two ahead, patterns of public spending and taxation, and hence the structure of the economy as a whole, may over a longer period have evolved in ways that perhaps were not intended; such developments might have been avoided had the medium-term implications of policy and developments been more fully traced through at the policy-for-mation stage. Moreover, formulation of macroeconomic policies in a medium-term perspective puts the process of achieving concord-ance between them and structural and microeconomic policies on to a more rational basis. The coordination of macro and micro policies is potentially of considerable significance for economic perform-ance in the years ahead, but the subject lies outside the scope of this book.

At the same time, however, recognition of the desirability of working out the likely medium-term implications of policy and the associated economic developments – in particular of guarding against reacceleration of inflation – does not mean that all that is required for satisfactory macroeconomic performance is to set policy once and for all in a medium-term context and then simply wait for everything to evolve satisfactorily. The evidence of the last ten years, as well for that matter of the decades before, is that satisfactory policy-making will generally call for more than that. Economies seem continually to be subjected to shocks, both internal and from abroad, and it would seem unlikely that any one setting of policy could be optimal for the whole range of potential shocks. That policy should not seek to 'fine tune' is no reason for it to become tone-deaf.

It is evidently necessary to be concerned with the evolving economic situation, to monitor developments as they occur, and continually to project the most likely outcome (through to the medium term) on the basis of present policies. Particularly when economies are afflicted by new shocks, it is necessary to update the projection; and if the shock is a novel one, this may be no easy matter. In such cases, it is generally useful to start by appealing to economic theory to determine the relevant potential effects – and then monitor incoming data with care in an attempt to assess the quantitative significance of those effects, as well as the lags with which they may work themselves out. Once the projection has been updated it will be necessary to reassess whether policy settings remain appropriate. It may well be judged on many occasions that they are, so that little or nothing would be gained by changing policy, particularly given uncertainty about the size and timing of policy effects. This applies all the more strongly when the act of changing policy may itself unsettle private sector expectations. It would seem that the safer course is to analyse each new shock as it occurs, and to consider carefully if policy settings should be altered. This need not, and in most cases probably would not, imply policy activism. But policy choices, even when they amount to a decision to leave policy settings unchanged, should always be conscious, informed by the best projections and the best analysis available.

This prescription perhaps sounds imprecise. How is the best possible policy setting to be determined? And how is it to be achieved? These are not easy questions to answer, but just as it is sometimes easier, and even perhaps more important, to know what not to do rather than what positively to do, so do many recent events give some guidance as to what is unlikely to represent an adequate basis for making policy.

Some principles of economic policy

Economies, individually and collectively, are complicated structures. This is true also, of course, of many other phenomena, such as those that scientific theory seeks to illuminate and even explain. But whereas experience in the natural sciences is that it is possible, at least on occasion, to secure a dramatic breakthrough in understanding and perhaps also control, in economics this is seldom if ever the case. Rather the reverse is true. Experience over the last decade would seem to confirm that it pays to beware the unique explanation, the uni-causal theory, the single-equation representation of an economy. The single-policy solution to an economy's problems should also be treated with circumspection, whether it be fiscal reflation, incomes policy or constant money growth. Not only are economies not that simple, but it is not generally illuminating or helpful to attempt diagnosis or prescription in that way. For example, inflation expectations may indeed be influenced, perhaps strongly, by announced money growth targets, but that is almost certainly not the only influence on wage claims and settlements. Work effort almost certainly is influenced by the level of taxation, but that is not the only influence. Exchange rates almost certainly are affected by inflation differentials, but there are other influences too.

It is sometimes helpful, for pedagogic purposes, to attempt to describe an economy in particularly simple terms, or to capture key features of an economic system by a handful of relationships. But when analysing an economy and economic behaviour for the purposes of formulating policy, it is inappropriate in general to ignore the range of other useful information that has come to be accepted over the years, and which there is no good immediate reason to stop accepting. Accordingly new relationships, as they become important, should be considered not in isolation but in conjunction with all the other relationships that have been substantiated in the past. This typically results in a system whose properties are too complex to arrive at by intuition, and the understanding of which can be aided considerably by computerized methods of solution. This is not to say that the results have to be taken on trust, just because they are obtained by a process that in some respects is more intricate than that of the unaided mind. Quite the contrary: model-generated results have to be scrutinized from all angles, to ensure their plausibility. Rather the point is that a satisfactory representation of an economy, or a group of economies, is more likely to be achieved when there is explicit representation of all the relationships thought to be at work than when the representation is arbitrarily restricted.

If these propositions are broadly correct for the single economy, they almost certainly apply with even greater force for the world economic system as a whole. Individual economies are nowadays so open to trade and financial flows that national developments are importantly – sometimes predominantly – influenced by developments that originate outside the domestic economy. This adds a further dimension to the task of forecasting and policy-making. The experience of attempts to model the international transmission of such influences, however, has been that while the broad elements are understandable and quantifiable, there is much that remains to be understood. But considerable strides are being made, just as they have been with the representation of relationships within individual economies; and as more evidence is collected, analysed and incorporated in international economic models, the state of knowledge and understanding should improve. However imperfect international economic models may be at present, their careful use, with the appropriate addition of judgement, provides a more rational basis for policy analysis than mere conjecture or hunch.

Where does this leave international cooperation in the formulation of national policies? At present, with a number of aspects of international economic interaction not yet fully understood, and the theory of cooperative and non-cooperative games as applied to the formulation of economic policy in an international context also at a relatively early stage of development, any judgement has to be based rather more upon simple observation of the past, and rather less upon rigorous quantified analysis, than would normally be thought desirable. Hence any conclusions have to be offered tentatively, in the recognition that they may well have to be reconsidered and perhaps at some later stage discarded. Moreover, even if the theory were robust, practical application would no doubt still face formidable difficulties. Having said all this, the discussion in chapter 12 suggests rather strongly that there are circumstances in which cooperative policy formulation can be beneficial to all participants.

Drawing together a number of the themes evoked above, it seems that, for the foreseeable future, national economic objectives are more likely to be achieved, taking one year with another, if countries:

- set their policies as far as possible in the light of their likely medium-term consequences, while continually assessing their appropriateness against high quality continually-updated economic forecasts;
- base their policy upon the widest possible understanding of how the economy works, which involves understanding the full range of quantified economic relationships that is available. However, this has to be supplemented throughout by other relevant extraneous quantitative information as well as by all-important non-quantitative judgement.

Given however the susceptibility of economies to developments that emanate from abroad, this implies that the appropriateness of each country's policies will depend *inter alia* upon the accuracy of the forecasts of developments in partner countries; and success in setting policies appropriately, and thereby realizing an acceptable domestic performance, will be the greater the more stable, satisfactory and well-predicted is economic performance in partner countries. For countries collectively, therefore, this implies on the one hand the need for the best possible set of internationally-consistent economic forecasts, and on the other hand the need for internationally compatible – perhaps cooperative – policy-making.

Notes

2 The contribution of policy in the 1950s and 1960s

1 See Musgrave and Musgrave (1976), Chapter 1.
2 See Boltho (1975).
3 For a more detailed description of this period, see for example Worswick and Ady (1962) pp. 212-213, and Flamant and Singer-Kérel (1968) pp. 83-92.
4 See Shapiro (1977), especially p. 270.
5 See for example Llewellyn and Potter (1982), pp. 141-149.
6 For a fuller discussion, see for example Maddison (1964), especially chapter 4.
7 McCracken et al (1977), p. 38.
8 See OECD (1968). The economists were Walter Heller (U.S.), Cornelis Goedhart (Netherlands), Guillaume Guindey (France), Heinz Haller (Switzerland), Jean van Houtte (Belgium), Assar Lindbeck (Sweden), Richard Sayers (U.K.), and Sergio Steve (Italy).
9 OECD (1975), p. 131.
10 For a recent survey of this episode, see Cairncross (1983).
11 Dow (1964), p. 5.
12 Prest (1968), p. 5.
13 Musgrave and Musgrave (1968), p. 44.
14 For a judgement on the role of monetary policy over this period, see Artis (1978), especially pp. 302-303.
15 p. 42.
16 p. 307.
17 pp. 15-16.
18 Hansen's approach was developed from earlier contributions by Brown (1956), Lindbeck (1956) and Musgrave (1964).
19 p. 933.
20 p. 16.

3 Policy successes and failures since the early 1970s

1 OECD (1970), p. 7.
2 See for example Cooper and Lawrence (1975) and Labys and Thomas (1975).

3 For an interesting discussion of these elements, see Bird (1982).
4 See for example Llewellyn, Ostry and Samuelson (1982).

4 The influence of international linkages

1 For an evaluation of national and international multiplier effects, under a variety of assumptions, see the technical annex to Larsen, Llewellyn and Potter (1983).
2 See also Koromzay, Llewellyn and Potter (1984).

5 The need for monitoring and forecasting

1 See, for example, Poole (1971), Okun (1972), Cooper and Fisher (1972), Battenberg et al (1975), Craine et al (1976), and Stekler (1976).
2 For an interesting elaboration of some of the principal differences between economic forecasting and weather forecasting, see Mason (1983).
3 *OECD Economic Outlook* 31, p. 13.
4 This, it turned out, was largely attributable to Libya which, short of foreign exchange earnings, slashed its imports by half. With a weight of 10 per cent in overall OPEC imports at the time, this reduced the growth of OPEC import volumes by around 5 per cent. There was no further fall in Libyan imports after the third quarter of 1982, but by that time most other OPEC countries were sharply cutting back the rate of their import volume growth.
5 McNees (1979) p. 3.
6 Op. cit. p. 20.
7 Levels nearly always change significantly when the base year is changed – rates of change sometimes are affected.

6 The dependability of economic forecasts

1 This chapter draws on material, including data, presented in Llewellyn and Arai (1984)
2 Recent post-mortems on single-country forecasts are to be found, for example, in Barker (1982), Cipolletta and de Roo (1981), Daub (1981), Fontenau (1982), Hatjoullis and Wood (1979), and McNees (1979 and 1981). For recent studies which include forecasts of country-groupings, generally made by the international organizations, see Barker (1983), Fontenau (1983), and MacFarlane and Hawkins (1983).
3 There are many other considerations too in the assessment of forecasting accuracy, although not of direct concern to this paper. For a useful recent review, see Klein and Young (1980), especially pp. 131 to 147.
4 These data are available from the authors upon request.
5 See especially Sapir (1949) and Zarnowitz (1979).

6 p. 313.
7 The model used here is described in Llewellyn and Arai (1984).
8 McCracken et al (1977), p. 47.
9 Imports of goods, for example, grew by nearly 22 per cent in volume, over 4 times as fast as the growth of GNP (4.7 per cent). Most import functions at the time would have predicted import growth of only about 10 per cent.
10 *OECD Economic Outlook* 4, December 1968, pp. 8-9.
11 *OECD Economic Outlook* 5, July 1969, p. 7.
12 *OECD Economic Outlook* 9, July 1971, p. 9.
13 *OECD Economic Outlook* 10, December 1971, p. 16.
14 McCracken et al (1977), p. 51.
15 See for example, in addition to the discussion in Chapter 3, *OECD Economic Outlook* 27, July 1980, pp. 128-130, *OECD Economic Outlook* 31, July 1982, pp. 139-140, Llewellyn, Ostry and Samuelson (1982) and Larsen and Llewellyn (1983).
16 Other years of rapid OECD real GNP growth were 1950 (8.3 per cent), 1951 (7.1 per cent), 1955 (6.8 per cent) and 1964 (6.2 per cent). All occurred before the Secretariat started forecasting – see Maddison (1982), p. 86.

7 Approaches to economic forecasting

1 See, for example, Mitchell (1913), and also Burns and Mitchell (1946), and Moore (1961).
2 It is intriguing to re-read the literature of the 1950s on applied macroeconomic models, where the term 'large model' applied to a system of only about twelve equations. Such a system would be simple to put up on any one of many personal computers on the market today – or even on some of the very recent pocket computers.

9 The INTERLINK system

1 Belgium and Luxembourg are, at this stage, taken together as one 'country'.
2 See OECD (1983) for a fuller description of the OECD country models.
3 See OECD (1983) for a fuller description of non-OECD regional models.
4 See OECD (1983) for a fuller description of trade linkage methods.
5 See Artus and Rhomberg (1973) and Rhomberg (1976).
6 See Tinbergen (1952) and Theil (1964).

11 Recent approaches to policy

1 For example Eilbott (1966), in simulations of the United States economy, estimated that automatic stabilizers would generally reduce fluctuations in GNP by 35 to 50 per cent in a decline, and by 25 to 40 per cent in a recovery. See also Balopoulos (1967), Chalmers and Fischel (1967) and Pearse (1962).
2 See, for example, Duesenberry, Eckstein and Fromm (1960) and Pack (1963).
3 All the figures quoted in this paragraph relate to so-called *general government*, which includes regional and local as well as central government. For the United States, the Federal budget alone was further into deficit than that of general government during the period in question, state and local administrations being in surplus.
4 See Friedman (1948), (1953), (1959), and also Shaw (1958). Even these do not represent the beginning of the debate, which goes back at least to the 1920s.
5 See, for example, his response to the U.K. House of Commons Committee on the Treasury and Civil Service (quoted in their Third Report, para. 4.34): 'I conclude that ... only a modest reduction in output and employment will be a side effect of reducing inflation to single figures by 1982.'
6 See, for example, Artis and Currie (1981), and OECD (1984).
7 For a brief history of supply-side theories and their importance in macroeconomics, including a diagram of Laffer's curve, see Keleher and Orzechowski (1982).
8 Chan-Lee and Kato (1984).

12 International cooperation in economic policy-making

1 pp. 470-475.
2 See Feldstein (1983).
3 Bryant (1980), pp. 464-468. In addition, see in particular Niehans (1968) and Hamada (1974 and 1976).
4 See OECD, Working Party No. 3 (1966).
5 A further-developed version of this work can be found in Boltho and Keating (1973).
6 The current account for this purpose was the balance on goods, services and private transfers; official transfers, at that time mainly aid, were in this context considered to belong with capital movements.
7 See Solomon (1977), Chapter XII.
8 See Artus and Rhomberg (1973).
9 See *Communiqué* of the Committee of Twenty following its meeting of 17-18 January 1974.
10 See *Communiqué* of the OECD Ministerial meeting in 1976: PRESS/-A(76)21.
11 *OECD Economic Outlook* 23, pp. v-xv, which laid out the 'concerted action' philosophy in detail.

12 De Menil and Solomon (1983), p. 47.
13 See PRESS/A(80)37.
14 'Pervasive economic linkages mean that the ability of individual
    countries to achieve domestic policy objectives depends importantly on
    the policies and performance of others. It is important for the
    consistency of policies that each Member country take account of the
    international implications of Member countries' policies taken
    together' – PRESS/A(83)25, p. 2.
15 See, in particular, McKinnon (1984).
16 See Olson (1971).
17 See Cooper (1968), p. 264.
18 p. 469.

Bibliography

Adams, F.G., H. Eguchi, and F. Meyer-zu-Schlochtern, *An Econometric Analysis of International Trade*, OECD, 1969.

Amano, A., E. Kurihara and L. Samuelson, 'Trade Linkage Sub-Model in the EPA World Economic Model', *Economic Bulletin* no. 19, Economic Research Institute, Economic Planning Agency, Japanese Government, Tokyo, 1980.

Artis, M.J., 'Monetary Policy – Part II', in Blackaby, F.T. (ed.), *British Economic Policy 1960-74*, The National Institute of Economic and Social Research, 1978.

Artis, M.J. and D.A. Currie, 'Monetary Targets and the Exchange Rate: A Case for Conditional Targets', in W.A. Eltis and P.J.N. Sinclair (ed.), *The Money Supply and the Exchange Rate*, Oxford University Press, 1981.

Artus, J. and R. Rhomberg, 'A Multilateral Exchange Rate Model', *IMF Staff Papers*, Volume 20, November 1973.

Artus, P., 'Capital, Energy and Labour Substitution', *OECD Department of Economics and Statistics Working Papers*, March 1983.

Ball, R.J. (ed.), *The International Linkage of National Economic Models*. North-Holland, 1973.

Balopoulos, E.T., *Fiscal Policy of the British Economy*, North-Holland, 1967.

Barker, K.M., 'World Economy Forecast Post Mortems: 1978-82', *National Institute Economic Review*, May 1983.

Barker, T.S., 'Forecasting the 1980-81 recession: The track records of Cambridge Econometrics, LBS, NIESR and CEPG', *Mimeo*, Department of Applied Economics, University of Cambridge, 1982.

Battenberg, D., J. Enzler and A. Havenner, 'MINNIE: A Small Version of the MIT-PENN-SSRC Econometric Model', *Federal Reserve Bulletin*, Washington, D.C., November 1975.

Beckerman, W., 'The World Trade Multiplier and the Stability of World Trade, 1930 to 1953', *Econometrica*, vol. 24, 1956.

Begg, D.K.H., *The Rational Expectations Revolution in Macroeconomics*, Philip Allan, 1982.

Bird, P.J.W.N., 'Speculation in Commodity Markets: The Case of the 1972 to 1975 Commodity Price Boom', *mimeo*, University of Stirling, 1982.

Boltho, A. and M. Keating, 'The Measurement of Domestic Cyclical

Fluctuations', *OECD Economic Outlook, Occasional Studies*, July 1973.

Boltho, A., *Japan An Economic Survey 1953-1973*, Oxford University Press, 1975.

Boltho, A., 'British Fiscal Policy, 1955-1971 – Stabilizing or Destabilizing?', *Oxford Bulletin of Economics and Statistics*, November 1981.

Boltho, A. (ed.), *The European Economy – Growth and Crisis*, Oxford University Press, 1982.

Box, G.E.P., and G.M. Jenkins, *Time Series Analysis: Forecasting and Control*, Holden-Day, 1970.

Brandsma, A.S. and A.J. Hughes Hallett, 'The Co-ordination Approach to Policymaking in Interdependent Economies', *mimeo*, Department of Economics, Erasmus University, Rotterdam, 1983.

Bristow, J.A., 'Taxation and Income Stabilization', *Economic Journal*, June 1968.

Brown, E.C., 'Fiscal Policy in the Thirties: A Reappraisal', *American Economic Review*, December 1956.

Bryant, R.C., *Money and Monetary Policy in Interdependent Nations*, The Brookings Institution, Washington, 1980.

Burns, A.F., and W.C. Mitchell, *Measuring Business Cycles*, National Bureau of Economic Research, New York, 1946.

Cairncross, A., 'Is Employment Policy a Thing of the Past?', *The Three Banks Review*, September 1983.

Chalmers, J.A. and W.A. Fischel, 'An Analysis of Automatic Stabilizers in a Small Econometric Model', *National Tax Journal*, December 1967.

Chan-Lee, J. and H. Kato, 'A Comparison of Simulation Properties of National Econometric Models', *OECD Economic Studies*, Spring 1984.

Cipolletta, I. and D. de Roo, 'Erreurs et Ajustments Successifs dans les Previsions Macroeconomiques en Europe', *Prévision et Analyse économique*, Vol. 2, No. 4, November/December 1981.

Cooper, J.P. and S. Fisher, 'Stochastic Simulation of Monetary Rules in Two Macroeconomic Models', *Journal of the American Statistical Association*, December 1972.

Cooper, R.N., *The Economics of Interdependence*, McGraw-Hill, 1968.

Cooper, R.N. and R.Z. Lawrence, 'The 1972-75 Commodity Boom', *Brookings Papers on Economic Activity* No. 3, 1975.

Craine, R., A. Havenner and P. Tinsley, 'Optimal Macroeconomic Control Policies', *Annals of Economic and Social Measurement*, 1976.

Daub, M., 'The Accuracy of Canadian Short-term Economic Forecasts Revisited', *Canadian Journal of Economics*, XIV, No. 3, August 1981.

Dhrymes, P.J. et al., 'Criteria for Evaluation of Econometric Models', *Annals of Economic and Social Measurement*, 1972.

Dow, J.C.R., *The Management of the British Economy 1945-60*, Cambridge University Press, 1964.

Duesenberry, J., O. Eckstein, and G. Fromm, 'A Simulation of the United States Economy in Recession', *Econometrica*, October 1960.

Eckstein, O., 'Econometric Models for Forecasting and Policy Analysis: the Present State of the Art', *Data Resources U.S. Review*, September 1979.

Eilbott, P., 'The Effectiveness of Automatic Stabilizers', *American Economic Review*, June 1966.

Fabritius, J.F.R., and C.E. Petersen, 'OPEC Respending and the Economic Impact of an Increase in the Price of Oil', *Scandinavian Journal of Economics*, Volume 83, No.2., 1981.

Feldstein, M.S., 'The World Economy Today', *The Economist*, 11th June 1983.

Flamant, M. and J. Singer-Kérel, *Modern Economic Crises*, Presses Universitaires de France, 1968. Published in English by Barrie and Jenkins Ltd., 1970.

Fontenau, A., 'La Fiabilité des Prévisions Macroéconomiques à Court Terme: 12 ans d'Experiences Françaises (1970-1981)', *Observations et diagnostics économiques*, No. 2, October 1982.

Fontenau, A., 'Les Erreurs des Prévisions Economiques pour 1982,' *Observations et diagnostics économiques*, No. 4, June 1983.

Friedman, M., 'A Monetary and Fiscal Framework for Economic Stability', *American Economic Review*, June 1948.

Friedman, M., 'The Effects of Full Employment Policy on Economic Stability: A Formal Analysis', in *Essays in Positive Economics*, University of Chicago Press, Chicago, 1953.

Friedman, M., 'The Goals and Criteria of Monetary Policy', in N.H. Jacoby (ed.), *A Program for Monetary Stability*, Fordham, 1959.

Goldberger, A.S., *Econometric theory*, Wiley, New York, 1964.

Hamada, K., 'Alternative Exchange Rate Systems and the Interdependence of Monetary Policies', in Aliber, R.Z. (ed.), *National Monetary Policies and the International Financial System*, University of Chicago Press, 1974.

Hamada, K., 'A Strategic Analysis of Monetary Interdependence', *Journal of Political Economy*, August 1976.

Hansen, A.H., *A Guide to Keynes*, McGraw-Hill, 1953.

Hansen, B., *Fiscal Policy in Seven Countries 1955-1965*, OECD, 1969.

Hatjoullis, G. and D. Wood, 'Economic Forecasts – An Analysis of Performance', *The Business Economist*, Society of Business Economists, Vol. 10, No. 2, Spring 1979.

Heller, W., et al., *Fiscal Policy for a Balanced Economy*, OECD, 1968.

Helliwell, J.F. and F. Gorbet, 'Assessing the Dynamic Efficiency of Automatic Stabilizers', *Journal of Political Economy*, July-August 1971.

Helliwell, J.F. and C.I. Higgins, 'Macroeconomic Adjustment Process', *European Economic Review*, 1976.

Hickman, B.G. and L.J. Lau, 'Elasticities of Substitution and Export Demands in a World Trade Model', *European Economic Review*, 1973.

Hicks, J.R., 'Mr. Keynes and the Classics – A Suggested Interpretation', *Econometrica*, April 1937.

Holtham, G.H., 'Multinational Modelling of Financial Linkages and Exchange Rates', *OECD Economic Studies*, Spring 1984.

Johnston, J., *Econometric Methods 2nd ed.*, McGraw Hill, 1972.

Keleher, R.E., 'Evidence Relating to Supply-Side Tax Policy', in Fink, R.H. (ed.), *Supply-Side Economics: a Critical Appraisal*, Aletheia

Books, University Publications of America Inc., 1982.

Keleher, R.E. and W.P. Orzechowski, 'Supply-Side Fiscal Policy: An Historical Analysis of a Rejuvenated Idea', in Fink, R.H. (ed.), *Supply-Side Economics: A Critical Appraisal*, Aletheia Books, University Publications of America Inc., 1982.

Klein, L.R., *Economic Fluctuations in the United States, 1921-1941*, John Wiley, 1950.

Klein, L.R., *The Economics of Supply and Demand*, Basil Blackwell, 1983.

Klein, L.R. and A.S. Goldberger, *An Econometric Model of the United States, 1929-1952*, North-Holland, 1955.

Klein, L.R. and A. van Peeterssen, 'Forecasting World Trade within Project LINK', in Ball (1973).

Klein, L.R. and R.M. Young, 'An Introduction to Economic Forecasting and Forecasting Models', *Lexington Books*, 1980.

Koopmans, T.C., (ed.), *Statistical Inference in Dynamic Economic Models*, John Wiley, 1950.

Koromzay, V., J. Llewellyn and S. Potter, 'Exchange Rates and Policy Choices: Some Lessons from Interdependence in a Multilateral Perspective', *American Economic Review, Papers and Proceedings*, May 1984.

Labys, W.C. and H.C. Thomas, 'Speculation, Hedging and Commodity Price Behaviour: an International Comparison', *Applied Economics*, December 1975.

Larsen, F. and J. Llewellyn, 'Simulated Macroeconomic Effects of a Large Fall in Oil Prices', *OECD Economics and Statistics Department Working Papers*, June 1983.

Larsen, F., J. Llewellyn and S. Potter, 'International Economic Linkages', *OECD Economic Studies*, Autumn, 1983.

Lindbeck, A., 'Stats budgetens verkningar pa konjunkturutvecklingen', *Statens Offentliga Utredninger*, Stockholm, 1956.

Little, I.M.D., 'Fiscal Policy', in Worswick, G.D.N. and P. Ady (eds.), *The British Economy in the Nineteen-Fifties*, Oxford University Press, 1962.

Llewellyn, J. and H. Arai, 'International Aspects of Forecasting Error', *OECD Economic Studies*, Autumn 1984.

Llewellyn, J., S. Ostry and L. Samuelson, 'The Cost of OPEC II', *OECD Observer*, No. 115, March 1982.

Llewellyn, J. and S. Potter, 'Competitiveness and the Current Account', in Boltho, A. (ed.), *The European Economy*, Oxford University Press, 1982.

Llewellyn, J. and L. Samuelson, 'The OECD International Linkage Model', *OECD Economic Outlook, Occasional Studies*, 1979.

Llewellyn, J. and L. Samuelson, 'Forecasting Experience at OECD', *Prévisions et Analyses Economiques (Economica)*, Volume II, 1981/04.

Lucas, R.E., 'Econometric Policy Evaluation: A Critique', in K. Brunner and A.H. Meltzer (eds.) *The Phillips Curve and Labor Markets*, North-Holland, 1976.

Machlup, F., *International Trade and the National Income Multiplier*, August M. Kelly, 1961.

MacFarlane, I.J. and J.R. Hawkins, 'Economic Forecasts and their Assessment', *The Economic Record*, December 1983.

Maddison, A., *Economic Growth in the West*, George Allen and Unwin, 1964.

Maddison, A., *Phases of Capitalist Development*, Oxford University Press, 1982.

Malinvaud, E., *Statistical Methods of Econometrics*, Rand McNally, 1970.

Mason, J., 'Predictability in Science and Society', Presidential Address to The British Association, Brighton, 1983.

Masson, P., A. Blundell-Wignall and P. Richardson, 'Domestic and International Effects of Government Spending Under Rational Expectations', *OECD Economic Studies*, Autumn 1984.

Matthews, R.C.O., 'Why has Britain had Full Employment Since the War?', *Economic Journal*, September 1968.

McCracken, P., et al, *Towards Full Employment and Price Stability*, OECD, 1977.

McKinnon, R.I., *An International Standard for Monetary Stabilization*, Institute for International Economics, 1984.

McMahon, C.W., *Techniques of Economic Forecasting*, OECD, 1965.

McNees, S.K., 'The Accuracy of Macroeconometric Models and Forecasts of the U.S. Economy', in Ormerod, P. (ed), *Economic Modelling*, Heineman, 1979.

McNees, S.K., 'The Forecasting Record for the 1970s', *New England Economic Review*, September/October 1979. Corrected, extended, and reprinted by the *Federal Reserve Bank of Boston*, September/October 1979.

McNees, S.K., 'The Recent Record of Thirteen Forecasters', *New England Economic Review*, September/October 1981. Corrected and reprinted by the *Federal Reserve Bank of Boston*, September/October 1981.

Menil, G. de, and A.M. Solomon, *Economic Summitry*, Council on Foreign Relations, 1983.

Metzler, L.A., 'Unemployment Equilibrium in International Trade', *Econometrica*, 1942.

Metzler, L.A., 'A Multiple Region Theory of Income and Trade', *Econometrica*, No. 18, 1950.

Meyer-zu-Schlochtern, F. and A. Yajima, 'OECD Trade Model 1970 Version', *Economic Outlook, Occasional Studies*, OECD, Paris, 1970.

Mitchell, W.C., *Business Cycles*, University of California Press, 1913.

Moore, G.H. (ed.), *Business Cycle Indicators*, Princeton University Press for NBER, 1961.

Moriguchi, C. 'Forecasting and Simulation Analysis of the World Economy', *American Economic Review*, 1973.

Musgrave, R.A., 'On Measuring Fiscal Performance', *Review of Economic Statistics*, May 1964.

Musgrave, R.A. and P.B. Musgrave, 'Fiscal Policy', in Caves, R.E. (ed.), *Britain's Economic Prospects*, George Allen and Unwin Ltd., 1968.

Musgrave, R.A. and P.B. Musgrave, *Public Finance in Theory and Practice*, McGraw-Hill, 1976.

Neisser, H. and F. Modigliani, *National Incomes and International Trade*,

University of Illinois Press, 1953.

Niehans, J., 'Monetary and Fiscal Policies in Open Economies Under Fixed Exchange Rates: An Optimising Approach', *Journal of Political Economy*, July/August 1968.

OECD Economic Outlook, various issues.

OECD, *Exchange Rate Management and the Conduct of Monetary Policy*, 1984.

OECD, *Fiscal Policy for a Balanced Economy*, 1968.

OECD, *Inflation – the Present Problem*, 1970.

OECD, *The INTERLINK System*, Technical Manual, 1983.

OECD, *The Role of Monetary Policy in Demand Management*, 1975.

OECD, Working Party No. 3, *The Balance of Payments Adjustment Process*, 1966.

Okun, A.M., 'Fiscal-Monetary Activism: Some Analytical Issues', *Brookings Papers on Economic Activity*, 1972.

Olson, M., *The Logic of Collective Action: Public Goods and the Theory of Groups*, Harvard University Press, 1971.

Oudiz, G. and J. Sachs, 'Macroeconomic Policy Co-ordination Among the Industrial Economies', *Brookings Papers on Economic Activity*, I., 1984.

Pack, H., 'Formula Flexibility: A Quantitative Appraisal', in Ando, A., E.C. Brown and A.F. Friedlander (eds.), *Studies in Economic Stabilization*, The Brookings Institution, Washington, D.C., 1963.

Pauly, P. 'Policy Co-ordination and Global Development', *mimeo*, Applied Econometric Association, Brussels, December 1983.

Pearse, P.H., 'Automatic Stabilisation and the British Taxes on Income', *Review of Economic Studies*, February 1962.

Polak, J.J., *An International Economic System*, Allen and Unwin, London, 1954.

Polak, J.J. and L. Boissonneault, 'Monetary Analysis of Income and Imports and its Statistical Application' *IMF Staff Papers*, 1960.

Poole, W., 'Alternative Paths to a Stable Full Employment Economy', *Brookings Papers on Economic Activity*, No. 3, 1971.

Prest, A.R., 'Sense and Nonsense in Budgetary Policy', *Economic Journal*, March 1968.

Price, R., and P. Muller, 'Structural Budget Indicators and the Interpretation of Fiscal Policy Stance in OECD Economies', *OECD Economic Studies*, Autumn 1984.

Rhomberg, R., 'Indices of Effective Exchange Rates', *IMF Staff Papers*, Volume 23, March 1976.

Roberts, P.C., 'The Breakdown of the Keynesian Model', *The Public Interest*, No. 52, 1978, reprinted in Fink, R.H. (ed.), *Supply Side Economics: a Critical Appraisal*, Aletheia Books, University Publications of America Inc., 1982.

Samuelson, L., 'A New Model of World Trade', *OECD Economic Outlook, Occasional Studies*, 1973.

Samuelson, L., 'The OECD World Trade Model: Some Recent Extensions', in Courbis, R. (ed.), *Commerce International et Modèles Nationaux*, Economica, 1976.

Samuelson, L., 'International Coordination of National Economic Policies', in Peschel, K. and J. Rohwedder (eds.), *International Dependence of Scandinavian Industries*, University of Kiel, 1977.

Samuelson, L. and E. Kurihara, 'OECD Trade Linkage Methods', *Economic Bulletin No. 18*, Economic Research Institute, Economic Planning Agency, Tokyo, 1980.

Sapir, M., 'Review of Economic Forecasts for the Transition Period', *Studies in Income and Wealth*, II, N.B.E.R., N.Y., 1949.

Shapiro, H.T., 'Inflation in the United States', in Krause, L.B. and W.S. Salant (eds.), *Worldwide Inflation*, The Brookings Institution, 1977.

Shaw, E.S., 'Money Supply and Stable Economic Growth', in *United States Monetary Policy*, Columbia University, 1958.

Sims, C., 'Policy Analysis with Economic Models', *Brookings Papers on Economic Activity, 1:1982*.

Smyth, D.J., 'Built-in Flexibility of Taxation and Automatic Stabilization', *Journal of Political Economy*, August 1966.

Snyder, W.W., 'Measuring Economic Stabilization: 1955-65', *American Economic Review*, December 1970.

Solomon, R., *The International Monetary System, 1945-1976*, Harper and Row, 1977.

Stekler, H.O., 'Economic Forecasting and Contracyclical Stabilization Policy', *Journal of Public Economics*, April/May 1976.

Theil, H., *Optimal Decision Rules for Government and Industry*, North-Holland, Amsterdam, 1964.

Tinbergen, J., *Statistical Testing of Business Cycle Theories, II. Business Cycles in the United States of America 1919-1932*, League of Nations, Geneva, 1939.

Tinbergen, J., *On the Theory of Economic Policy*, North-Holland, Amsterdam, 1952.

Wallich, H.C., 'Institutional Cooperation in the World Economy', lecture at University of Chicago, 5th May 1983.

Wallis, K.F., 'Econometric Implications of the Rational Expectations Hypothesis', *Econometrica*, Vol. 48, 1980.

Worswick, G.D.N., 'Fiscal Policy and Stabilization in Britain', in Cairncross, A. (ed.), *Britain's Economic Prospects Reconsidered*, The Brookings Institution, 1971.

Worswick, G.D.N. and P.H. Ady, *The British Economy in the Nineteen-Fifties*, Oxford University Press, 1962.

Zarnowitz, V., 'An Analysis of Annual and Multiperiod Quarterly Forecasts of Aggregate Income, Output and the Price Level', *Journal of Business*, Vol. 52, No. 1, 1979.

Index of names

Index of subjects